The Best-ever Book of
100 Incredible Thi
to Make, Do and P

The Best-ever Book of
100 Incredible Things to Make, Do and Play

Petra Boase   Clare Bradley

Marion Elliot   Judy Williams

LORENZ BOOKS

PUBLISHER'S NOTE

Crafts and nature projects are great fun to do, but a few guidelines should be followed for general safety and care of the environment.
When outdoors:
• *Always ask permission before going exploring, and always make sure you have a reliable person with you. Let others know when you are expected to return.*
When indoors:
• *Always ask permission before borrowing materials used in the projects.*
• *Use non-toxic materials wherever possible, for instance paint, glue and varnishes. Where this is not possible, use materials in a well-ventilated area, and always follow manufacturers' instructions.*
• *Needles, scissors and all sharp tools must be handled with care. Please pay attention to all safety notes and warnings as marked by the sign* !

This edition first published in 1998 by Lorenz Books

© Anness Publishing Limited 1998

Lorenz Books is an imprint of
Anness Publishing Limited
Hermes House
88–89 Blackfriars Road
London SE1 8HA

All rights reserved. No part of this publication may be reproduced, stored in a retrieval system, or transmitted in any way or by any means, electronic, mechanical, photocopying, recording or otherwise, without the prior written permission of the copyright holder.

ISBN 1 85967 728 2

A CIP catalogue record for this book is available from the British Library

Publisher: Joanna Lorenz
Project Editor: Zoe Antoniou
Designers: Peter Laws, Lilian Lindblom, Alan Marshall and Adrian Morris
Jacket designer: Ian Sandom
Photographers: James Duncan and John Freeman
Stylists: Petra Boase, Madeleine Brehaut, Susan Bull and Judy Williams
Extra recipes: Sam Dobson
Illustrations: Lucinda Ganderton and Andrew Tewson

Printed and bound in Hong Kong

1 3 5 7 9 10 8 6 4 2

Contents

Introduction	6
Basic Techniques	8
Recycling Fun	10
Fun with Toys	46
Dressing-up Fun	82
Gardening Fun	114
Cooking Fun	152
Templates	186
Index	190

INTRODUCTION

It's always great fun to make something, and this book is full of all kinds of brilliant ideas. Whatever you like to do, there is something special here for everyone.

There are lots of toys to make and play with, from rag dolls to robots. Or, if you like to play outside, this book can show you how to explore your garden. It is really interesting planting seeds and watching them grow into plants. If you want to impress your friends, cook them a fantastic meal or throw a wild fancy dress party! Show everyone how to make up their faces so they look like spooky monsters or wild animals.

Next time it's a friend's birthday, make a special badge or bracelet using a jamjar lid or plastic bottle. Recycling things that you find around the house is very cheap and fun to do. It's amazing what you can do with a few plastic straws or coloured paper clips!

Some of the projects you can make yourself, following the step-by-step pictures and the simple instructions. You may need to ask an adult to help you to make some of the toys, or when you are in the kitchen. Always be very careful if you are using sharp tools or are cooking on a hot stove.

Indoors and outdoors, summer and winter – there's always something incredible to make, do or play!

Basic Techniques

Tracing

Some of the projects in this book have patterns that you can transfer directly to paper or use to make templates. Tracing is the quickest way to make copies of a pattern so that you can easily transfer it to another piece of paper or cardboard.

 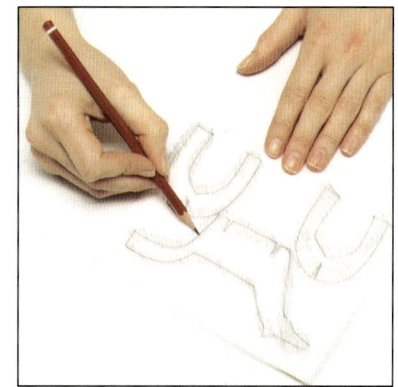

1 Lay your piece of tracing paper on the pattern and use a soft pencil to draw over the image, making a dark line. Turn the sheet of tracing paper over and place it on a scrap of paper. Scribble over the lines with your pencil.

2 Turn the tracing right-side up again and place it on an appropriate piece of paper or cardboard. Carefully draw over the lines to transfer the tracing to the paper or cardboard.

3 Lift up the tracing paper and you will see that your outline is now on the paper or cardboard.

Scaling-up

Sometimes you will want to make a project bigger than the template given. It's easy to make it larger. This is known as scaling-up. Use a scale of, say, one square on the template to two squares on the graph paper. You can use a different scale depending on the size you want.

1 If you wish to copy a template that is not printed on a grid, trace it and transfer it to graph paper. If the template you have chosen does appear on a grid, proceed directly to step 2.

2 Using an appropriate scale, enlarge the template onto a second piece of paper, copying the shape from each smaller square to a larger square.

3 Cut out the template and transfer it to card (posterboard) or paper.

8

BASIC TECHNIQUES

Papier-mâché

Papier-mâché is made by shredding paper, usually old newspapers, and combining it with glue. The paper can be used in a number of ways to make a huge variety of objects which are either useful or just for decoration.

1 For most projects, paper should be torn into fairly short strips approximately 2 cm (¾ in) wide.

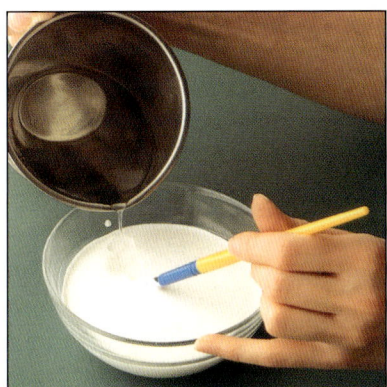

2 Mix some non-toxic PVA (white) glue with water to the consistency of single (light) cream.

3 Papier-mâché can be pressed into lightly greased moulds or wrapped around cardboard shapes like this.

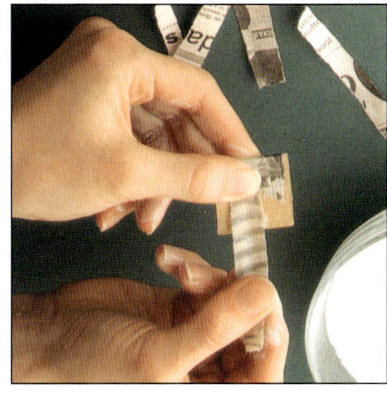

4 To cover smaller shapes, use small, thin pieces of newspaper.

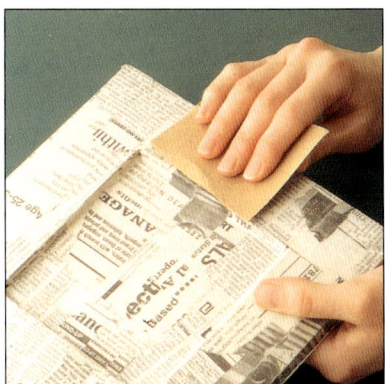

5 Your papier-mâché object may have a slightly rough surface when it has dried out. To make it uniformly smooth, lightly rub the paper with fine sandpaper.

6 Prime your papier-mâché with two coats of non-toxic white paint to conceal the newsprint surface before decorating.

RECYCLING FUN

Materials

These are just some of the materials you will need. Some you will already have, others you can buy.

Cardboard tubes
These come in a variety of sizes in the centres of toilet rolls, kitchen-paper rolls and rolls of silver foil.

Coloured cord, thin
This is very strong and is good for necklaces and mobiles.

Coloured sticky-paper dots
These come in a variety of colours and sizes and are available from most stationers.

Corks
Corks are good for making small dolls, animals and other toys.

Cotton thread
This comes in lots of bright colours and thicknesses and is used for patchwork and sewing.

Darning needles
These are wide needles with large eyes and rounded ends that are not very sharp. Use them for sewing, for stringing beads and for threading elastic.

Elastic
It is possible to buy thin elastic in different colours, such as silver, gold and glitter-effect.

Fabric and felt scraps
Scraps of fabric and felt are useful for making fabric pictures, toys' clothes and patchwork. Felt comes in lots of lovely colours and doesn't fray.

Felt-tipped pens
These must be non-toxic. They are good for adding decoration to paper and card (posterboard).

Masking tape
Masking tape is made from paper and is easy to remove after it has been stuck down.

Measuring tape
You sometimes need this for measuring fabric.

Natural objects
These include twigs, acorns and fir cones, which can be picked up in parks and during country walks. Always show an adult what you have found before you use it, to make sure that it is safe.

Paintbrushes
Paintbrushes come in a variety of sizes. Use a medium-thick brush for general painting and for applying glue. Use fine brushes to paint more detailed designs.

Paints
These must be non-toxic. Poster paints are good because they come in lots of lovely colours.

Palette
A palette is a useful container for paint. If you don't have one, use an old saucer or carton.

Paper clips
Paper clips may be plain or patterned and come in lots of sizes. They are meant for holding pieces of paper together, but some are very colourful and attractive and can be used as decoration as well.

Paper glue
This must be non-toxic and comes in liquid or a solid stick.

Pencils
A soft pencil is useful for making tracings and transferring them to card (posterboard) and paper.

PVA (white) glue
This must be non-toxic. PVA (white) glue is very sticky and is good for gluing cardboard and fabric. It can also be mixed with poster paints to make them stick to plastic surfaces. It is useful as a varnish and, if you dilute it, you can use it to make papier-mâché.

Rubber bands
These come in lots of colours and different lengths.

Ruler
A ruler is useful for measuring and drawing straight lines.

Scissors
These should be specially for children with rounded blades.

Silver and coloured foil
Silver foil comes on long rolls and is good for making jewellery. Coloured foil covers sweets (candy) and biscuits (cookies).

Sticky tape
This can be used for sticking paper, card (posterboard) and foil.

Strong glue
This must be non-toxic and solvent-free. Strong glue is useful for sticking heavy cardboard and holding awkward joints together.

coloured sticky-paper dots

coloured foil

sweet (candy) wrappers

corks

10

Recycling Fun

Printing with Foam Rubber Stamps

Simple stamps can be cut from sheets of thin foam rubber and stuck onto cardboard bases. Use these recycled stamps to make your own special greetings cards, or even to decorate your walls.

1 To make the stamps, cut several rectangles of heavy cardboard measuring 5 x 6 cm (2 x 2¼ in). Cut an equal number of smaller rectangles measuring 1.5 x 6 cm (⅝ x 2¼ in) to form the handles. Stick the handles to the tops of the bases with strong glue.

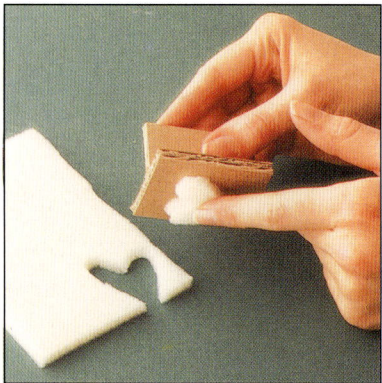

2 Draw the stamp motif onto foam rubber. Cut it out with scissors and glue it to the cardboard base. Leave aside to dry thoroughly.

3 Mix paint with water to a stiff consistency. Gently dip the stamp in the paint and then press it onto medium-weight paper or thin card (posterboard).

Painting on Plastic

Sometimes you may want to paint plastic bottles and yogurt cartons but ordinary poster paint will not stick to plastic. However, if you add glue to the paint it will become sticky and will cover the plastic well.

1 Put some ordinary poster paint into a palette or small dish.

2 Pour in a little PVA (white) glue. Carefully mix the paint and the glue, until they are thoroughly mixed together.

3 Wash your plastic bottle in warm soapy water and dry thoroughly. Apply the paint mixture over the surface of the bottle, taking care to spread the paint smoothly. Wash your brush thoroughly, as soon as you have finished.

RECYCLING FUN

Flattening and Cutting Up a Box

Cardboard can be used for papier-mâché frames among other things. Old boxes are the best source, and you can flatten them out easily.

1 Remove any tape that is holding the box together and press it flat.

2 Cut the box into pieces, ready for use in your various projects.

Removing a Label From a Bottle

Plastic bottles can be used for all kinds of projects. You will need to wash them thoroughly.

1 Fill a washing-up bowl with warm soapy water.

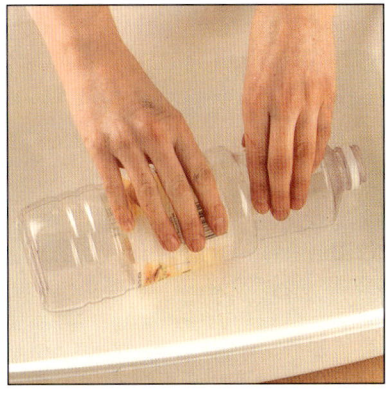

2 Soak the bottle in the water for approximately 10 minutes.

Re-using Foil Wrappers

Coloured foil is great for decorations, and you don't have to buy it specially. Save old sweet (candy) wrappers and cases made of pretty colours, and cut them into different shapes.

1 Flatten the wrappers and cases and smooth them out. Cut them up for use in your projects.

3 Peel the label off the bottle. If the label is still sticking to the bottle, soak it in the water for a little longer.

RECYCLING FUN

Junk Robot

All you need to make this fabulous robot is a washing-powder box, a plastic cup, some washing line, washing-up sponges and toilet-roll tubes. Its features and control panel are added with various bits and pieces, such as bottle tops, yogurt pots and a safety pin, so keep an eye on the kitchen bin for useful robot parts!

RECYCLING TIP
Silver foil can be used more than once. If it has been used for food wash it carefully with soapy water and a sponge and leave it to dry.

YOU WILL NEED
PVA (white) glue
4 toilet-roll tubes
washing line
rubber bands
plastic cup
silver foil
scissors
sticky tape
washing-powder box
washing-up sponges
2 small yogurt pots
2 thick sponge scourers
3 round plastic scourers
bottle caps and other
 plastic bits and pieces
foil pie dishes (pans)
2 metal washers
safety pin

toilet-roll tubes

washing-up sponge

foil dishes (pans)

plastic scourer

sticky tape

1 Put a little glue on the tops and bottoms of the toilet-roll tubes. Wrap washing line around the tubes. Hold it in place with rubber bands while the glue dries. Do the same to the plastic cup.

2 Cut a piece of silver foil that is large enough to cover the washing-powder box. Loosely crumple the foil, to give it a crinkly surface, and tape it around the box.

3 Cut two circles from washing-up sponge and glue them to one end of two of the toilet-roll tubes. Glue a small yogurt pot to the other end of both tubes to make the robot's arms.

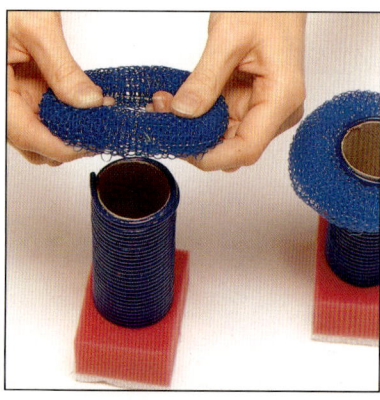

4 To make the robot's legs, glue a thick scourer to one end of the two remaining toilet-roll tubes. Stretch a round plastic scourer over each end of the tubes.

5 Glue bottle caps, foil dishes and other bits and pieces to the front of the box to make the controls. Glue two metal washers and a safety pin to the front of the plastic cup to make the face.

6 Glue the cup to the top of the box and put a plastic scourer over it to make the neck. Glue the legs to the bottom and one arm to each side; hold in place with rubber bands until the glue dries.

14

Peg Cowboys

These cowboys are ready to ride the range on their dappled horses. They are made from old-fashioned wooden pegs (clothespins) and look very smart in their gingham shirts and spotted neckerchiefs. The horses are made from thin card (posterboard) and they can stand upright.

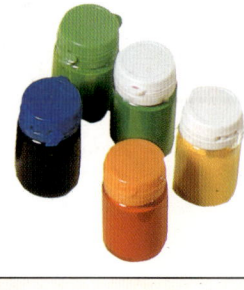

YOU WILL NEED
white, dark blue and red
   poster paints
paintbrushes
paint-mixing container
wooden clothes pegs (clothespins)
scissors
yellow, red and white
   paper scraps
non-toxic strong glue
tracing paper
pencil
thin white card (posterboard)
felt-tipped pens

1 Paint the top of a peg (clothespin) white. Paint the bottom half dark blue to make the cowboy's jeans.

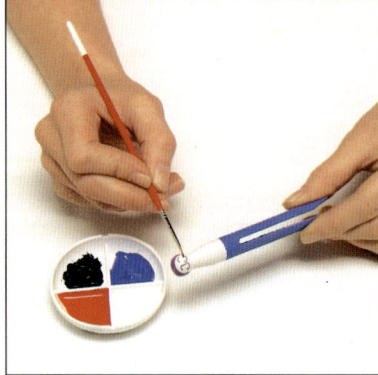

2 When the first coat of paint has dried, add details, such as the cowboy's face and the checks on his shirt, using poster paints.

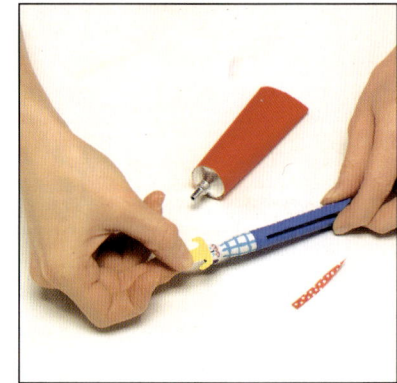

3 Cut a hat from yellow paper. Fold up the edges and then glue the hat to the front of the cowboy's head. Cut a neckerchief from red paper and add spots with white paint. Glue the neckerchief around the cowboy's neck.

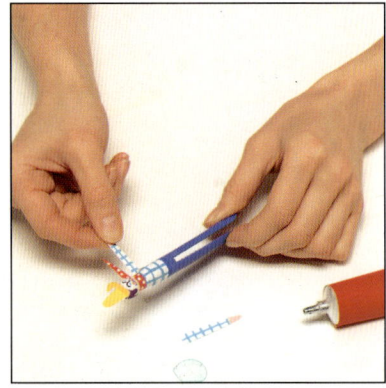

4 Cut two strips of white paper to make the cowboy's arms. Paint a hand at the end of each strip and add checks. Glue the arms to the cowboy's sides.

5 Trace the horse templates from the back of the book. Lay the tracings face-down on thin white card (posterboard) and draw over the lines to transfer them. Cut out all the pieces.

6 Using felt-tipped pens, draw in the horse's face and its markings. Push the body into the slots in its legs. Sit the cowboy on his horse.

RECYCLING FUN

Snake Sock Puppets

One good way to give your old socks a new lease of life is to make them into puppets. These snakes are decorated with brightly coloured felt. Once you've made a snake, why not make some other characters to keep it company?

YOU WILL NEED
scraps of coloured felt
scissors
non-toxic strong glue
1 sock

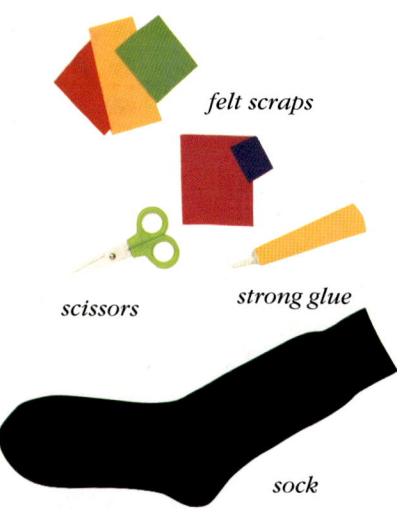

felt scraps

scissors *strong glue*

sock

1 To make the snake's eyes, cut two circles of felt. Cut two smaller circles of a different colour and glue them to the middle of the larger circles.

2 Glue the snake's eyes in position at the top of the sock.

3 Cut diamonds and strips of felt in various colours. Glue the strips at equal distances along the length of the sock. Glue the diamonds between the strips.

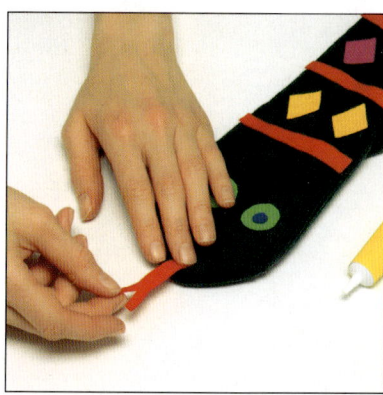

4 Cut a forked tongue from red felt. Glue the tongue to the top of the toe of the sock, in the centre. Allow the glue to dry thoroughly before you play with your sock puppet.

RECYCLING FUN

Wooden Spoon Puppets

You can make puppets from all sorts of things, but wooden spoons are especially good because they are just the right shape to make a head and a body. Gather a piece of fabric to hide the spoon handle, paint a face at the top and away you go!

YOU WILL NEED
wooden spoon
pink, blue, brown and yellow poster paints
paintbrush
paint-mixing container
pencil
ruler
fabric
scissors
darning needle
matching thread
non-toxic strong glue
satin ribbon scrap
gold and coloured foil

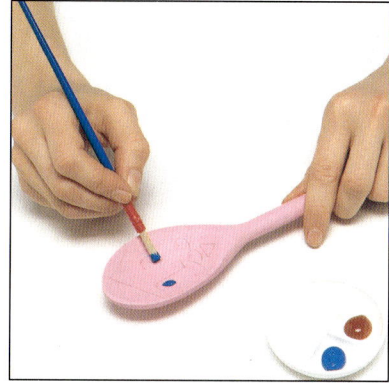

1 Paint the top half of the wooden spoon pink and leave it to dry. Draw the puppet's eyes, nose, mouth and hair in pencil on the spoon and then fill in its features using poster paints.

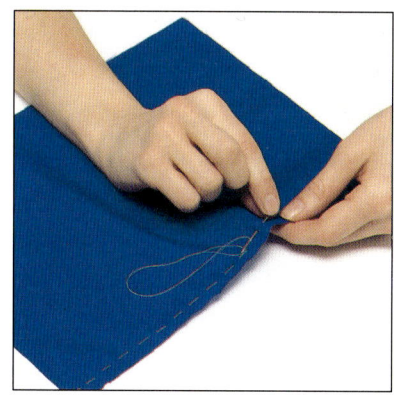

2 Cut a piece of fabric as long as the spoon handle and 30 cm (12 in) wide. Sew two lines of running stitches along the top edge of the fabric and pull the threads tight to gather the material. Knot the ends of the threads together.

3 Glue the gathered edge of the fabric around the spoon handle, below the puppet's face. Glue a short scrap of satin ribbon around the puppet's neck, to cover the top of the gathered fabric.

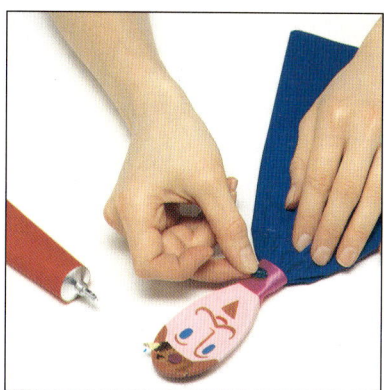

4 Cut a crown from gold foil and glue it to the top of the head. Cut two circles of coloured foil and glue one to the middle of the crown and one at the centre of the satin ribbon, as 'jewels'.

Catch-the-ball Game

Test your skill with this bat-and-ball game. It takes quite a lot of practice to catch the ball in the cup but it's good fun while you are learning! Use a plastic bottle with a long neck, because this makes a better handle to hold on to.

YOU WILL NEED
coloured tissue paper
PVA (white) glue
mixing bowl
clear plastic bottle
scissors
yogurt pot
non-toxic strong glue
thin coloured cord

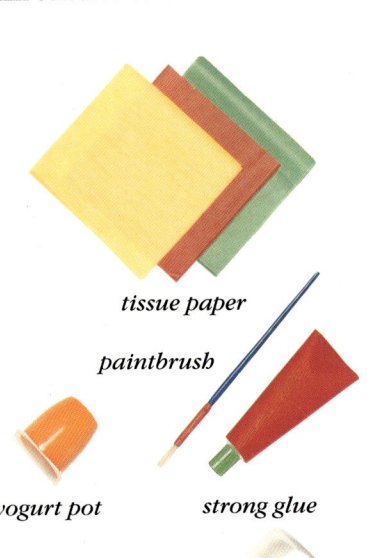

tissue paper
paintbrush
yogurt pot
strong glue
cord
plastic bottle

1 Take two sheets of different coloured tissue paper and tear them into strips and circles.

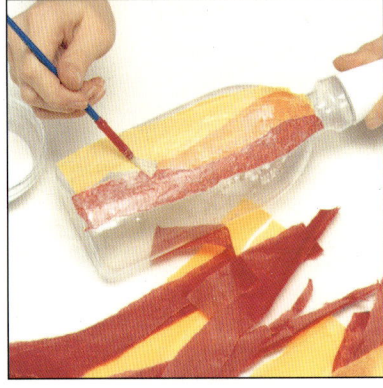

2 Mix some PVA (white) glue with a little water. Coat each strip of tissue paper with glue. Cover the bottle with the paper. Add some circles of paper on top of the strips. Leave to dry thoroughly.

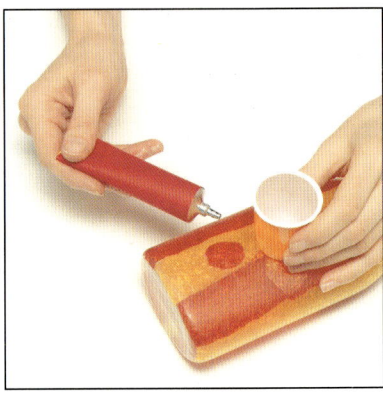

3 Carefully cut the corners from the top of the yogurt pot. Glue the pot to the centre of the bottle.

4 Roll a sheet of tissue paper tightly into a small ball. It should be small enough to fit inside the yogurt pot.

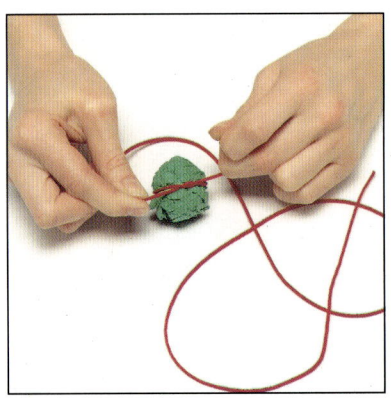

5 Cut a long piece of coloured cord. Tie one end of the cord tightly around the ball of tissue paper.

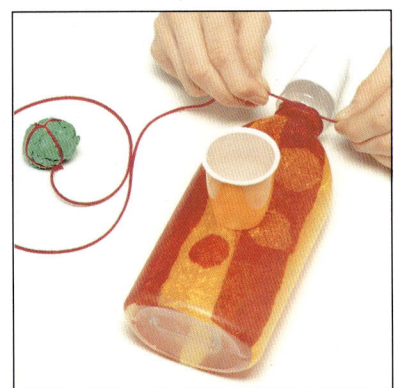

6 Tie the other end of the thin coloured cord around the end of the neck of the bottle.

RECYCLING FUN

Shaker

This shaker is filled with beads and buttons, but you can use rice or dried beans.

YOU WILL NEED
clear plastic bottle, with cap
small beads and buttons
large and small coloured
    sticky-paper dots
non-toxic strong glue

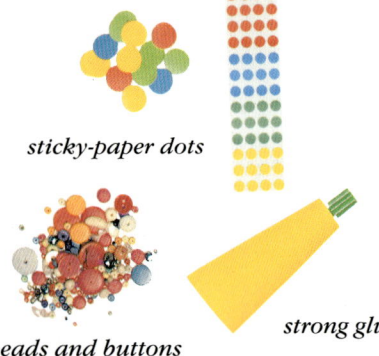

sticky-paper dots

beads and buttons   *strong glue*

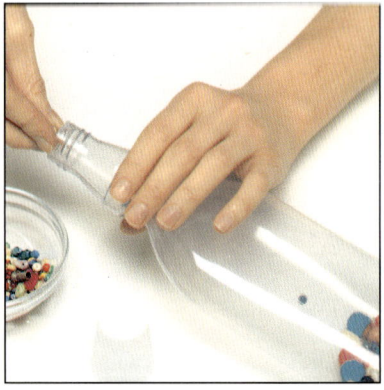

1 Wash and carefully dry the bottle. It should be dry inside as well. Pour a mixture of small beads and buttons into the bottle. A couple of handfuls will make a good noise.

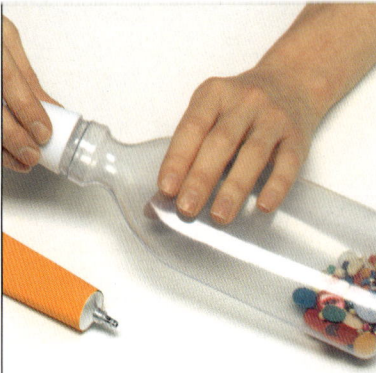

2 Spread a line of glue around the inside of the bottle top. Screw the top back onto the bottle. Stick large coloured sticky-paper dots to the outside to make a bright and decorative pattern.

3 Stick a row of small coloured sticky-paper dots around the lower edge of the bottle top to make a pattern.

Tambourine

Two foil pie dishes (pans) can quickly and easily become a shiny tambourine.

YOU WILL NEED
ruler
thin satin ribbon
scissors
small bells
sticky tape
2 foil pie dishes (pans)
non-toxic strong glue

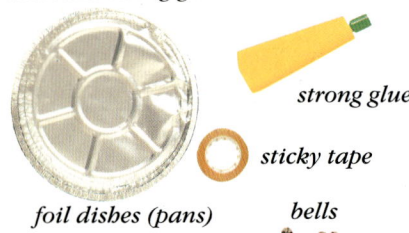

foil dishes (pans)   *strong glue*   *sticky tape*   *bells*

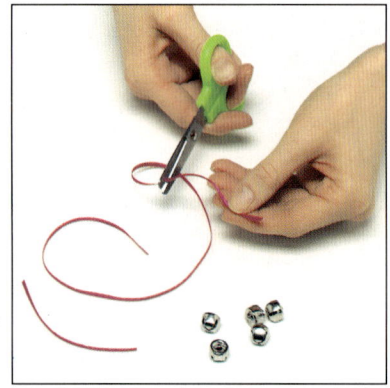

1 Cut 10 cm (4 in) lengths of ribbon, and tie a bell to each piece.

2 Tape the bells around the inside edge of one of the foil dishes (pans), making sure to space them evenly.

3 Spread glue around the rim of the second foil dish. Glue the two dishes together, rim to rim, covering the ends of the ribbons. Leave the glue to dry.

Drum

Drums are good fun to play and this one is portable, so you can play it wherever you are. The drum is made from an old plastic ice-cream tub and the drumsticks are knitting needles, with wooden beads on the ends.

YOU WILL NEED
ice-cream tub, with lid
yellow poster paint
paintbrush
paint-mixing container
PVA (white) glue
paper glue
scissors
coloured paper
thick coloured cord
dried rice
non-toxic strong glue
2 large wooden beads
2 knitting needles

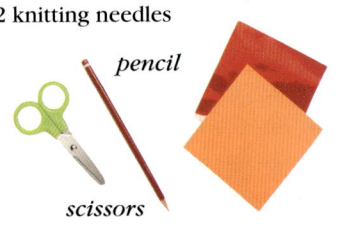

1 Paint the outside of the ice-cream tub with bright poster paint mixed with a little PVA (white) glue. When the paint is dry, cut out squares of red paper and glue them around the tub.

2 Ask an adult to punch a hole in both sides of the tub. Cut a length of thick coloured cord and poke the ends through the holes. Tie a double knot in each end of the cord.

3 Put a handful of dried rice inside the tub and replace the lid. The rice will make a swishing sound when you beat the drum.

4 Cut a circle of red paper and glue it to the top of the lid of the drum.

5 Cut diamonds of coloured paper. Glue one on top of each coloured square of paper around the sides of the drum and one to the top of the lid.

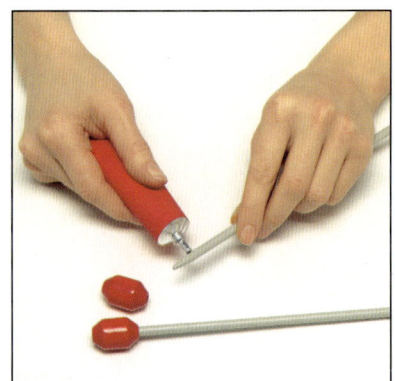

6 To make the drumsticks, use the strong glue to attach a large wooden bead to the end of each knitting needle. Let the glue dry thoroughly before you play your drum.

RECYCLING FUN

Pom-pom Hat

Beat the cold with this fun pom-pom hat. It's made by cutting down an old pair of wool tights. Leftover balls of wool are used to make two pom-poms to decorate the top of the hat. It looks so stylish that no one will be able to guess what it is made from.

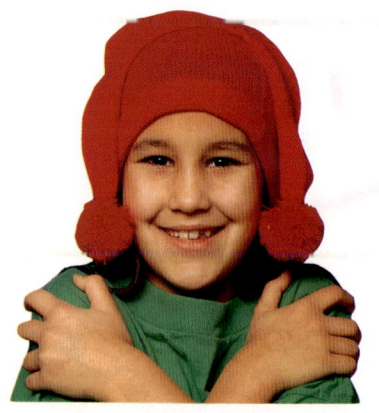

YOU WILL NEED
tape measure
pair of wool tights
scissors
darning needle
thin knitting wool (yarn)
pencil
pair of compasses
thin cardboard
knitting-wool oddments

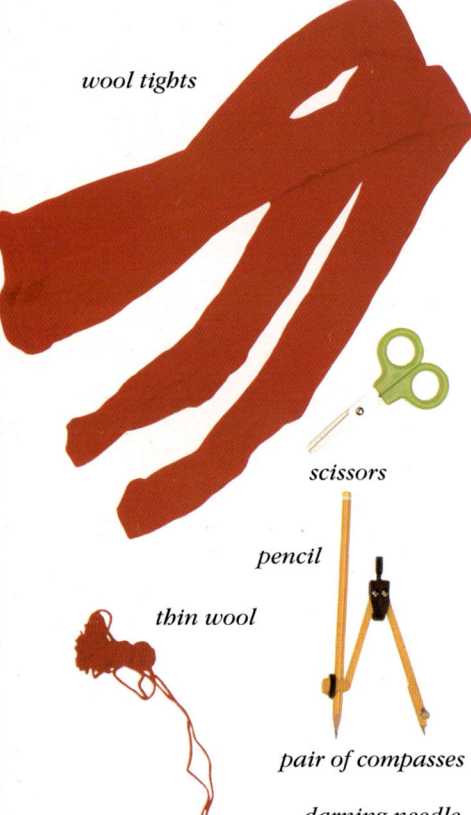

wool tights

scissors

pencil

thin wool

pair of compasses

darning needle

1 Measure 15 cm (6 in) down from the top of each leg of the tights. Cut off the legs at this point and discard them.

2 Thread the needle with the wool. Sew across the top of the cut ends, using small running stitches. Pull the stitching tight. Sew two more stitches to keep the ends gathered. Cut the thread.

3 Draw two identical circles with the pencil and pair of compasses on the cardboard. Draw smaller circles inside. Cut out the larger circles. Ask an adult to help you to cut out the smaller ones.

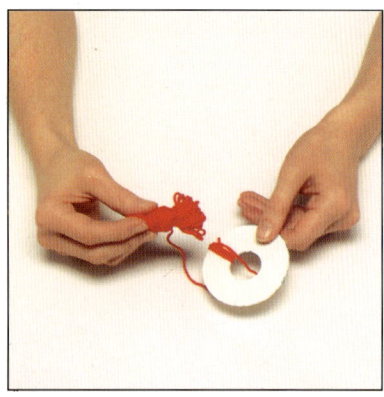

4 Place the circles together. Tie the end of a length of wool around the circles. Wrap the wool around and around the circles, passing it through the central hole, until the hole is filled in.

5 Snip through the wool at the edge of the circles. Pull the circles slightly apart and tie a short piece of wool around the centre of the wool between the circles, to keep it all together. Pull the circles off and trim any uneven wool.

6 Make a second pom-pom, then sew one to the end of each gathered leg. To wear the hat, roll up the waistband a couple of times to make a brim, and tie the legs loosely together.

26

RECYCLING FUN

Squeezy Bottle Dog Book-ends

These book-ends are made by covering two squeezy bottles with small pieces of papier-mâché and then painting them. The legs are made from corks, and the ears and tails are cut from scraps of thin card (posterboard).

YOU WILL NEED
2 squeezy bottles
funnel
dried rice
masking tape
newspaper
diluted PVA (white) glue
8 corks
white, red, yellow, brown and black poster paints
paintbrushes
paint-mixing container
pencil
thin white card (posterboard)
scissors
strong non-toxic glue

1 Wash and dry the squeezy bottles. Put a funnel in the top of each bottle and half-fill it with rice. Seal the top of each bottle with a strip of masking tape.

2 Tear the newspaper into strips. Dip each strip in the PVA (white) glue and cover the bottles completely with two layers of paper. Leave the bottles to dry.

3 With PVA (white) glue, stick four corks to one side of each squeezy bottle to make the legs. Leave the book-ends to dry thoroughly.

4 Paint the book-ends white. You may have to use two coats of paint to cover up the newsprint completely.

5 Draw in the dogs' faces, collars and markings with the pencil. Decorate the dogs using poster paints.

6 Draw four ears and two tails on the card (posterboard) and cut out. Bend back the edges of each shape and glue ears and a tail onto each dog, using the strong glue.

Nail Chimes

Make beautiful music with these nifty nail chimes. They are suspended from a cardboard tube and they make a lovely, clear, ringing sound when you strike them. You will need to find bolts in various sizes, so that your chimes make different notes.

YOU WILL NEED
scissors
coloured paper
cardboard tube
paper glue
coloured sticky-paper dots
strong coloured cord
bolts of various sizes
1 long bolt

paper

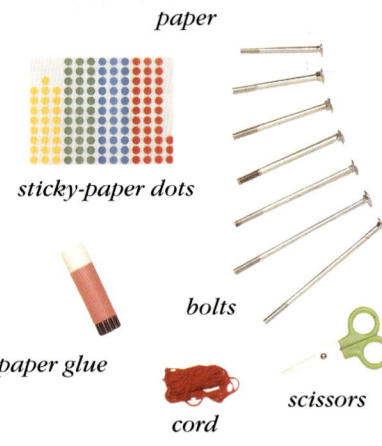
sticky-paper dots
paper glue
bolts
scissors
cord
cardboard tube

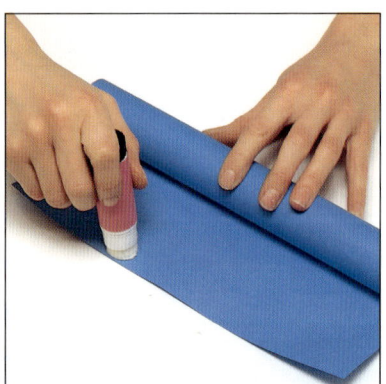

1 Cut a rectangle of coloured paper as long as the cardboard tube and wide enough to fit around it. Stick the paper to the tube.

2 Stick a row of sticky-paper dots around each end of the cardboard tube, as decoration.

3 Cut a long length of coloured cord. It must be strong enough to bear the weight of all the bolts.

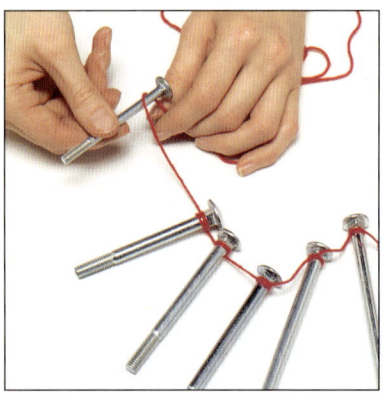

4 Tie the length of cord around the head of each bolt. Make sure that the bolts are evenly spaced along the cord.

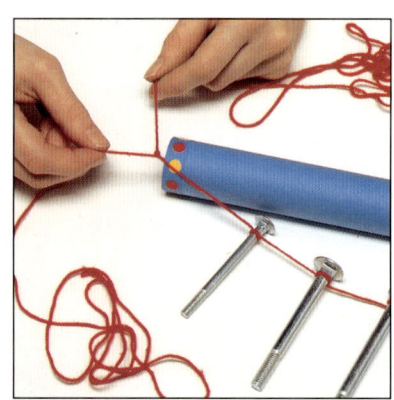

5 Thread the free ends of the coloured cord through the cardboard tube. Tie them together at one end.

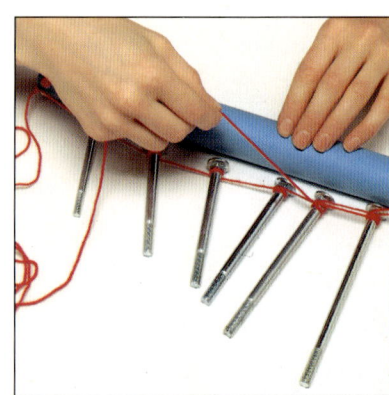

6 Loop one of the cords two or three times around the head of each bolt again, then pass it back through the tube. Tie the ends tightly together. Play the chimes using the long bolt.

Groovy Guitar

Make yourself a groovy, twanging guitar from a cardboard tube and a washing-powder box. The strings are made from elastic bands and they rest on half a toilet-roll tube, which gives them quite loud different sounds.

Recycling Tip
You could cover the guitar with silver foil if you have some spare.

YOU WILL NEED
washing-powder box
felt-tipped pen
scissors
long cardboard tube
brown-paper tape
toilet-roll tube
non-toxic strong glue
yellow and orange poster paints
paintbrush
paint-mixing container
6 rubber bands
5 small cotton reels (spools)
silver foil
thick cord

toilet-roll tube

brown-paper tape

silver foil

strong glue

poster paints

paintbrush

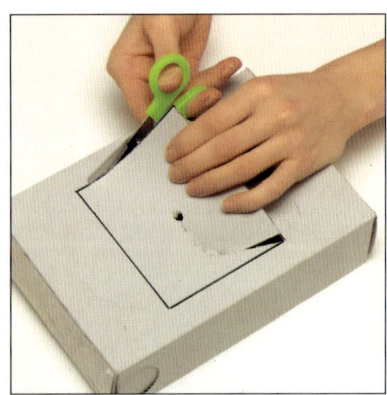

1 Draw a square on the front of the washing-powder box. Ask an adult to help you to cut the square out of the box.

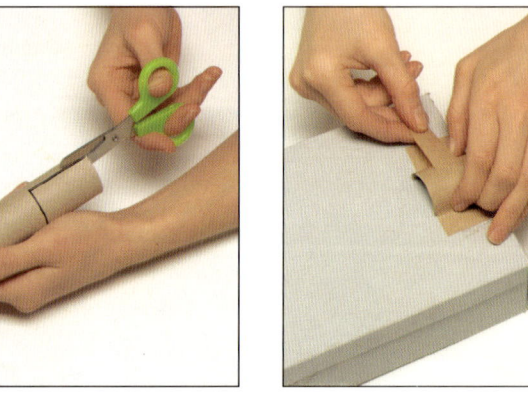

2 Draw a rectangle on one end of the cardboard tube. Ask an adult to help you cut the shape out of the tube, so that it will fit on the end of the box.

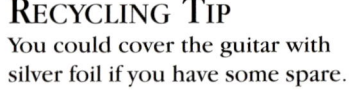

3 Put the tube on the end of the box and tape it in place with brown-paper tape to make the neck of the guitar.

4 Cut a toilet-roll tube in half. Glue the half-tube below the hole in the front of the guitar.

5 When the brown-paper tape and glue have dried, paint the guitar, using poster paints. Leave the guitar to dry thoroughly before stringing.

RECYCLING FUN

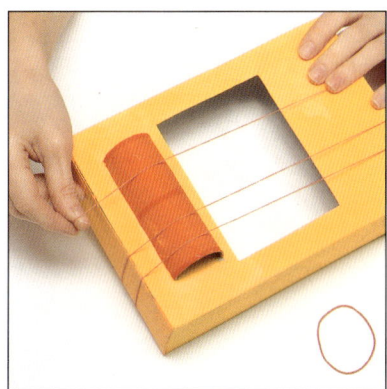

6 Stretch six rubber bands around the body of the guitar. Rest the rubber bands on the half toilet-roll as this will make them louder.

7 Cover five small cotton reels (spools) with silver foil, then glue four reels to the neck of the guitar to make pegs. Glue the other reel to the end of the guitar. Tie a length of cord from the neck of the guitar to the reel at the base of the guitar to make a strap.

RECYCLING FUN

Storage Chest

This small storage chest is great for keeping little treasures safe. It is made from large, empty matchboxes and is covered with scraps of sticky-backed plastic. You can make the chest as large as you want – just keep adding more matchboxes. You can also use large and small matchboxes, so you have different-size compartments.

RECYCLING TIP
This is an ideal storage place for those buttons, beads, pins and paper clips that all good recyclers collect and keep.

YOU WILL NEED
green and red sticky-backed plastic
scissors
6 large matchboxes
non-toxic strong glue
tracing paper
pencil
thin card (posterboard)
6 coloured plastic beads

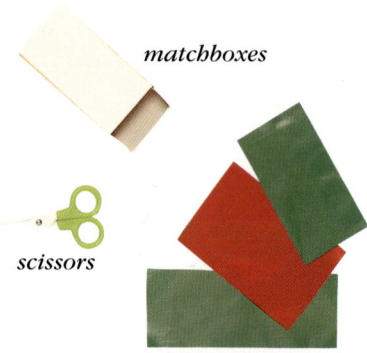

matchboxes
scissors
sticky-backed plastic
strong glue
pencil
plastic beads

1 Cut three green and three red pieces of sticky-backed plastic the same width and long enough to fit around a matchbox. Glue them on.

2 Cut six thin strips of red and six of green sticky-backed plastic. Glue them to the front and back of the box trays: red in green boxes and green in red boxes.

3 Spread glue along the long side of one green box and glue it to a red box. Repeat so that you have three rows of two boxes.

4 When the glue has dried, glue the three rows of boxes on top of each other to make the storage chest. Make sure that the edges of the boxes line up.

5 Trace the template at the back of the book. Lay it face-down on a piece of card (posterboard), draw over the lines to transfer it and cut out. Cover with sticky-backed plastic and trim.

6 Cut out a small red heart and stick it to the front of the card (posterboard). Bend back the base and glue it to the top of the chest. Glue a bead to the front of each tray for handles.

RECYCLING FUN

Nature Box

If you go for an autumn walk in the countryside or a park you will probably find some twigs, seed pods, fir cones and so on, which make lovely decorations. This plain cardboard box is decorated with rows of acorns, seed pods and small and large fir cones have been added to make it really attractive. Always ask an adult to look at what you have found to see that it is safe. Carefully wash everything before you use it.

YOU WILL NEED
green poster paint
paintbrush
paint-mixing container
small, round cardboard box, with lid
acorns, fir cones and seed pods
non-toxic strong glue

1 Paint the lid and base of the cardboard box with poster paint and leave it to dry thoroughly.

2 Arrange a row of acorns around the edge of the lid of the box and glue them in position.

3 Glue a large fir cone to the middle of the lid. Glue small fir cones to the top of the lid, between the acorns and the large fir cone.

4 Glue a row of seed pods at equal distances around the sides of the box. Let the glue dry thoroughly before you use your box.

36

RECYCLING FUN

Sponge-flower Hairband

Washing-up sponges come in such pretty colours that it seems a pity not to use them in new ways. Here, pink, yellow and green sponges have been used to make a flower to decorate and brighten up a plain hairband.

YOU WILL NEED
tracing paper
pencil
thin card (posterboard)
scissors
yellow, pink and green
　washing-up sponges
thin black felt-tipped pen
darning needle
pink, yellow and green or
　blue threads
hairband

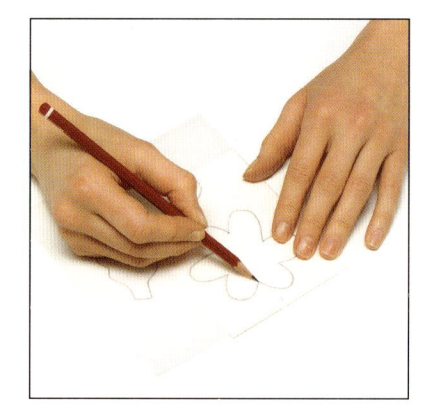

washing-up sponges

hairband

threads

scissors

felt-tipped pen

1 Trace the flower patterns from the back of the book. Lay the tracings face-down on the card (posterboard) and draw over the lines again. Cut out the shapes to make templates.

2 Place the flower template on the yellow sponge, the flower centre on the pink sponge and the leaves on the green sponge. Draw around the templates with the felt-tipped pen. Cut out the shapes.

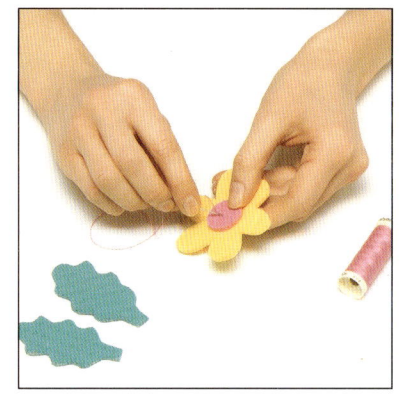

3 Place the pink flower centre in the middle of the flower. Sew the centre to the flower with three or four small stitches, using pink thread.

4 Place the leaves, pointing outwards, on the front of the hairband. Sew the leaves to the hairband with small stitches in blue or green thread. Lay the flower on top of the leaves, and sew its centre and edges to the band with yellow thread.

Straw Mobile

Drinking straws come in wonderful bright colours and you can use them to make lots of different projects. This mobile is made from pieces of straw threaded together.

YOU WILL NEED
scissors
coloured drinking straws
ruler
coloured cotton cord
non-toxic strong glue
large buttons
wooden beads

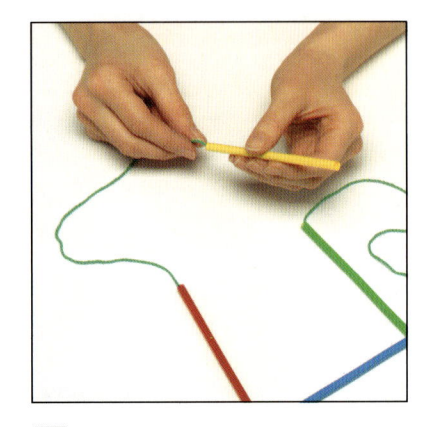

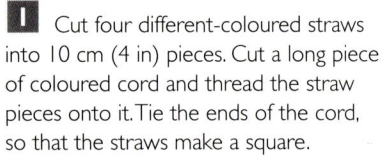

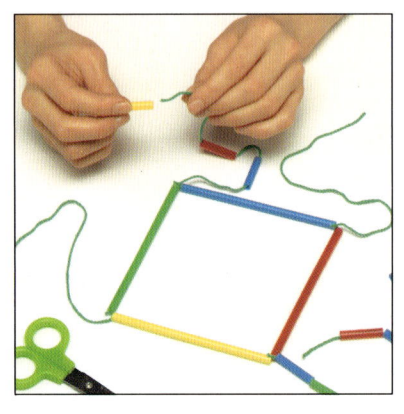

beads
buttons
scissors
drinking straws
cord
strong glue

1 Cut four different-coloured straws into 10 cm (4 in) pieces. Cut a long piece of coloured cord and thread the straw pieces onto it. Tie the ends of the cord, so that the straws make a square.

2 Cut more straws into 2.5 cm (1 in) lengths. Tie a length of coloured cord at each corner of the straw square. Thread the pieces of straw onto the cotton.

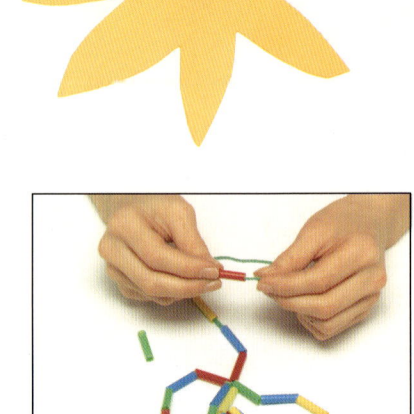

3 Tie the pieces of cotton together at the top. Tie another length of cord to the top of the mobile and thread some more short lengths of straw onto it.

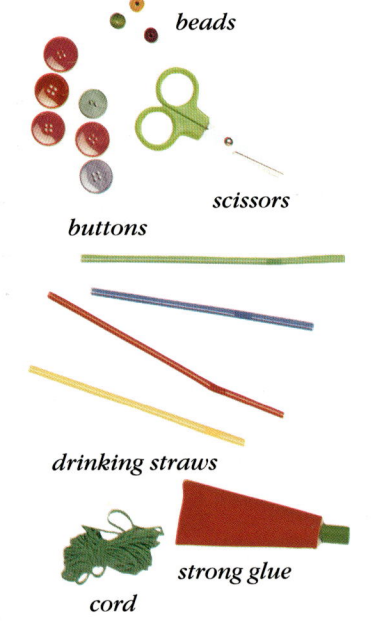

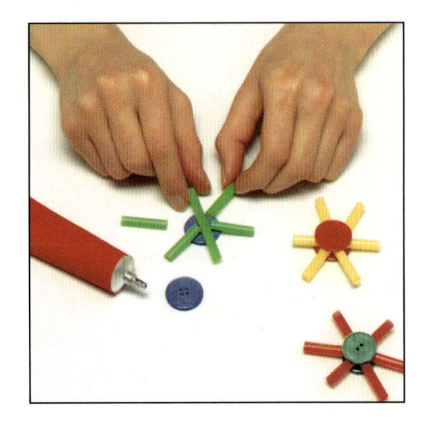

4 Cut four 2.5 cm (1 in) pieces and one 5 cm (2 in) piece of the same coloured straw. Glue the longer piece of straw to the back of a large button. Glue two short pieces of straw on each side of the long piece. Glue another button on top to make a star. Make four more stars in different colours.

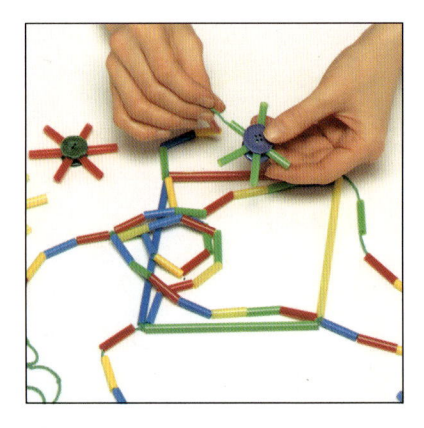

5 Cut four different lengths of coloured cord and tie one to each corner of the square, so that they hang down. Cut 2.5 cm (1 in) lengths of straw and thread them onto the cotton. Thread a star onto the end of each cord and one on the top of the mobile.

6 Thread a wooden bead on the end of each piece of cord, to keep the stars in place. Knot the ends of the four cords that hang down and trim the ends. Leave a long cord at the top of the mobile to hang it up.

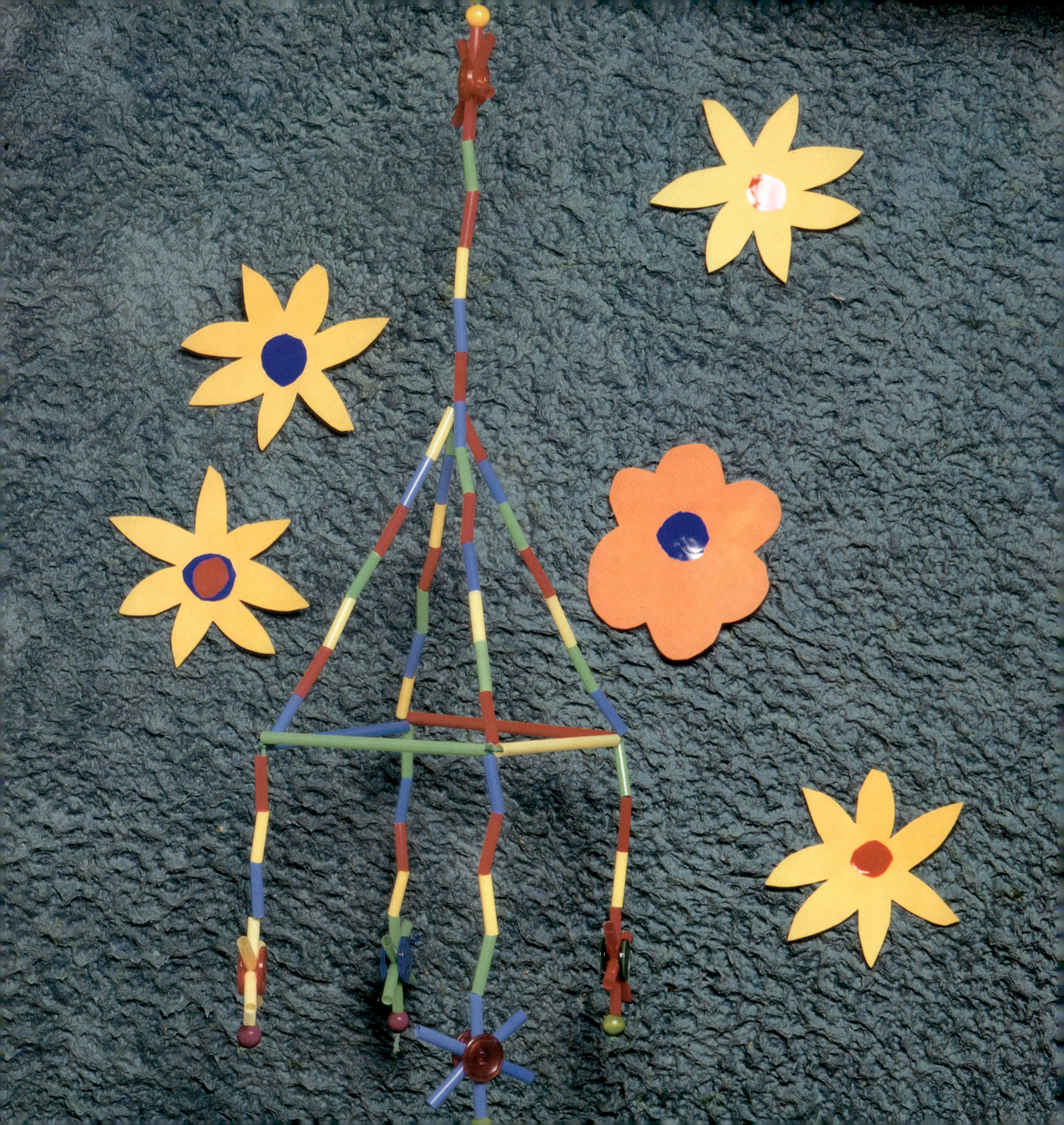

Paper Clip Christmas Decorations

These shiny Christmas decorations will add a sparkle to your Christmas tree. Decorate them with scraps of bright foil from sweet (candy) wrappers, and sandwich paper clips between them to make the decorations look like icicles.

YOU WILL NEED
pencil
pair of compasses
thin card (posterboard)
scissors
silver and coloured foil
non-toxic strong glue
silver paper clips
thin silver elastic

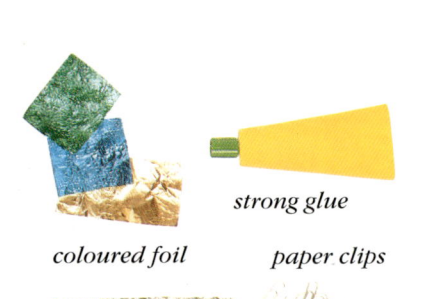

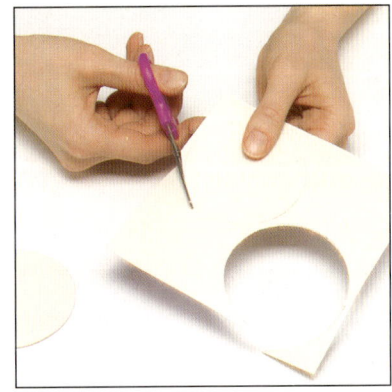

coloured foil   *strong glue*

silver foil   *paper clips*   *silver elastic*

scissors

1 Using a pencil and a pair of compasses, draw two circles exactly the same size on the card (posterboard). Cut them out.

2 Cut two squares of silver foil about 4 cm (1½ in) bigger all the way around than the circles of card (posterboard). Place a circle in the middle of each piece of foil. Wrap the edges of the silver foil over the card (posterboard).

3 Cut a circle of coloured foil and snip small triangles from its edges to make a 'star' shape. Glue the star to the front of one of the card (posterboard) circles. Cut two circles from coloured foil and glue them to the middle of the star.

4 Glue a row of paper clips to the back of the other circle. Glue the two circles together. Tie a length of thin silver elastic to the top of the decoration to hang it from the tree.

Pasta-shape Christmas Tree Decorations

These Christmas tree decorations are made from plastic pudding cartons. They are painted in bright colours and then decorated with pieces of dried pasta, which comes in lots of lovely shapes and sizes. Mix the paint with PVA (white) glue first, so that it sticks to the plastic.

YOU WILL NEED
2 plastic pudding cartons
PVA (white) glue
green, pink and gold
  poster paints
paintbrush
dried pasta shapes
2 gold pipe-cleaners
non-toxic strong glue

strong glue

poster paint

paintbrush

gold pipe-cleaner

dried pasta shapes

1 Wash and dry the cartons. Mix a little glue with green poster paint and paint one carton. Repeat with pink paint and the second carton. When dry, paint the top and bottom edges gold.

2 Paint the pasta shapes you have chosen with gold poster paint. Leave them to dry thoroughly.

3 Ask an adult to help you to make a hole in the top of the cartons. Push both ends of the pipe-cleaners through the holes. On the inside of the cartons, bend the ends of the pipe-cleaners outwards to keep them in place.

4 Spread a little glue around the edge of each pasta shape. Glue the shapes around the sides of the cartons. Thread a pasta shape over the top of each pipe-cleaner and glue it to the top of the decoration.

RECYCLING FUN

Jamjar Lid Badges

Next time you finish a jar of jam, keep the lid to make a fun badge. Cover the lids in silver foil and then cut shapes from scraps of bright foil, saved from sweet (candy) wrappers. You can buy special badge pins but a safety pin is fine.

YOU WILL NEED
scissors
silver foil
non-toxic strong glue
jamjar lid
scraps of gold and coloured foil
safety pin
sticky tape

safety pin

sticky tape

foil scraps

jamjar lid   *silver foil*

strong glue

scissors

1 Cut a square of silver foil that is about 4 cm (1½ in) larger all the way round than the jamjar lid. Spread glue on the back of the lid and then wrap it in the foil. Squash the foil down on the inside of the lid.

2 Cut a circle of gold foil and glue it to the inside of the lid. Cut shapes from scraps of coloured foil and glue them on top of the gold circle.

3 As a change, snip the edges of the gold foil circle to make a 'star'.

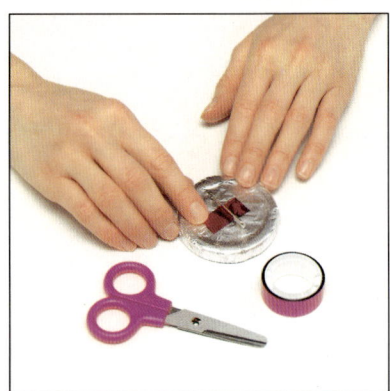

4 Turn the badge over and put a safety pin in the centre. Tape the pin in place to make a fastener.

RECYCLING FUN

Squeezy Bottle Bracelets

Sections of a squeezy bottle are perfect for making bracelets and bangles, and you can decorate them in lots of different ways. Scraps of coloured foil saved from sweet (candy) wrappers make really bright, cheerful stripes and you can also roll the foil to make glittery fake jewels.

YOU WILL NEED
squeezy bottle
scissors
sticky tape
silver foil
coloured foil scraps
non-toxic strong glue

silver foil

scissors

foil scraps

strong glue

squeezy bottle

1 Wash and dry an empty squeezy bottle. Ask an adult to help you to cut a 2.5 cm (1 in) wide section from the bottle that is long enough to go round your wrist comfortably. Join the ends of the section together, using sticky tape, to make a bracelet.

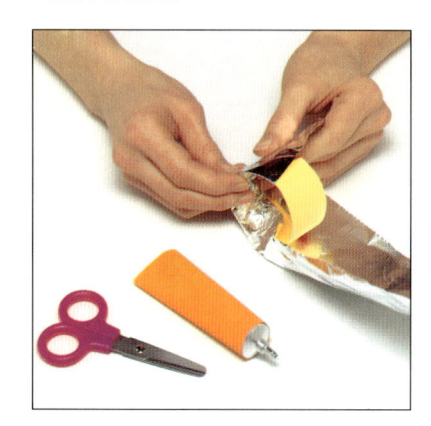

2 Cut a piece of silver foil about twice the width of the bracelet. Place the bracelet on the foil and press the foil around the bracelet to cover it.

3 Smooth the scraps of coloured foil with your fingers. Cut several strips of foil long enough to fit around the bracelet. Glue the strips around the bracelet at equal distances.

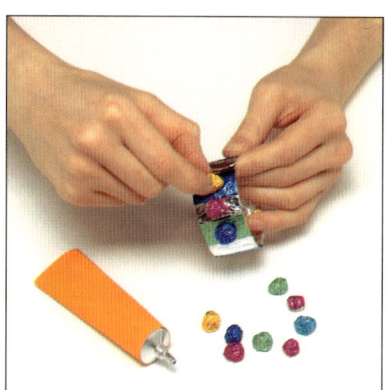

4 Roll more scraps of different-coloured foil into small beads and glue them around the outside of the bracelet to make 'jewels'.

43

RECYCLING FUN

Paper Bag Animal Masks

Plain paper bags are great for making masks quickly and easily. You can cut them into all sorts of different shapes and use felt-tipped pens to add exciting decoration. Collect brown-paper carrier bags to make masks too – they're stronger than paper bags and will last longer.

YOU WILL NEED
pencil
2 large paper bags
scissors
paper glue
orange, red and black felt-tipped pens

felt-tipped pens

paper bag

pencil

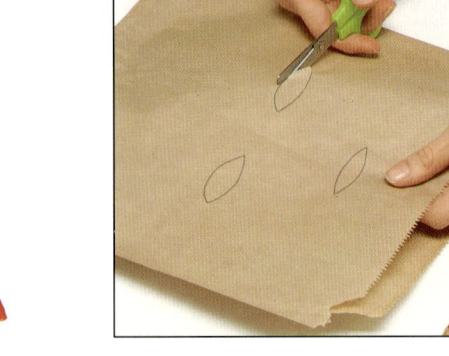

scissors

paper glue

1 Draw three holes on the front of one paper bag, for your eyes and mouth. Cut out the holes.

2 Draw two ears along the top edge of the bag and cut them out. Glue the top edges of the bag together again.

3 Draw the animal's face on the front of the bag, using felt-tipped pens. Draw red lines around the eyes so that they stand out strongly.

4 Cut three wide strips from another paper bag. Make long cuts along one long edge of each strip. Glue the uncut edges of the strips to the sides and top of the animal's head to make a mane.

44

RECYCLING FUN

Foil Robot

This robot is made from cotton reels (spools) and foil pie dishes (pans). Cotton reels (spools) are great because the holes in the middle mean they can easily be threaded together.

YOU WILL NEED
scissors
silver foil
17 small cotton reels (spools)
1 large cotton reel (spool)
sticky tape
darning needle
thin elastic
4 small foil pie dishes (pans)
paper clips
press studs
non-toxic strong glue

strong glue
paper clips
press studs
silver foil
scissors
foil dishes (pans)
cotton reels (spools)

1 Cut strips of silver foil about 1.5 cm (⅝ in) wider than the reels (spools) and long enough to fit around them. Cover the reels (spools) with foil.

2 Thread a darning needle with elastic and tie a big knot in the end. Ask an adult to make a hole in the centre of two dishes (pans) and two holes in a third. Thread a dish (pan) onto the elastic; then three small reels (spools); then the dish (pan) with two holes; then three reels (spools); then a dish (pan). Tie a knot in the end and cut the elastic.

3 Ask an adult to make a hole in the centre of the last dish (pan). To make the upper body, tie a knot in the end of a piece of elastic. Thread on three small reels (spools) and a large reel (spool) for the head. Secure with a paper clip.

4 To make an arm, tie a paper clip to elastic, thread on four small reels (spools) and tie a knot in the end. Glue the dishes (pans) together. Attach the arms below the head. Use paper clips and press studs for the face and controls.

45

FUN WITH TOYS

Materials

These are some of the materials you will need. Many of these projects will require an adult's help, particularly when you see the sign **!**

Bottles
Only use plastic bottles for the projects. Save bottle tops for decoration. However, they are not suitable for decorating babies' toys.

Card (posterboard) and paper
Card (posterboard) comes in a range of thicknesses. It sometimes needs to be cut with a craft knife rather than scissors, and you must ask for help with this. Newspaper is the core material used for papier-mâché.

Decorations
These are incredibly wide-ranging and the only curb on your imagination is making absolutely sure that the decoration you have chosen for a toy is suitable for your age. All decorations should be very firmly attached. Choose from buttons (look in charity shops for unusual examples), furnishing fringing, coloured pipe-cleaners and pretty ribbons, including ribbon roses, sticky shapes or even shoelaces.

Fabrics
The choice of colours, patterns and textures is as wide as you could wish for. You may prefer to choose natural materials, such as cotton and linen. Felt is beautifully soft and has the added advantage of being easy to cut without fraying. It is also available with an adhesive backing for covering objects.

Fasteners
Paper fasteners can be used to join two pieces of card (posterboard) or paper together, while still allowing them to move. Poppers (snap fasteners) or press studs are used for fastening fabric. Velcro is also a quick and easy fastener for fabric.

Glues and tapes
Double-sided tape can be used instead of glue to stick paper or card (cardboard). Electrical tape is very strong and can be used to fasten heavy materials. It can also be used for decoration and it comes in a wide range of bright colours. Masking tape is very useful for reinforcing card (posterboard) shapes and for marking out areas before painting. PVA (white) glue is a water-based, non-toxic glue ideal for sticking wood or paper. It can also be diluted with water and used in papier-mâché or as a quick and easy varnish.

Paints
Water-based paints are non-toxic and ideal for babies' and children's toys. Choose from either poster, acrylic or emulsion (latex) paints. Enamel paints are oil-based paints that will adhere to metal, wood or plastic. Spray paints are mostly toxic when wet, so use them outdoors or in a well-ventilated room and always wear a mask.

Polymer clay
This is a modelling medium that is available in a range of colours. Always follow the manufacturer's instructions, as products do vary.

Safety pin
Use this to help thread ribbon or cord through a fabric tube.

Screw eyes
These are screwed into the back of a piece of wood (for example, a picture frame) and cord can be attached to them for hanging.

Stuffing (batting)
This is used to fill toys and shapes made from fabric.

Ties
Cord is stronger than either string or ribbon and can be threaded through a drawstring bag to pull it shut. Rope is stronger still, although nylon rope does tend to unravel at the ends unless you seal them by burning (with an adult's help).

Threads
Embroidery threads are used in hand sewing to make colourful, detailed stitches. For ordinary hand or machine sewing choose either cotton or rayon thread.

Wood
Balsa wood is a very soft wood that can be bought from model shops. Medium-density fiberboard, or MDF, is a manmade wood. Wear a mask when sawing as it produces a fine dust.

Velcro spots
fabric
matchsticks
coloured paper
strong glue
safety pin
newspaper
sticky stars

cord

rope

balsa wood

masking tape

MDF (fiberboard)

screw eyes

electrical tape

spray paint

double-sided tape

felt

enamel paints

paper bauble (ball)

stuffing (batting)

paints

bottle top

varnish

buttons

threads

pipe-cleaners

ribbon roses

squeaker

dowel

poppers (snap fasteners)

zip (zipper)

ribbon

paper fasteners

polymer clay

embroidery threads

PVA (white) glue

shoelaces

fringing

cardboard

bottle

Sanding Wood

It is very important to smooth the surface and corners of wood before painting as this will avoid splintering.

1 Use sandpaper to smooth any rough edges on sawn wood.

! Drilling Wood

Make sure that you ask an adult to drill or saw any wood that you work with.

1 Place an old piece of wood under the piece you want to drill.

! Sealing Rope Ends

Some of the projects use plastic rope and the ends can be burnt to prevent them unravelling.

1 Ask an adult to carefully burn the rope ends for you, and then put them outside on a stone or concrete surface to cool.

Stuffing Soft Toys

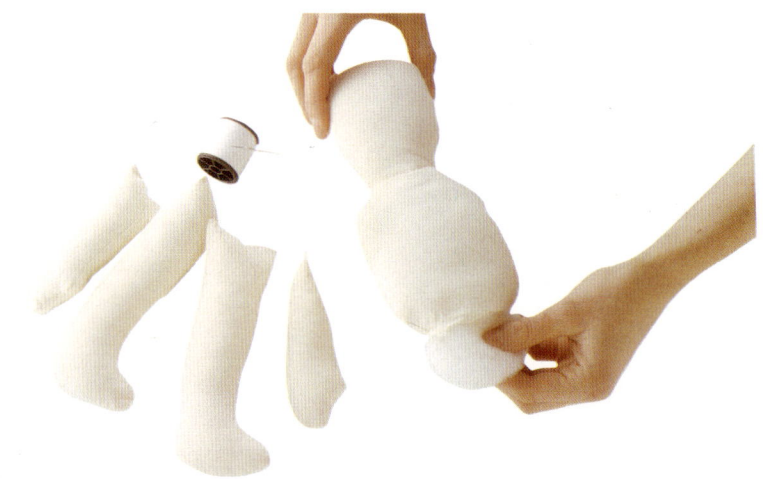

1 Push stuffing (batting) to the ends of toy pieces, using a knitting needle or the end of a wooden spoon to reach small or awkward shapes.

FUN WITH TOYS

Stitches

Several of the needlework projects use decorative stitches. Some of them you may be familiar with.

French knots

1 Tie a knot at the end of the sewing thread then stitch through to the right side of the fabric. Using the needle, make a knot close to the fabric.

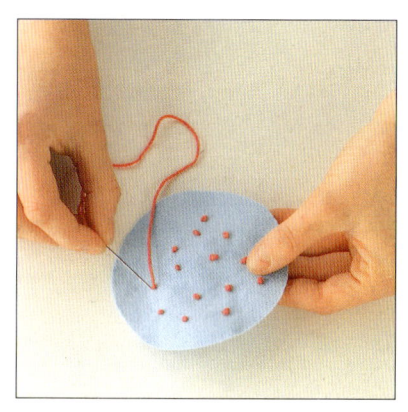

2 Pass the needle back through the fabric again close to the knot.

Blanket stitch

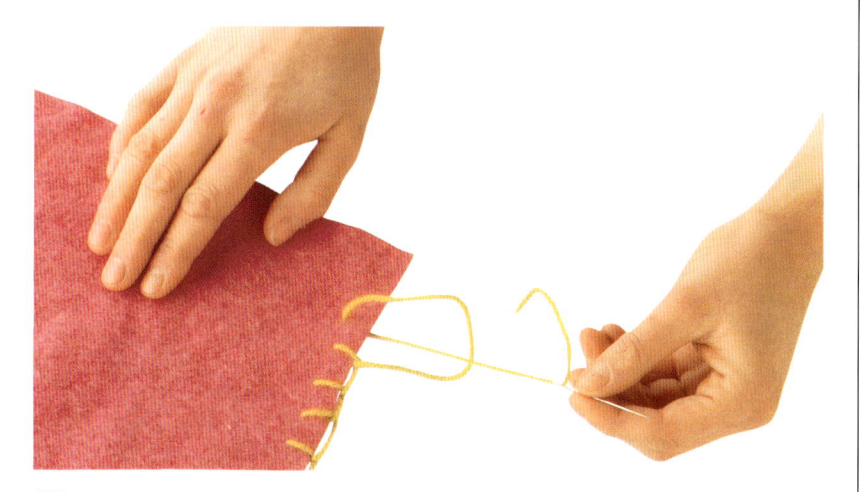

1 Use this stitch for edging fabric to prevent it from fraying. Tie a knot at the end of the sewing thread or wool (yarn), and pass it through the fabric from the wrong side. Push the needle through the right side of the fabric 1 cm (½ in) farther on and place the needle over the loop to form a stitch. Repeat.

! Bending Wire

1 Ask an adult to help you use a pair of pliers to bend a piece of wire into shape.

2 To secure the two ends of the wire together, twist them and press hard with the tips of the pliers.

! Making a Hole in a Can

1 An adult must help you with this technique. Place a ball of softened modelling clay on the can where you want to make a hole then pierce it with a bradawl. The modelling clay will prevent the bradawl from slipping.

49

FUN WITH TOYS

Rag Doll

Every little girl needs a calico doll like this as a best friend. First make the doll, then make her a special outfit to wear, such as a dress and matching pantaloons.

YOU WILL NEED
tracing paper
pencil
paper
scissors
50 cm x 1 m (20 in x 39 in) calico
matching sewing thread
needle
stuffing (batting)
knitting needle, optional
blue and pink scraps of felt
blue, pink, brown and red embroidery threads
tapestry needle
yellow knitting wool (yarn)
ribbon

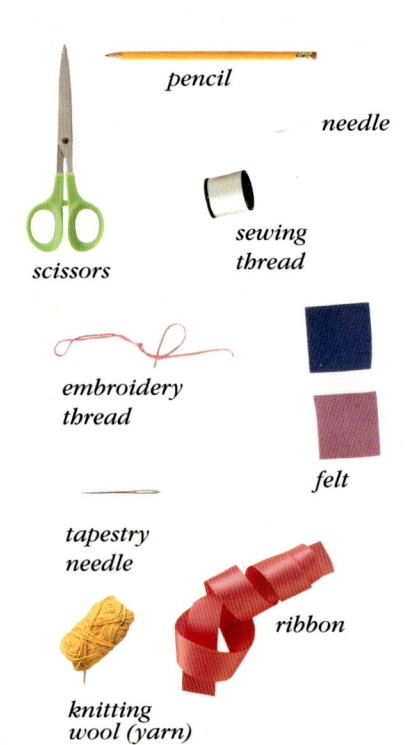

pencil
needle
scissors
sewing thread
embroidery thread
felt
tapestry needle
ribbon
knitting wool (yarn)

1 Trace the doll templates from the back of the book and cut out. Fold the calico in half and draw round the shapes. Cut the body shape out once and the arm and leg shapes twice. Stitch the shapes together in pairs, leaving an opening in each.

2 Turn all the pieces right side out and fill with stuffing (batting) until firm. Use a knitting needle if necessary to push the stuffing (batting) into the furthest corners. Slip stitch the openings to close them.

3 Pinch the tops of the arms and legs, then stitch.

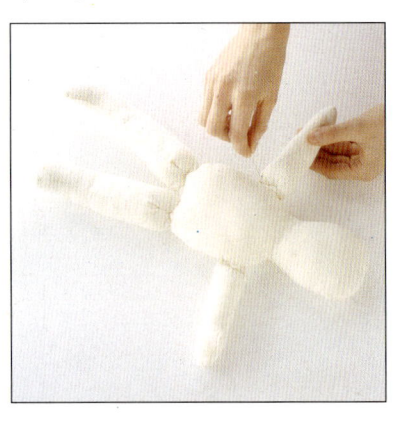

4 Stitch the arms and legs securely to the body.

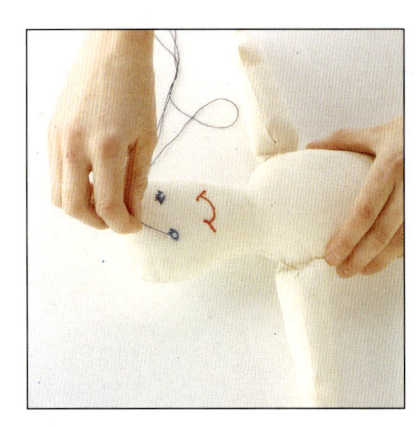

5 Cut two small circles out of blue felt for the doll's eyes, and two slightly larger circles out of pink felt for her cheeks. Stitch on to her face, using matching embroidery threads. Embroider her eyebrows in brown and her mouth in red in running stitch.

6 Stitch short lengths of yellow wool (yarn) through the top of the doll's head, using a tapestry needle. Tie each length of wool in a knot close to her head. Give her hair a neat trim. Tie the ribbon in a bow and stitch in place.

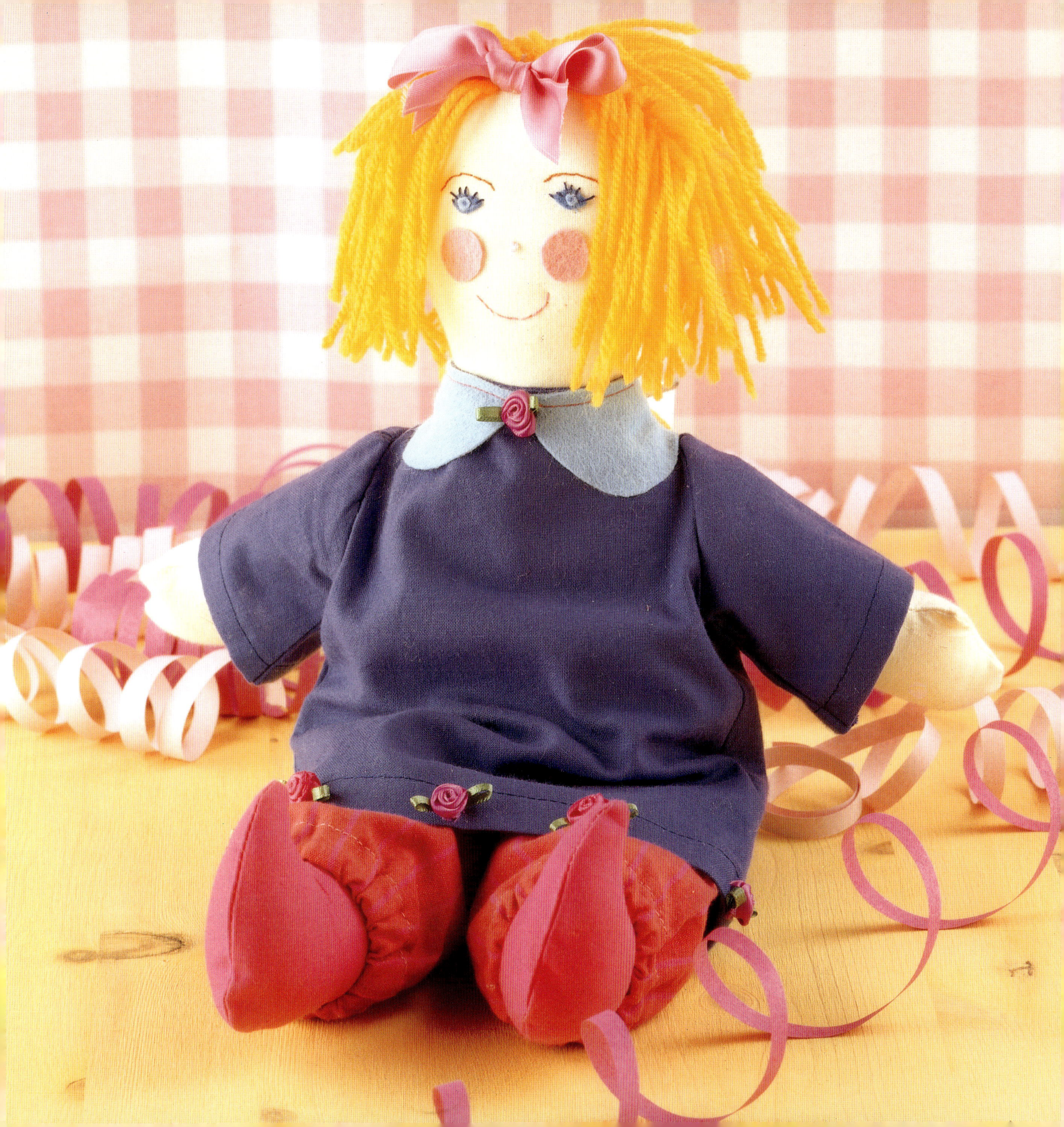

Rag Doll's Dress

The dress is decorated with a double felt collar and ribbon roses, which you can buy in craft and needlework shops. It fastens at the back with a row of poppers (snap fasteners), so is ideal for dressing and undressing the doll.

YOU WILL NEED
tracing paper
pencil
paper
scissors
50 cm x 1 m (20 in x 39 in) dress fabric
matching sewing thread
needle
felt
ribbon roses
poppers (snap fasteners)

dress fabric
scissors
ribbon roses
needle
poppers (snap fasteners)
pencil
sewing thread

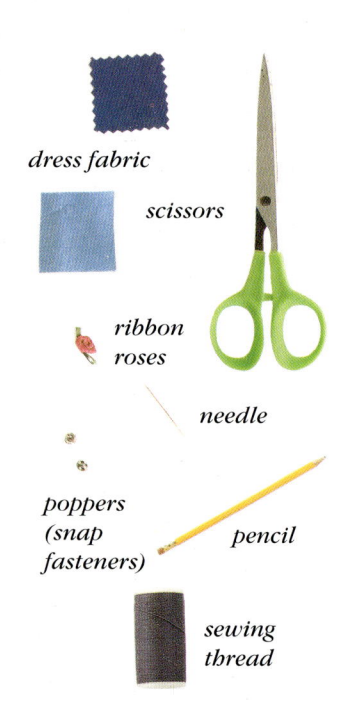

1 Trace the dress templates from the back of the book onto paper. Fold the fabric in half, place the pattern piece for the front on the fold and cut out. Cut two sleeves and two back pieces. Stitch the sleeve seams and hem the cuffs. Leave 6 mm (¼ in) seam allowance.

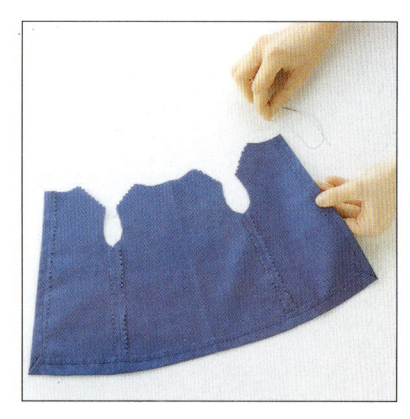

2 Stitch the two back pieces to the front piece, right sides together. Turn under 6 mm (¼ in) and hem.

3 Right sides together, stitch the shoulder seams. Turn the dress right side out. Place the sleeves through the armholes as shown and tack (baste) in position, then stitch.

4 Turn over 6 mm (¼ in) round the neck edge to the right side and stitch. Trace the collar template on to paper and cut out twice from felt. Stitch both collars round the neck edge. Decorate the dress with ribbon roses as shown. Turn the raw edges of the back opening under 2 cm (¾ in) to the wrong side and stitch. Stitch poppers (snap fasteners) to either side of the opening at the back.

Fun with Toys

Rag Doll's Pantaloons and Boots

Make the pantaloons in plain or patterned fabric to contrast with the rag doll's dress. Her boots are easily made out of scraps of fabric.

YOU WILL NEED
tracing paper
pencil
paper
scissors
matching sewing threads
needle
FOR THE BOOTS
scrap of fabric
FOR THE PANTALOONS
70 cm x 1 m (27½ in x 39 in) dress fabric
60 cm (24 in) narrow elastic
safety pin

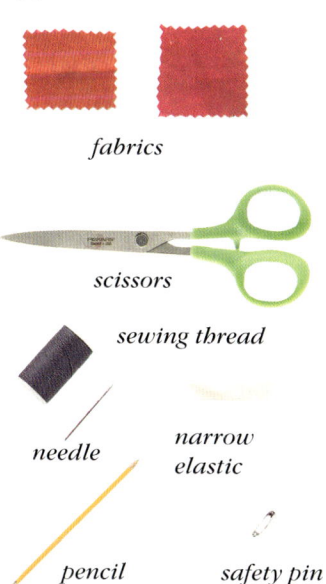

fabrics

scissors

sewing thread

needle   *narrow elastic*

pencil   *safety pin*

1 Trace the boot template from the back of the book onto paper. Fold a small piece of fabric in half, draw round the shape twice and cut out. Stitch two boot shapes together, right sides facing, leaving the top open. Hem the top and turn right side out. Make the other boot.

2 Trace the pantaloons template. Fold the fabric in half, right sides facing, then place the pattern piece on the fold as marked. Cut out twice. Keeping the fabric folded in half, stitch along the inside leg.

3 Turn one pantaloon leg right side out and place inside the other leg, with raw edges matching along the crotch seam. Stitch the crotch seam and turn right side out. Fold the waist edge over 3 cm (1¼ in) to the wrong side then stitch round the waist 1 cm (½ in) from the top, leaving a small opening. Repeat at the bottom of each leg.

4 Cut the elastic into one piece of 30 cm (12 in) and two pieces of 15 cm (6 in). Pin a safety pin to one end of the long piece and thread it through the waistband. Pull both ends to gather the waist and stitch firmly together. Repeat for the pantaloon legs.

FUN WITH TOYS

Activity Blanket

Tiny fingers will love playing with this blanket, and at the same time they will learn how to use zips (zippers), buttons and shoelaces. Make sure all the pieces are securely attached, especially the buttons.

YOU WILL NEED
coloured blanket
tapestry wool (yarn), in bright
  colours
tapestry needle
scissors
coloured zips (zippers)
dressmaker's pins
scraps of contrast-coloured
  blanket or felt
buttons
pom-poms
shoelaces

felt
tapestry needle
zip (zipper)
button
pom-poms
scissors
shoelaces
tapestry wool (yarn)

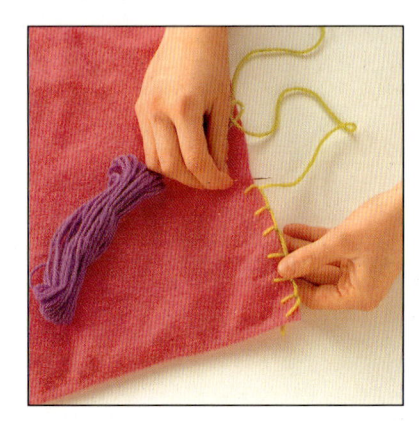

1 Cut the blanket if necessary to the size you want. Fold under the edges and blanket stitch, using contrasting tapestry wool (yarn).

2 Position the zips (zippers) on the blanket and pin in place. Secure with running stitch, using contrasting tapestry wool (yarn).

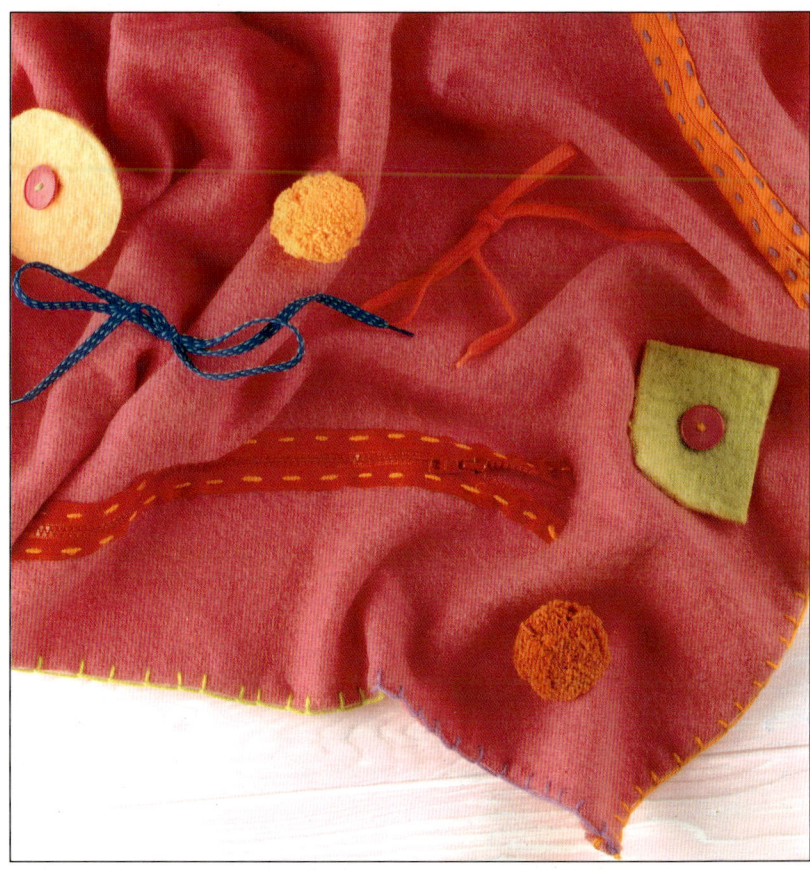

3 Cut out simple shapes, such as squares, circles and triangles, from coloured blanket or felt. Cut a slit in the centre of each shape for a button to go through. Stitch the buttons onto the blanket and fasten on the shapes.

4 Sew on pom-poms and shoelaces as more shapes to play with.

54

FUN WITH TOYS

Fridge Magnets

There are several modelling mediums you could use in this project, such as polymer clay, which can be purchased from craft and hobby shops. Whichever material you use, it is important to follow the instructions on the packet.

YOU WILL NEED
modelling medium
rolling pin (optional)
modelling tools (optional)
acrylic paints, in
 assorted colours
paintbrush
magnets
non-toxic strong glue

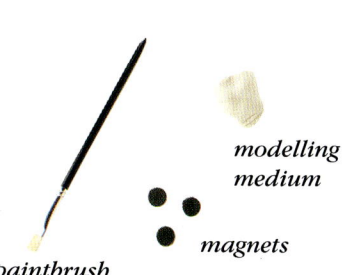

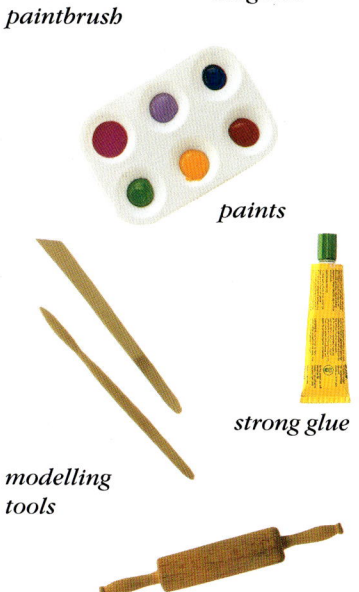

paintbrush
modelling medium
magnets
paints
strong glue
modelling tools
rolling pin

1 To make the teapot and the cups and saucers, mould each shape with your fingers, adding small pieces of the modelling medium for the details. If you are using polymer clay, you will need to roll it out first and cut out the shapes with modelling tools.

2 For the snail, roll out a length of modelling medium approximately 15 cm (6 in) long and coil it round. Add on small pieces for the antennae and tail.

3 Paint the shapes and leave the paint to dry. If you are using polymer clay, you do not need to paint it.

4 Glue a magnet onto the back of each shape with strong glue. Leave the glue to harden before placing the magnets on the fridge.

Fun with Toys

Bottle Maracas

Hold one of these in each hand and shake them in time to music – they make a great sound! For instructions on how to cover the bottles with papier-mâché, see the section at the beginning of the book.

YOU WILL NEED
FOR THE PAPIER-MÂCHÉ
newspaper
diluted PVA (white) glue
large bowl
FOR THE MARACAS
2 small, empty plastic bottles
emulsion (latex) paints, in assorted colours
paintbrush
buttons
non-toxic strong glue
A4 (11¾ x 8½ in) sheet of paper
100 g (4 oz) lentils or other dried pulses (legumes)
2 pieces of balsa wood, each 12 cm (4¾ in) long
craft knife
coloured electrical tape

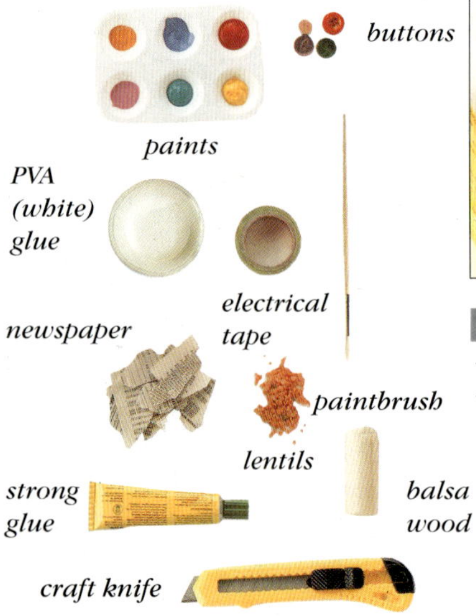

1 Make sure the bottles are clean and dry. Cover both bottles with two layers of papier-mâché.

2 When the papier-mâché is dry, paint the bottles all over in a base colour or two. Leave to dry.

3 Paint colourful patterns on top of the base colour. Leave the paint to dry.

4 Glue buttons round the bottom of the bottles with strong glue. Leave to dry.

5 Roll the sheet of paper into a cone and fit into the top of one of the bottles. Pour half the lentils or pulses (legumes) into the bottle. Repeat for the second bottle.

56

FUN WITH TOYS

6 ! Ask an adult to shave one end of the pieces of balsa wood with a craft knife until they fit snugly into the bottles.

7 Glue the balsa wood into the bottles with strong glue. When dry, wind coloured tape round the handles, and paint the ends of the handles.

57

FUN WITH TOYS

Felt Picture Book

The great thing about this colourful book is that you don't have to worry about the pages getting torn or crumpled. Make up a bedtime story to go with the pictures, or invent your own story and pictures.

YOU WILL NEED
tracing paper
pencil
paper
scissors
scraps of felt, for the pictures
5 pieces of felt, 6 cm (2½ in) square, in different colours
fabric glue and brush
6.5 cm (2¾ in) strip of felt, for the spine
embroidery thread
needle

brush
needle
fabric glue
felt
scissors
embroidery thread
pencil

1 Trace the templates at the back of the book onto paper and cut out. Lay the paper shapes on scraps of different coloured felt and cut out.

2 Position the felt shapes on the felt squares to make the pictures. Glue in place. Leave the glue to dry.

3 Place the felt squares on top of each other, with the pictures facing upwards. Place a plain felt square on top. Cut the felt spine to the length of the book, fold in half and glue round the edge, trapping the pages inside. Leave to dry.

4 Finally, to secure the spine, stitch through all the layers with embroidery thread, using a contrasting colour and neat blanket stitch.

58

FUN WITH TOYS

Skipping Rope

The simplest toys provide the most fun, and you can play skipping games for hours. Adjust the length of the rope as necessary.

YOU WILL NEED
34 cm (13½ in) coloured plastic tubing
craft knife
sandpaper
approximately 2 m (2¼ yd) smooth coloured rope
lighter

plastic tubing

coloured rope

craft knife

sandpaper

1 ! Ask an adult to help you cut the plastic tubing in half, using a craft knife. Smooth the edges with sandpaper.

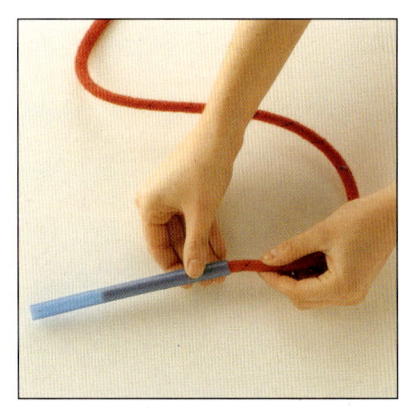

2 Thread each end of the rope through the tube.

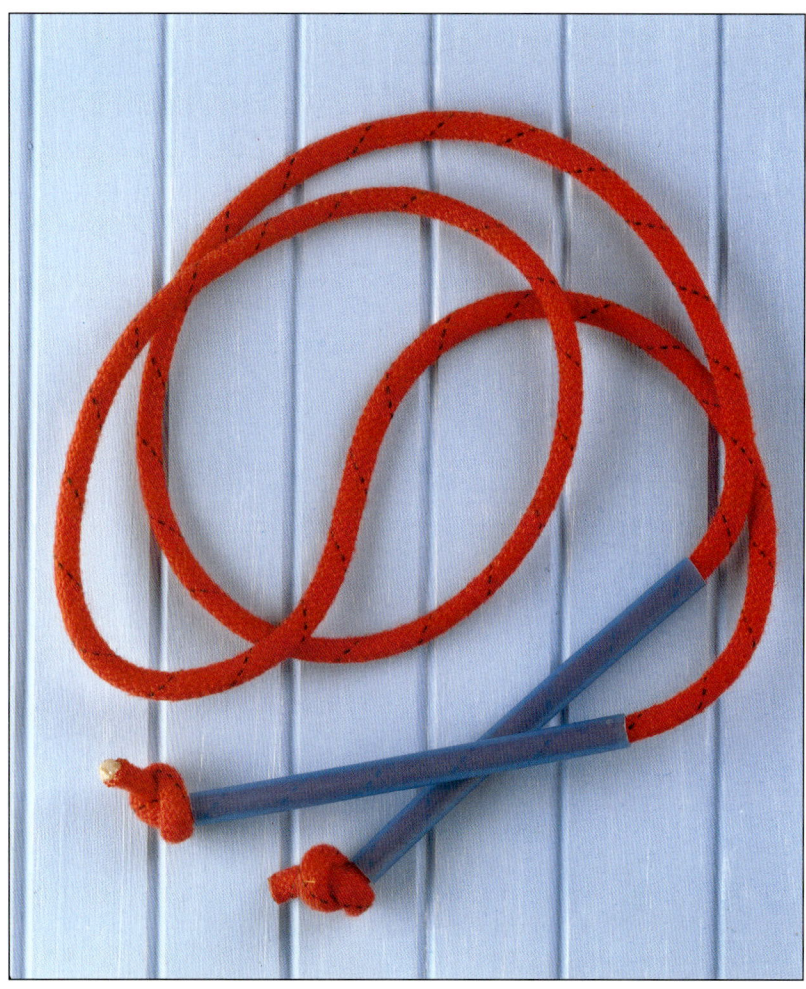

3 Check the length of the rope then knot the ends securely.

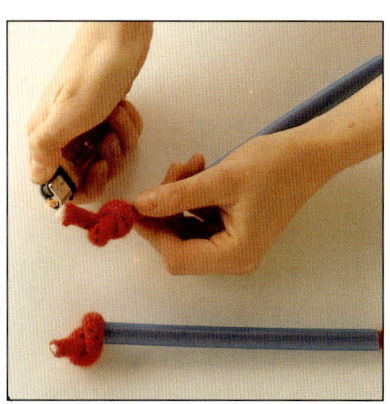

4 ! Burn the ends of the rope to prevent them from fraying if the rope is plastic.

59

FUN WITH TOYS

Character Skittles

Plastic bottles make excellent skittles, especially if you paint them to look like people. You can play the game indoors as well as outside if you use a soft ball.

! SAFETY NOTE
Ask an adult to remove the top of each bottle for you using a fretsaw.

YOU WILL NEED
clean, empty plastic bottles
fretsaw
newspaper
diluted PVA (white) glue
large bowl
paper baubles (balls)
non-toxic strong glue
acrylic paints, in assorted colours
paintbrush
ribbons, in various colours and patterns

newspaper
brush
plastic bottle
paper bauble (ball)
PVA (white) glue
ribbon
paints
fretsaw
strong glue

1 ! Remove the labels from the bottles by soaking them in water. Saw off the top of each bottle as shown.

2 Cover the bottles in papier-mâché. Leave to dry.

3 Glue a paper bauble on top of each bottle, using strong glue.

4 Paint the bottles and the bauble faces with a base coat. Leave the paint to dry.

5 Give each skittle a different character by painting different-coloured hair and clothes. Leave to dry.

6 Tie a piece of ribbon in a bow round the neck of each skittle.

60

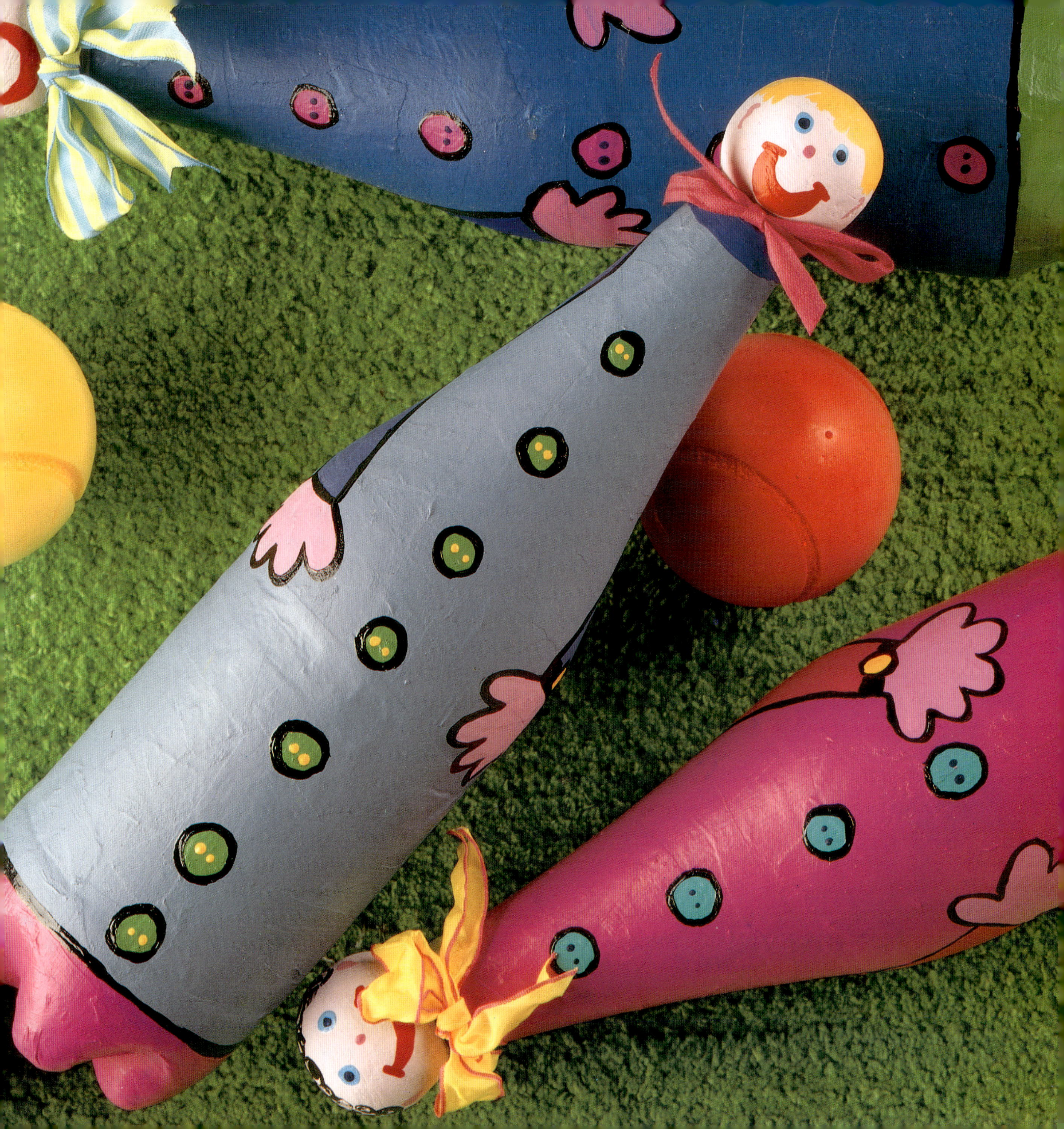

Fun with Toys

Felt Game

This popular game, known as Noughts and Crosses (Tic-tac-toe), is ideal for train or car trips. The felt shapes are attached to the board with Velcro so they can't fall off. Instead of adhesive felt, you can cut out the shapes from ordinary felt and stick them on with fabric glue.

YOU WILL NEED
30 x 30 cm (12 x 12 in)
  thick card (cardboard)
2 squares of adhesive felt,
  32 x 32 cm (13 x 13 in)
  and 30 x 30 cm (12 x 12 in)
adhesive felt, in 3 contrasting
  colours
tracing paper
pencil
ruler
scissors
thin card (posterboard)
9 Velcro spots
fabric glue and brush

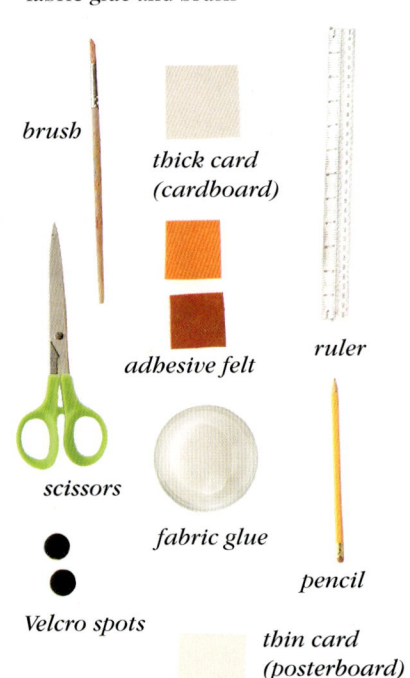

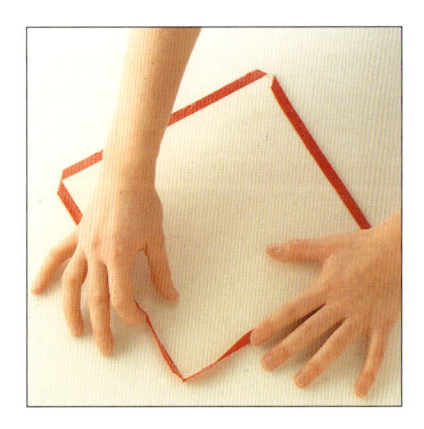

1 Position the 32 cm (13 in) square of felt in the centre of the thick card (posterboard). Stick down, folding the edges over to the back.

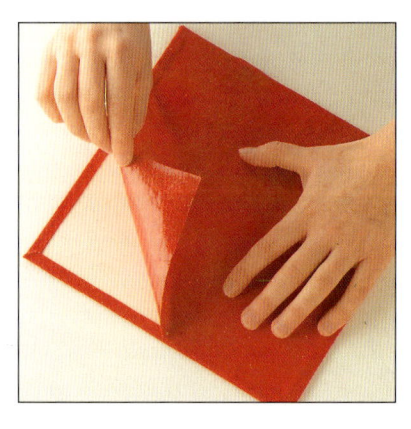

2 Stick the 30 cm (12 in) square of felt to cover the back of the card.

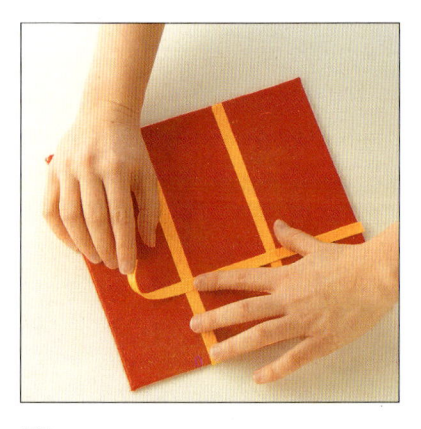

3 Cut four narrow strips of contrast-coloured felt 2 x 32 cm (¾ x 13 in). Stick them across the board to make nine equal squares.

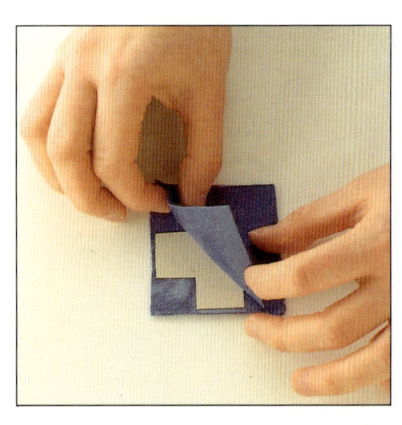

4 Trace the templates from the back of the book onto card (posterboard). Cut out four of each shape. Cover each shape with felt on both sides. Use a different colour for the noughts (0s) and the crosses (Xs).

5 Cut out the felt shapes, leaving the card (posterboard) inside.

6 Glue the furry side of the Velcro spots onto the centre of the noughts and crosses. Glue the looped side in the centre of the squares on the board.

62

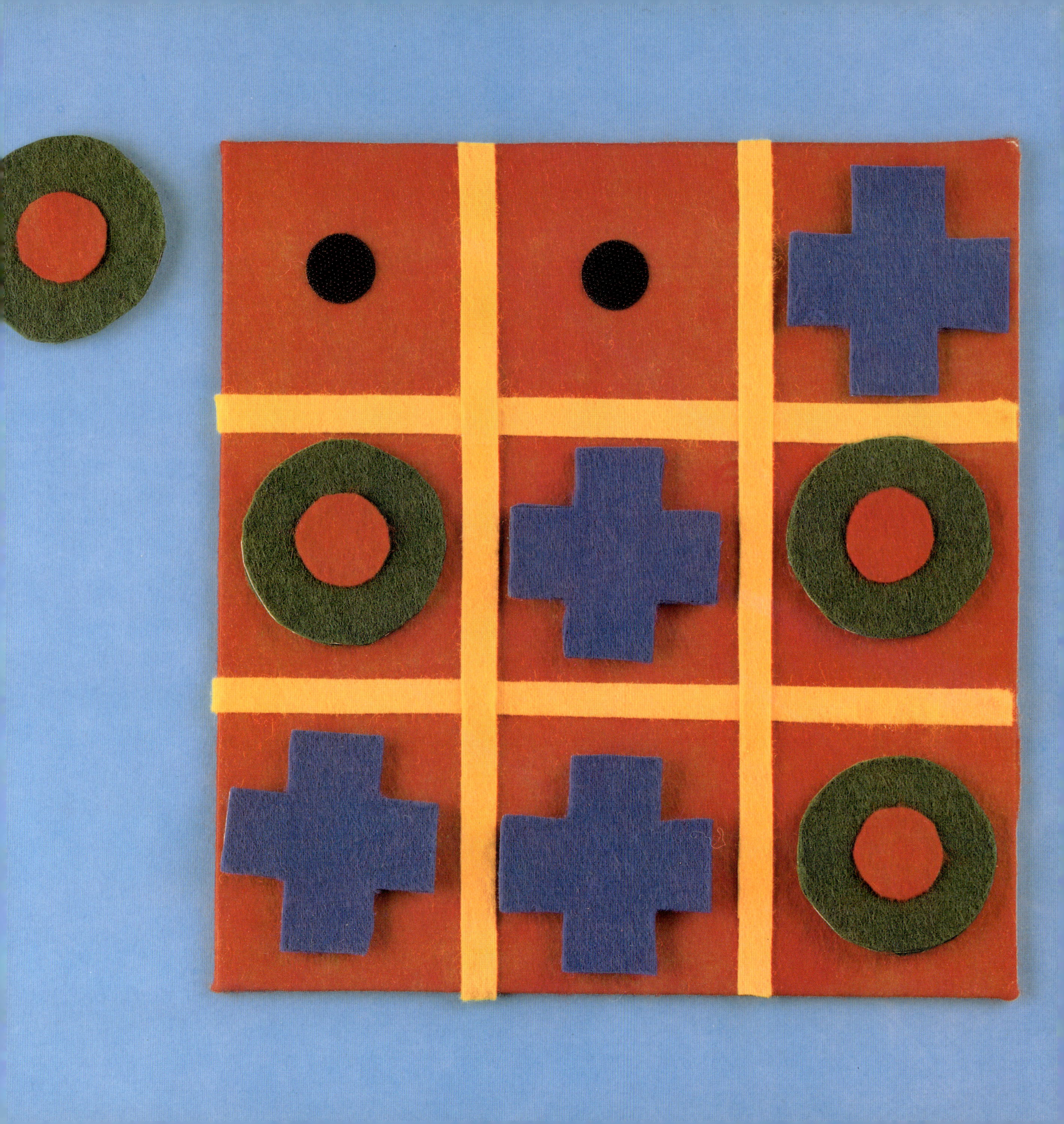

#Fun with Toys

Magnetic Fish

See how many goldfish you can catch – the highest score wins the game. To make a fishing rod, tie a piece of coloured string to a magnet. Tie the other end to a garden stick or cane.

YOU WILL NEED
tracing paper
pencil
paper
thin card (posterboard)
scissors
paints, in assorted colours
paintbrush
coloured metal paper clips
shallow box
magnet

thin card (posterboard)
paper clips
magnet
paints
paintbrush
scissors
pencil

1 Trace the fish template at the back of the book onto paper. Draw round the shape five or six times on card (posterboard) and cut out.

2 Paint the fish. Leave to dry then paint a different number on each fish.

3 Attach a paper clip to the mouth of each fish.

4 Paint the box blue and leave to dry. Using a darker blue, paint wavy lines round the edge to represent water.

FUN WITH TOYS

Dog Jigsaw

It is very easy to make your own simple, large-scale jigsaw. A template for the dog is supplied, but you could also make a jigsaw of your own pet or another favourite animal, or choose a completely different shape.

YOU WILL NEED
graph paper
pencil
card (posterboard)
craft knife
acrylic paints, in assorted colours
paintbrush
ruler
about 20 self-adhesive Velcro spots
45 x 35 cm (18 x 14 in) piece of thick card (cardboard)
40 x 30 cm (16 x 12 in) piece of adhesive-backed felt

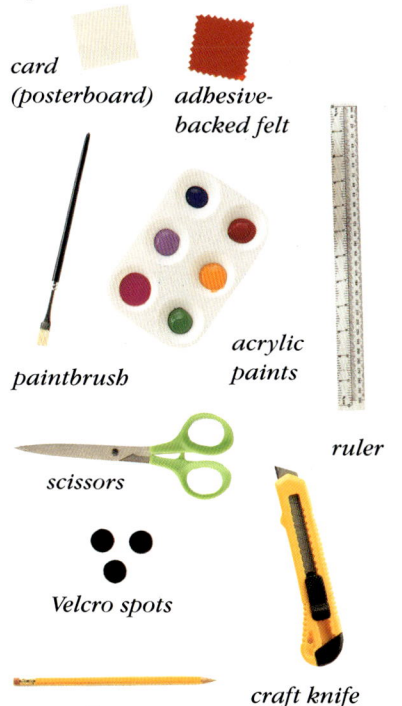

card (posterboard)
adhesive-backed felt
paintbrush
acrylic paints
ruler
scissors
Velcro spots
pencil
craft knife

1 ! Enlarge the template at the back of the book to 36 cm (14 in) long. Draw round the shape onto card (posterboard). Cut out with a craft knife.

2 Paint the dog as illustrated, or use your own colours. Leave the paint to dry.

3 ! Using a ruler, divide the dog into four or five simple pieces. Ask an adult to help you cut along the lines with the craft knife. Stick three or four Velcro spots on the back of each piece.

4 Make the base by placing the thick card (cardboard) in the middle of the felt. Fold over the edges and stick down.

FUN WITH TOYS

Toy Clock

Recycle your breakfast cereal packet to make a friendly clock, as a fun way of learning how to tell the time. Paint the clock face in sunny daytime colours, and surround it with a night sky painted with stars.

YOU WILL NEED
card (cardboard)
pencil
scissors
emulsion (latex) paint, in assorted colours
paintbrush
craft knife
paper fastener
cereal box
blue and yellow adhesive plastic
double-sided tape

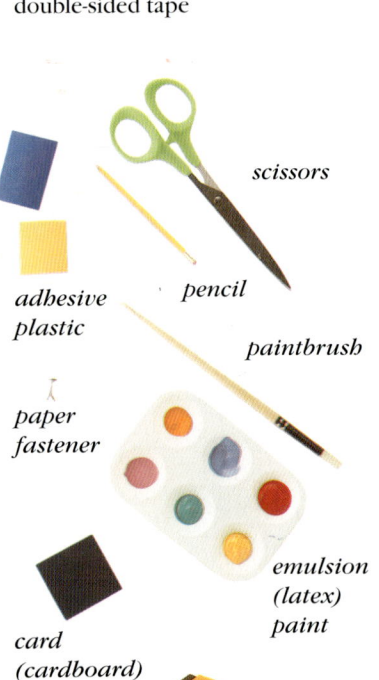

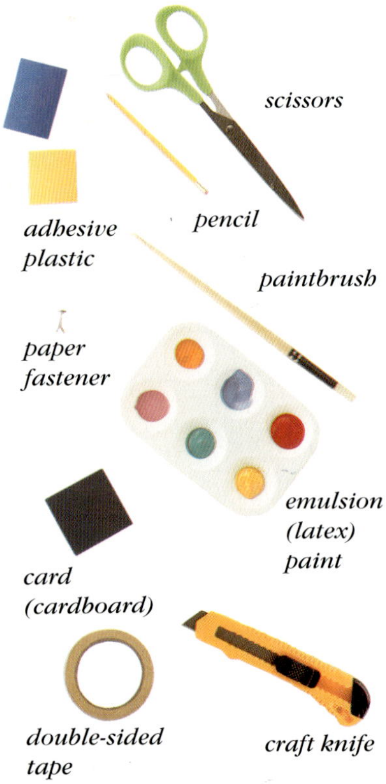

1 Draw round a small plate on to card (cardboard) and cut out. Find the centre of the circle and carefully pierce a hole using the tip of the scissors.

2 Paint the card circle in a sunny colour and leave to dry. Paint the numerals in contrasting colours with an inner circle of twelve dots. Leave to dry.

3 Draw two clock hands in the shape of arrows, one longer than the other, onto card and cut out. Paint and attach the arms to the clock with a paper fastener.

4 Cover the cereal box with blue adhesive plastic and smooth down, trying to avoid air bubbles.

5 Stick the clock face on to the box with double-sided tape. Cut out stars from yellow adhesive plastic and stick on to the sides of the box.

6 Stick more stars on the front of the clock round the face.

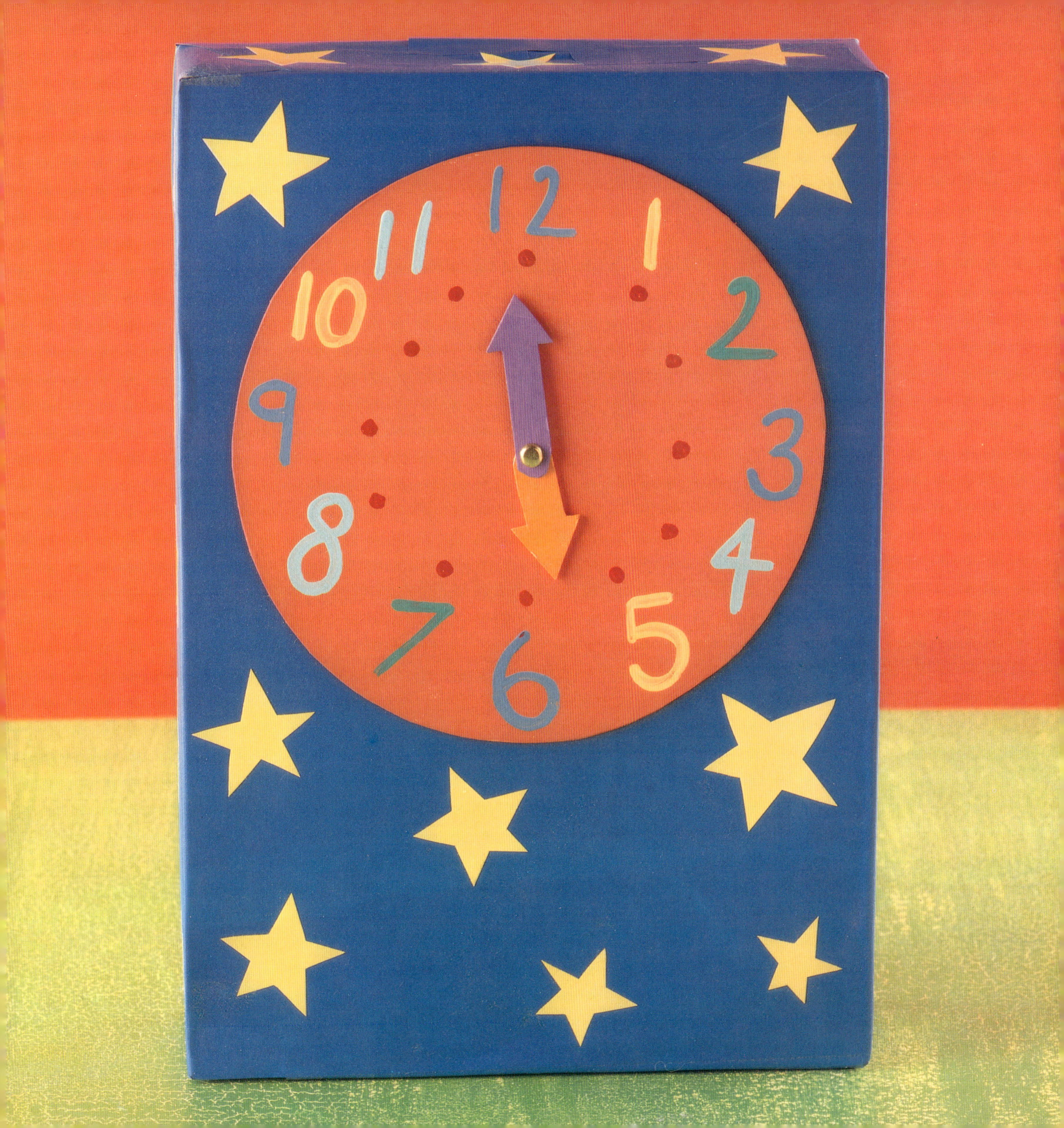
12
1
2
3
4
5
6
7
8
9
10
11

Fun with Toys

Dog and Bone Mobile

This witty mobile is great fun. As it swings around in the breeze, the Scottie dog chases the bone and the cat chases the fish! Trace the shapes from the templates supplied, cut them out of card (cardboard) and paint them in bright colours. Hang the rods up before tying on the shapes, as it will be easier to balance them.

! SAFETY NOTE
Ask an adult to drill, saw and cut with a craft knife for you.

YOU WILL NEED
2 x 45 cm (18 in) pieces of dowel, 5 mm (3/16 in) diameter
saw
sandpaper
drill
craft knife
poster paints, in assorted colours
paintbrush
cord
sticky tape (optional)
tracing paper
pencil
card (cardboard)
scissors
single-hole punch
thread, in assorted colours

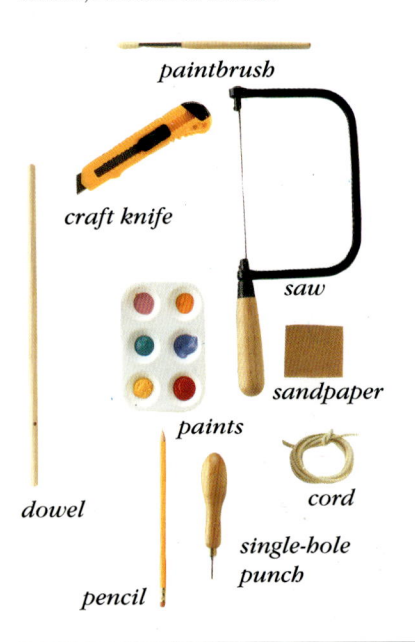

1 ! Cut the dowel to size and smooth the ends with sandpaper. Drill a hole in the centre of each dowel rod.

2 ! Using a craft knife, shave a 'V' shape round the hole on one of the dowel rods. This will help the rods to sit comfortably at right angles to each other. Paint each rod using a different colour. Leave to dry.

3 Thread a piece of cord through the holes and tie in a knot either side of the dowel rods. If you have trouble threading the cord through the holes, wrap a piece of sticky tape tightly round the end.

4 Trace the mobile templates at the back of the book and transfer them to card (cardboard). Cut out the shapes. Punch a hole on each shape where marked on the templates.

5 Paint the shapes on both sides.

6 Hang up the dowel rods and tie on each shape, using a different-coloured thread.

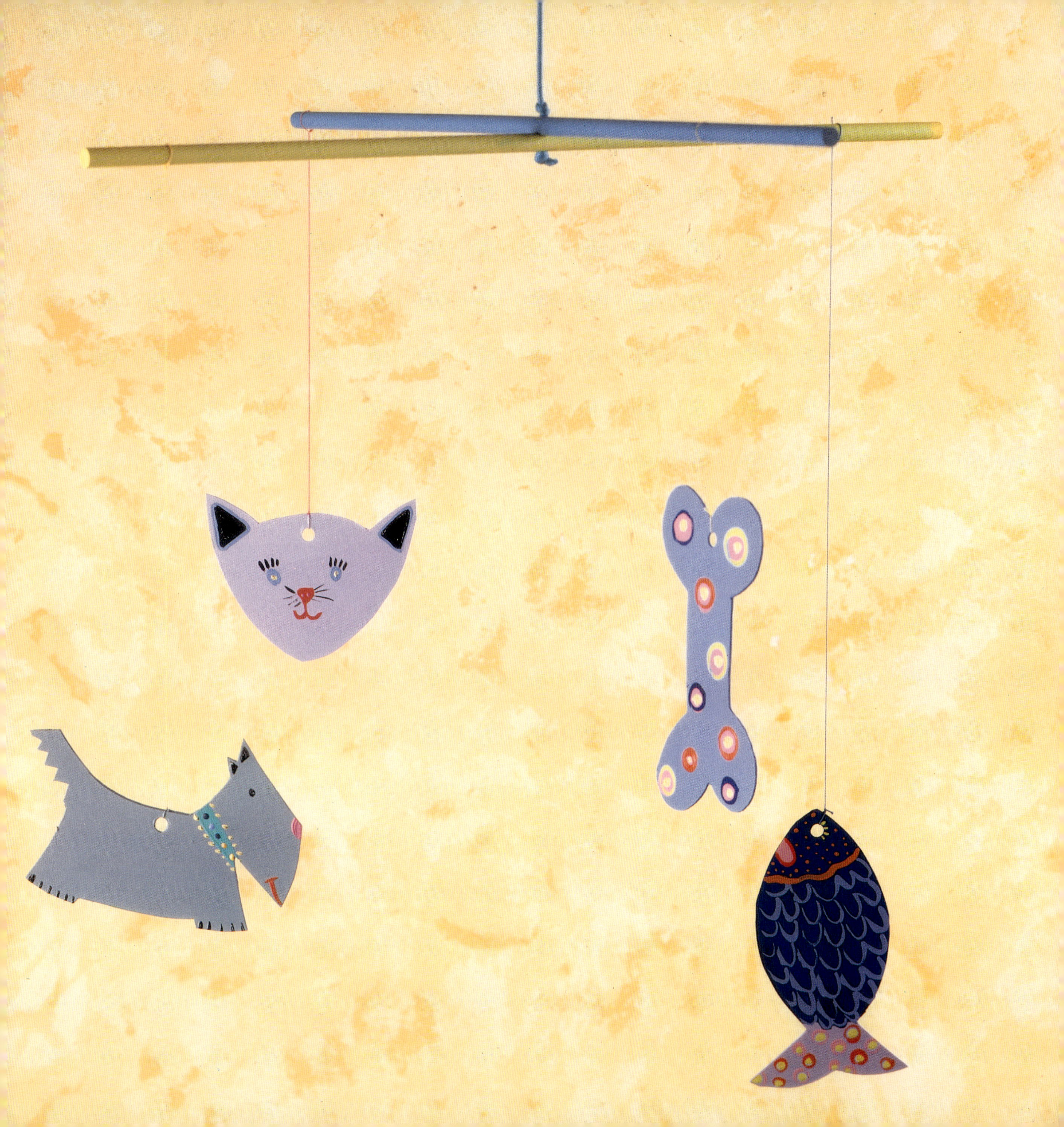

Flower Power Cushion

This checkerboard patchwork cushion is decorated with bright, sunny flowers, just right for small fingers to hold on to. The flowers are attached with Velcro so you can move them about to make a different design.

YOU WILL NEED
tracing paper
pencil
paper
scissors
scraps of felt in assorted
   colours, for the flowers
embroidery threads, in assorted
   colours
needle
16 cm (6½ in) Velcro
4 pieces of felt, each 22 cm
   (8½ in) square, in different colours
pins
stuffing (batting)
2 pieces of fabric, each 40 x 30 cm
   (16 x 12 in), for the cushion back
40 cm (16 in) square cushion pad
zip (zipper) (optional)

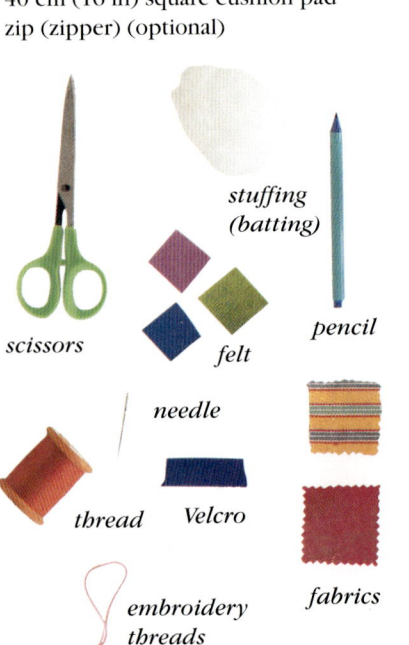

1 Trace the flower template at the back of the book. Draw round it four times on different colours of felt. Cut out four circles for the flower centres in contrast colours, and embroider with French knots.

2 Cut the Velcro into four equal pieces. Stitch one half of each piece to the back of each flower. Stitch the other half to the centre of each of the felt squares.

3 Position the flower centres on top of the flowers, trapping a small ball of stuffing (batting) in between. Pin in place then stitch round the flower centres in running stitch.

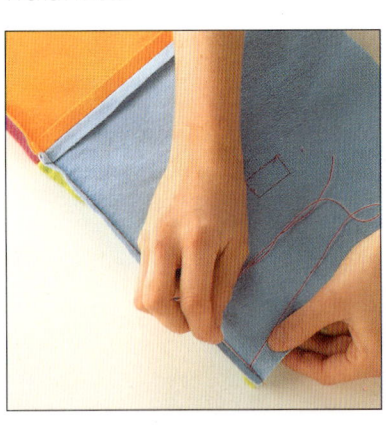

4 For the patchwork, place two of the felt squares together. Hand or machine stitch, leaving a 1 cm (½ in) seam allowance. Join the other two squares the same way, then stitch the two sets of squares together to make a large square.

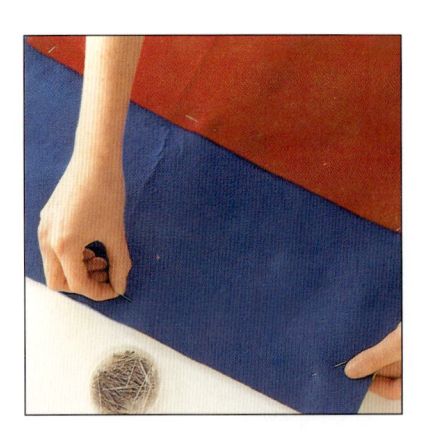

5 Place the two pieces of fabric for the cushion back on the felt, right sides together. Pin then stitch round all four sides, leaving a 1 cm (½ in) seam allowance. Fold back the raw edges of the back pieces and attach in the seam.

6 Turn the cushion cover right side out and insert the cushion pad. Stitch the opening or insert a zip (zipper). Attach the flowers onto the front, using the Velcro.

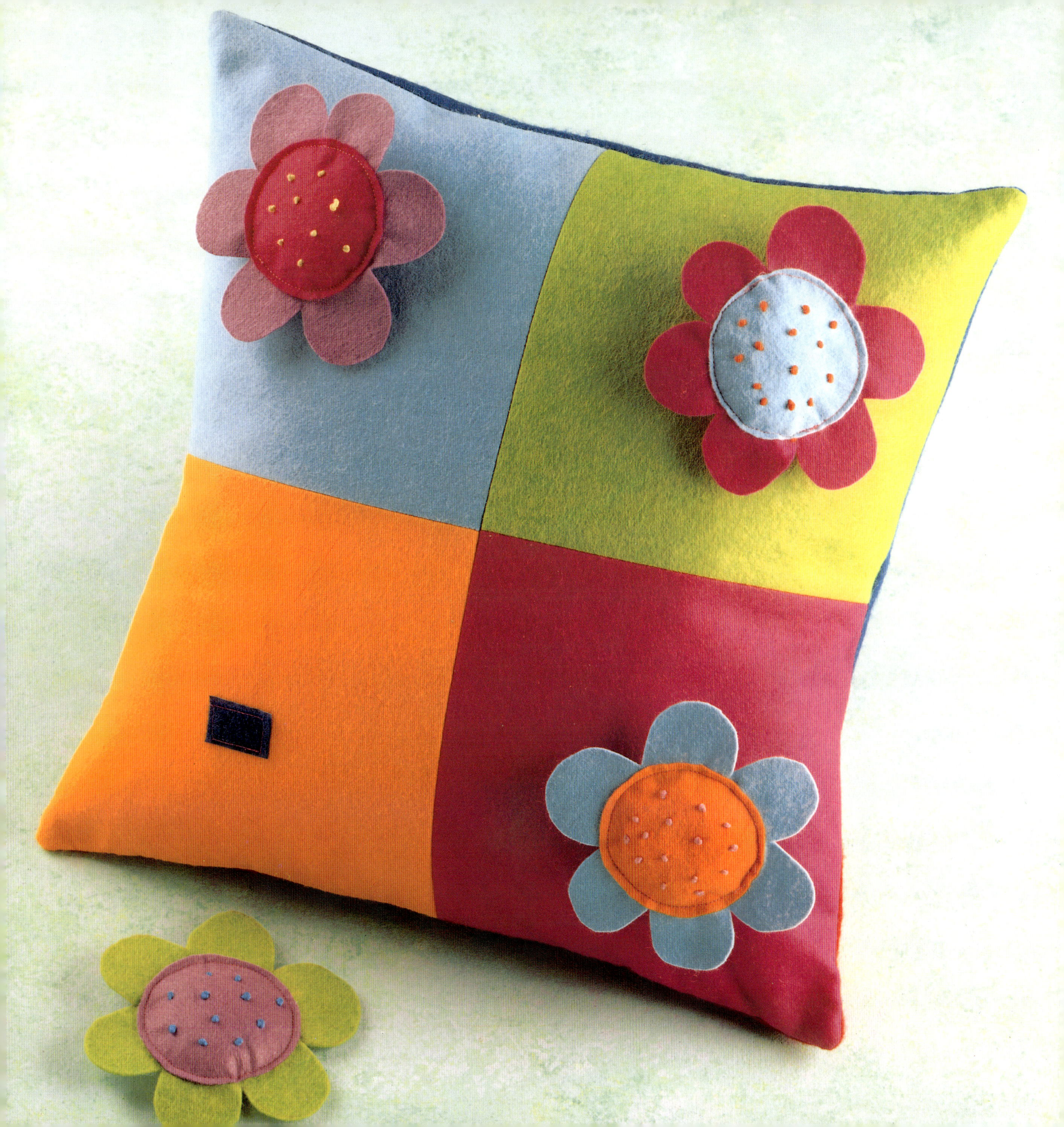

Toy Bag

This bag is a real star! It is big enough to store plenty of toys in at home or if you are going out for the day. Position the star so that it will be in the centre of one side of the bag when the fabric is folded in half.

YOU WILL NEED
tracing paper
pencil
paper
scissors
scraps of fabric, for the star
fabric glue and brush
needle
matching sewing threads
52 x 110 cm (20½ x 43 in) hardwearing fabric, for the bag
pins
1 m (1 yd) coloured tape
1.5 m (1½ yd) ribbon or cord
safety pin

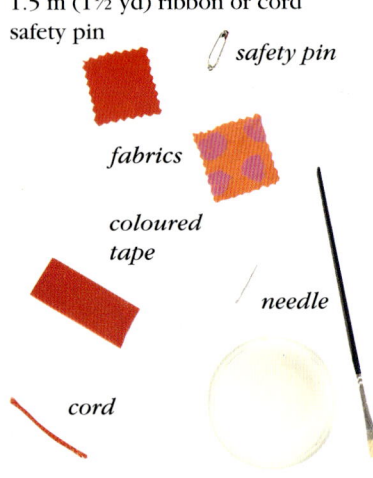

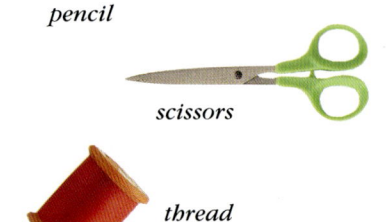

1 Trace the star template at the back of the book onto paper. Place on the reverse side of a piece of fabric and cut out. Cut out spots in a contrasting colour and glue them on to the right side of the star. Stitch the star onto the right side of the bag fabric.

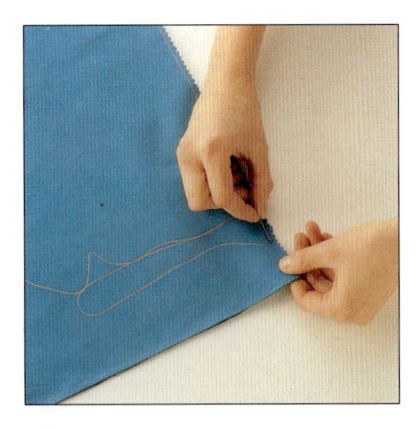

2 With right sides facing, fold the bag fabric in half to make a square. Hand or machine stitch along three sides, leaving a 1 cm (½ in) seam allowance.

3 Fold over the open side by 5 cm (2 in), then stitch round the top of the bag. Turn the bag right side out.

4 Starting at a side seam, pin the tape round the outside of the bag 3 cm (1¼ in) from the top. Fold in the raw ends then stitch along either side of the tape. Attach a safety pin to the end of the ribbon or cord and thread it through the tape. Tie the ends in a knot.

Fun with Toys

Paper Fastener Puppet

It's amazing what you can do with basic, everyday equipment such as paper fasteners. Here they are used to joint the limbs of this smartly dressed puppet, so that you can make him wave and dance. Hang him up on the back of a bedroom door or on the wall.

You will need
tracing paper
pencil
card (posterboard)
scissors
paints, in assorted colours
paintbrush
4 paper fasteners
electrical tape
embroidery thread

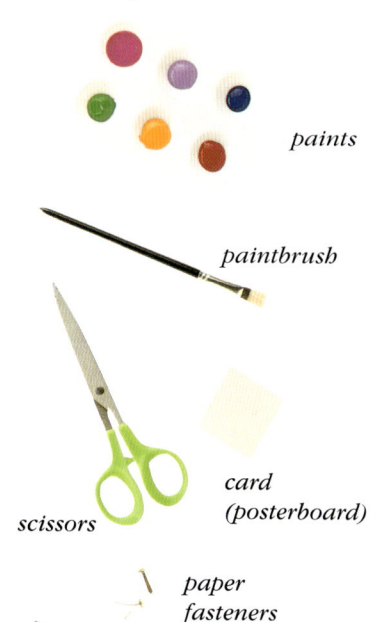

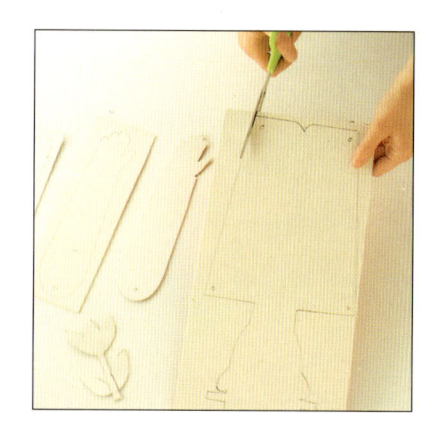

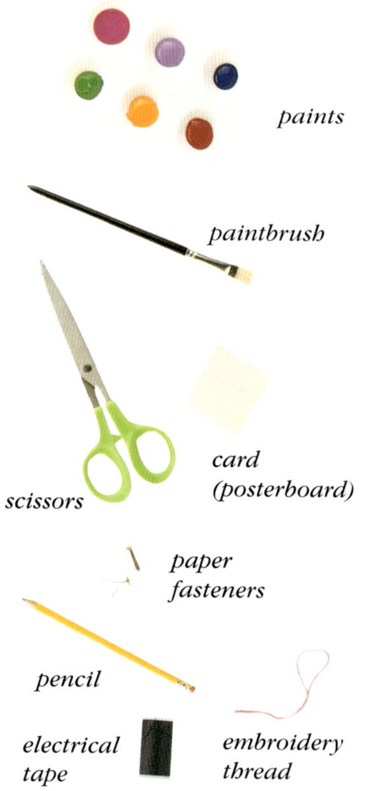

1 Trace the puppet templates from the back of the book. You will need two arms and two legs. Draw round the shapes onto card (posterboard) and cut out using scissors.

2 Paint the shapes in background colours and leave to dry. Then carefully paint the details of the man's checked suit and his face.

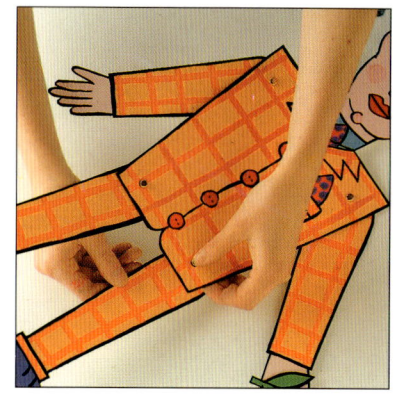

3 Ask an adult to help you make holes on the arms and legs, as shown on the templates. Make four holes on the body, as shown. Attach the limbs to the body with the paper fasteners.

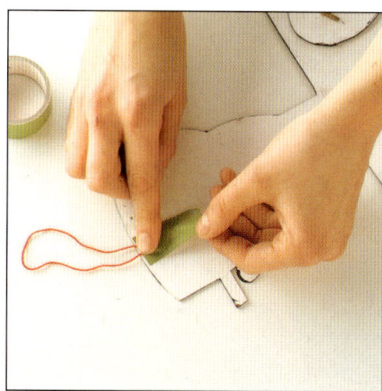

4 Using electrical tape, stick a double length of embroidery thread behind the top of the puppet's head so that you can hang him up.

FUN WITH TOYS

Big Foot Stilts

Children will love walking about on these giant feet! If possible, ask the child for whom the stilts are intended to stand on the cans so that you can measure the length of rope needed.

YOU WILL NEED
2 large, empty cans, the same size
plasticine
bradawl
spray paint
enamel paint, in contrasting colour
paintbrush
sticky stars
rope

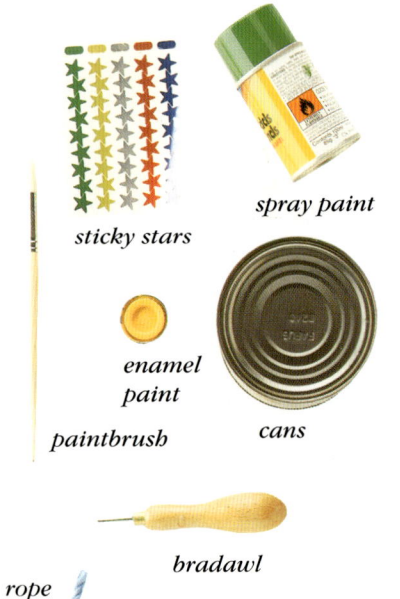

sticky stars

spray paint

enamel paint

paintbrush

cans

bradawl

rope

plasticine

1 ! Remove the labels from the cans. Place a ball of softened plasticine on either side of the top of each can. Ask an adult to pierce a hole through the plasticine with a bradawl then remove the plasticine.

2 Place the cans on a well-protected surface, preferably outdoors. Spray with spray paint and leave to dry. Spray on a second coat if necessary.

3 Paint the top of the cans with enamel paint. Leave to dry.

4 Decorate the cans with sticky stars.

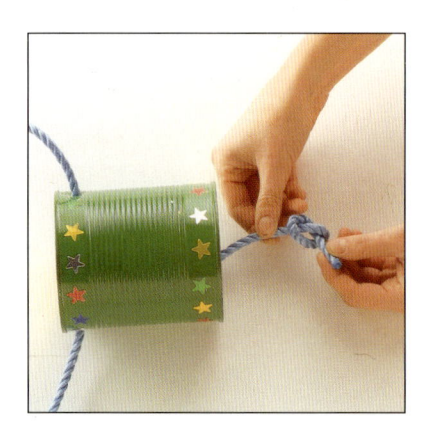

5 Stand on the cans. Measure the length of rope needed to suit your height then thread through the holes on each can. Tie the ends together in a knot.

6 ! Burn the ends of rope to prevent them from fraying

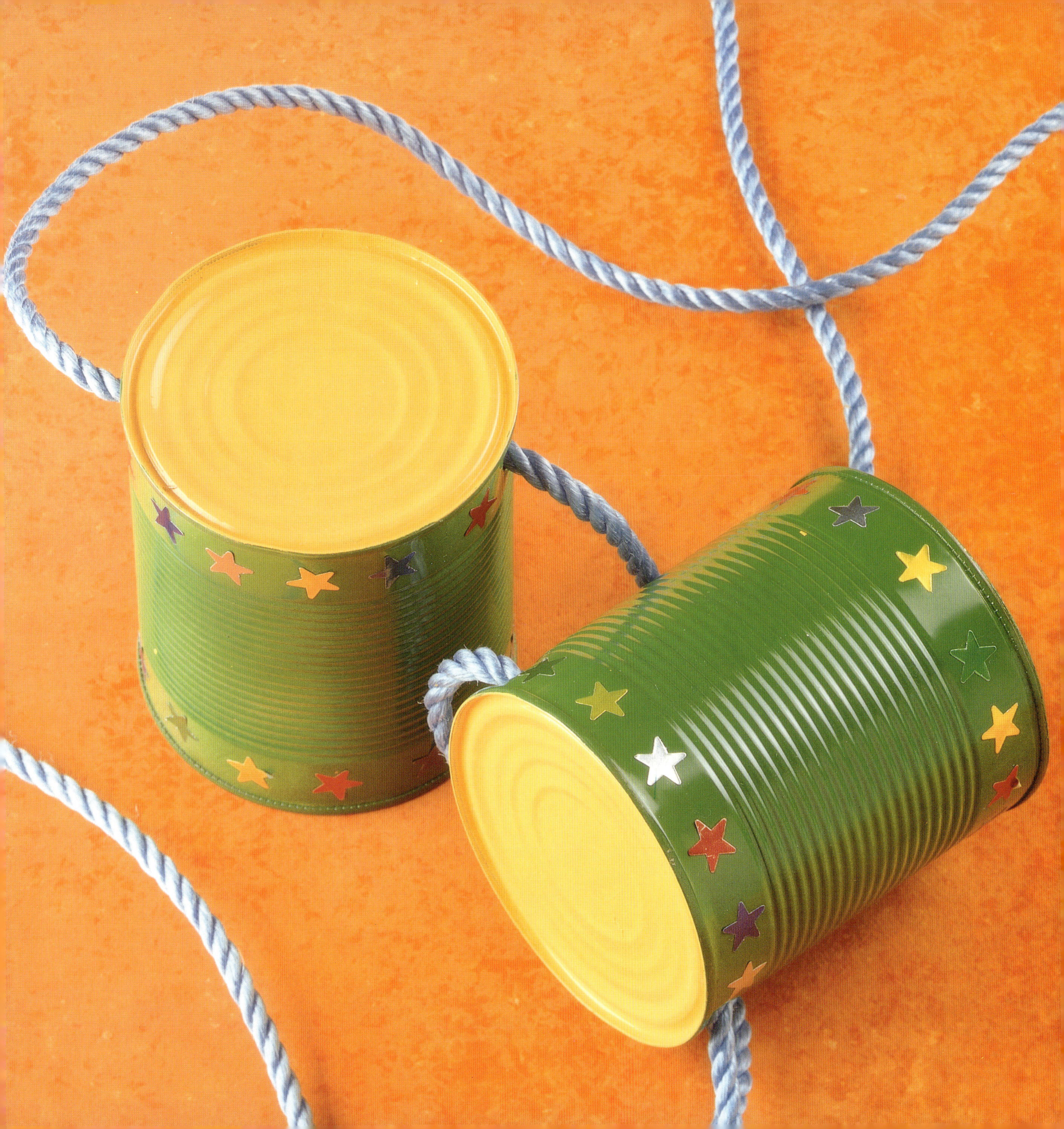

FUN WITH TOYS

Mexican Clay Doll

This doll is made in the traditional Mexican way, with the arms and legs tied to the body with threads. It is very fragile so this toy is best kept on a shelf as an ornament.

YOU WILL NEED
self-hardening clay
modelling tools
acrylic paints, in assorted colours
paintbrush
strong embroidery thread

self-hardening clay

embroidery thread

acrylic paints

paintbrush

modelling tools

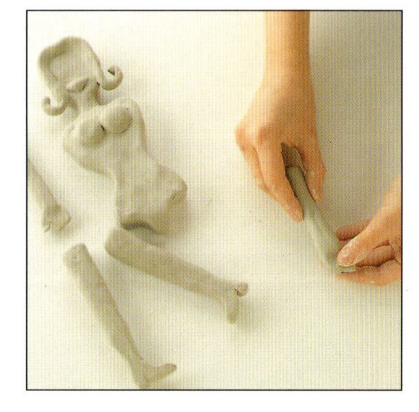

1 Shape the body, arms and legs out of the clay. The arms and legs should be the same size. Lay the pieces on a board or other flat surface.

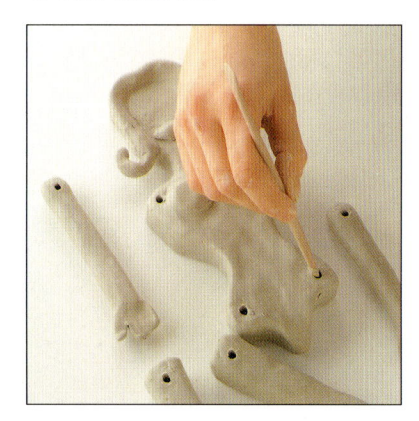

2 Using a modelling tool, pierce a hole at the top of each limb and at each corner of the body. Leave to dry in a warm place overnight, or as directed on the packet.

3 When the pieces have fully hardened, paint them in bright colours. Leave the paint to dry.

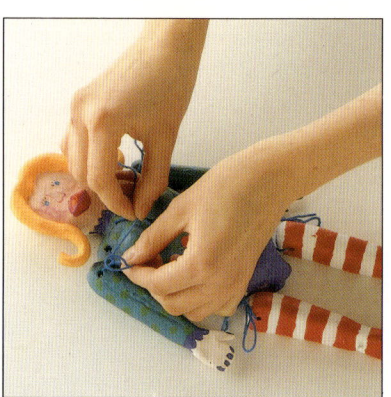

4 Tie the arms and legs to the body with lengths of thread, leaving enough slack for them to move freely.

FUN WITH TOYS

Star Board Game

Make your own painted board for this fun game, then make a set of star playing pieces to match using any small pastry cutter shape. Play the game the same way as traditional draughts (checkers).

YOU WILL NEED
52 x 52 cm (20 x 20 in)
  MDF (fiberboard)
metal ruler
pencil
emulsion (latex) or acrylic paints,
  in 2 contrasting colours
paintbrush
masking tape (optional)
varnish and brush
polymer clay, in 2 colours to
  match board
rolling pin
small star pastry cutter

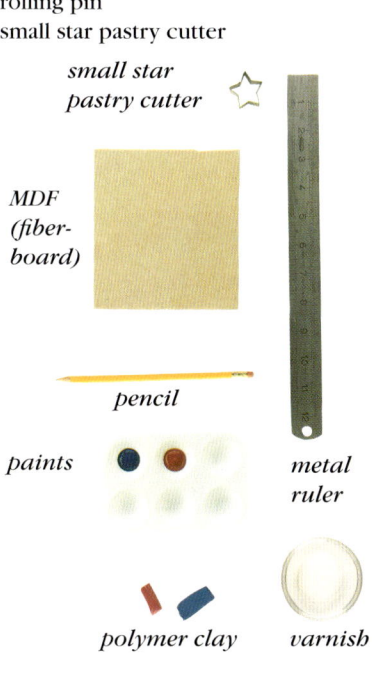

small star pastry cutter

MDF (fiber-board)

pencil

paints

metal ruler

polymer clay

varnish

paintbrush

masking tape

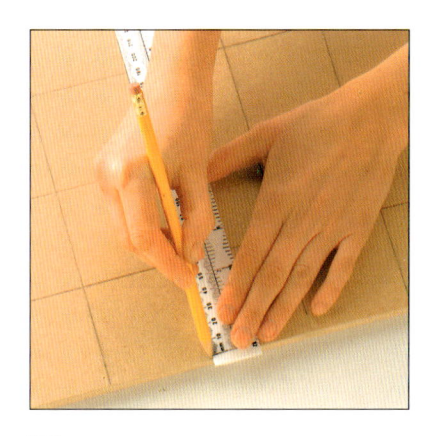

1 Using a metal ruler, divide the MDF (fiberboard) into 64 squares, each measuring 6.5 x 6.5 cm (2½ x 2½ in).

2 Paint alternate squares in the first colour. To help paint straight lines, you can mark out the squares with masking tape and remove it when the paint is dry.

3 Paint the remaining squares with the second colour. When dry, apply a coat of varnish.

4 For the pieces, roll the polymer clay approximately 5 mm (¼ in) thick. Using the pastry cutter, cut out twelve shapes from each colour. Bake the pieces following the manufacturer's instructions, and allow to cool.

77

Sunny Flower Blackboard

This novel blackboard should make sums and spelling more fun! Make it as large as you like, to fit your wall. If you have an electric jigsaw you can use it to cut out the flower shape, otherwise use a coping saw.

YOU WILL NEED
MDF (fiberboard)
pencil
string
saw
sandpaper
emulsion (latex) paints, in assorted colours
paintbrush
blackboard paint
bradawl
2 screw eyes
screwdriver

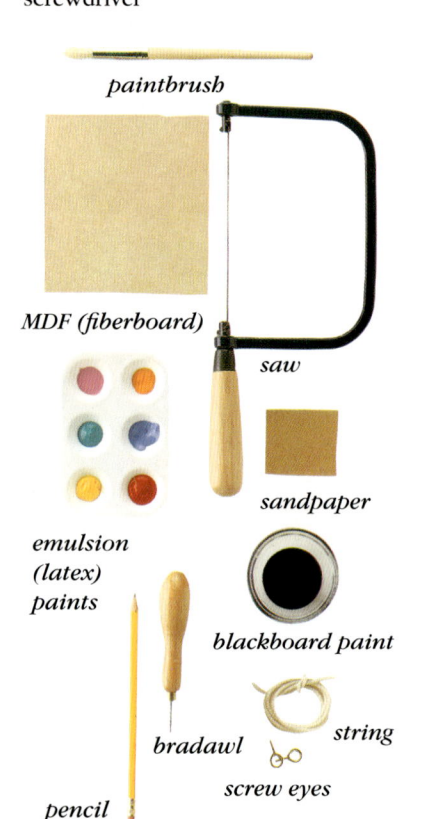

1 ! Draw the flower on the MDF (fiberboard) and ask an adult to cut it out. For the centre, use a pencil and string to draw a circle or draw round a plate. Smooth the edges with sandpaper.

2 Paint each petal a different colour, leave to dry then paint a second coat. Leave to dry.

3 Paint the centre of the flower with two coats of blackboard paint. Leave to dry.

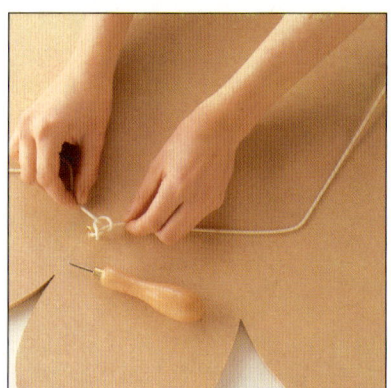

4 ! Turn the flower over. Mark two points, one on each side, and make small holes with a bradawl. Screw the screw eyes into the holes until they are tight. Tie a piece of string securely to each screw eye, allowing some slack for hanging.

FUN WITH TOYS

Glove Puppets

Make a different puppet for each hand, so they can perform together. If your hands are a different size to the template, simply draw round the hand and add a generous seam allowance.

YOU WILL NEED
tracing paper
pencil
paper
scissors
felt, blanket or wool fabric
blue and red embroidery threads
tapestry needle
knitting wool (yarn)
buttons

tapestry needle

scissors

buttons

felt

knitting wool (yarn)

embroidery thread

pencil

1 Trace the glove template from the back of the book onto paper and cut out. Draw round it onto the felt or fabric and cut out two glove shapes. Embroider blue eyes and a red mouth on one shape.

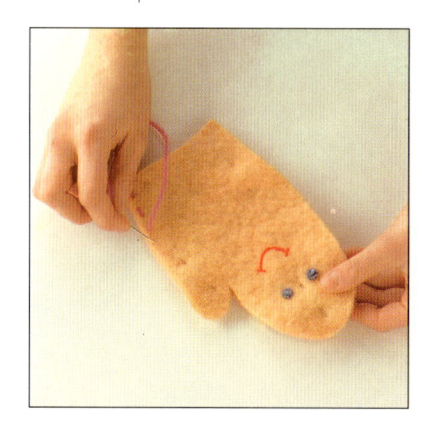

2 Place the two shapes together, wrong sides together, and stitch round the edge in running stitch. Leave the bottom edge open.

3 For the hair, stitch short lengths of knitting wool (yarn) through the top of the glove and knot.

4 Finally stitch a row of buttons down the centre front.

FUN WITH TOYS

Decoupage Toy Box

Jazz up an old, or boring, toy box with a splash of paint and some fun cut-outs. Decoupage is very cheap and simple to do – you simply cut out shapes from wrapping paper and paste them on. A layer of varnish means the paper shapes will not rub off and the finished decoration is very hardwearing.

YOU WILL NEED
wooden toy box
sandpaper
emulsion (latex) paint, in several colours
paintbrush
wrapping paper
scissors
PVA (white) glue and brush
varnish and brush

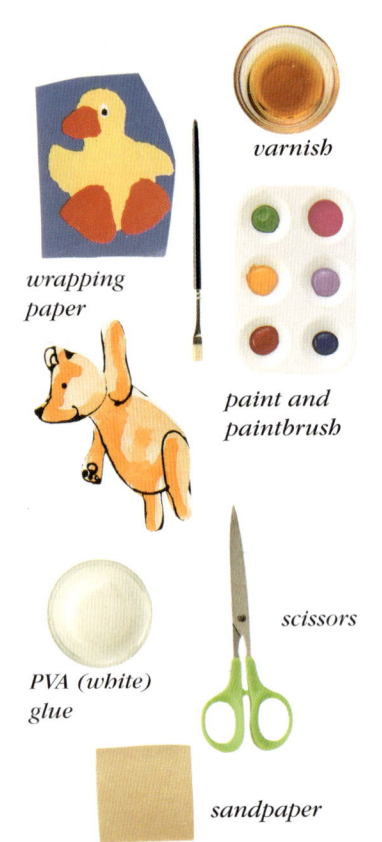

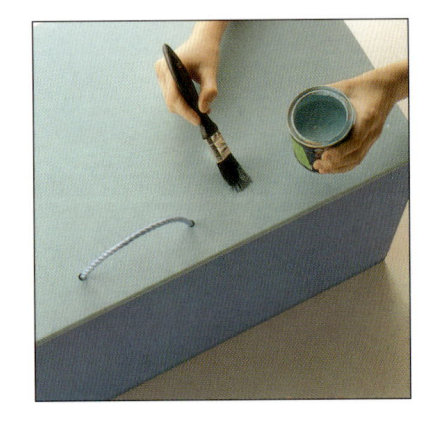

wrapping paper

varnish

paint and paintbrush

scissors

PVA (white) glue

sandpaper

1 First sand down the toy box. Paint the box with emulsion (latex) paint, using a different colour for each side. Leave the paint to dry then apply a second coat.

2 When the paint is dry, cut out shapes from the wrapping paper.

3 Arrange the paper shapes on the box to make a good design. Using the PVA (white) glue, paste them in place.

4 When the glue is dry, varnish the box and fill with toys.

Monster Feet

Disguise your hands with these colourful monster feet! They're great fun for parties and, as they cover only the backs of your hands, you will still be able to eat and drink a monstrous amount!

YOU WILL NEED
heavy coloured paper
pencil
scissors
thin paper in contrasting colours
non-toxic paper glue
paper clips (optional)

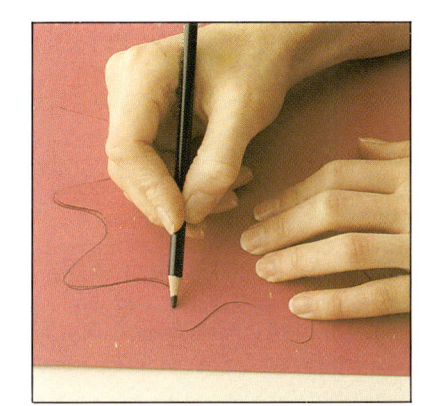

1 Draw a five-toed monster foot on the heavy paper. Cut it out and use it as a template to make a second foot. Remember to cut an extension of paper from each ankle to form a fastening band.

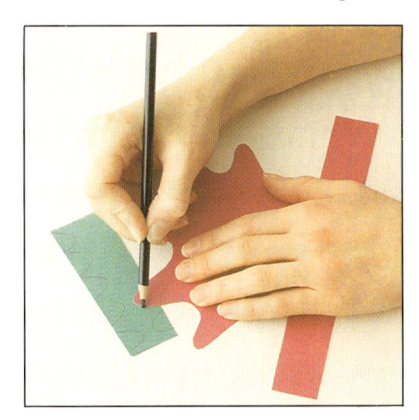

2 Place the monster feet on thin coloured paper. Draw around the tip of each toe and cut out the shapes to make toenails. Stick each toenail to its corresponding toe.

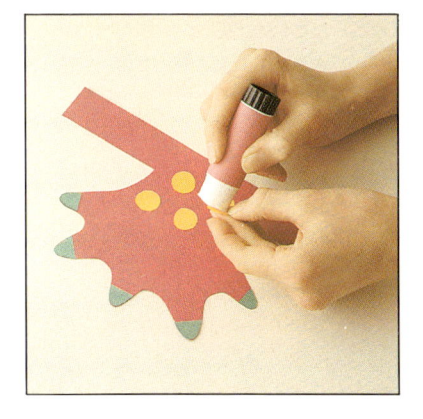

3 Cut out polka dots from a third coloured paper. Stick these in position on the fronts of the feet.

4 Wrap the fastening bands around your wrists and ask a friend to mark the point where they overlap. Trim if necessary and cut notches to form a fastening, or attach with paper clips.

Dressing-up Fun

Materials

There is an enormous range of face painting materials available at a range of different prices. Toy and novelty shops often stock a range of face paints, as well as theatrical suppliers.

Child's make-up kit
This is a good starter kit. It includes a bright range of coloured face paints, sponges, brushes, and a well for water. It is available from most toy shops.

Cleansing towels
These are ideal for removing the last traces of face paint.

Cold cream cleanser
Even though most water-based face paints come off with soap and water, you can also use a cream cleanser with soft tissues or cotton wool.

Cotton buds
These are used to apply and remove make-up around the eye.

Eyebrow brush
This is used for combing eyebrows and eyelashes.

Fake blood
This is great for special effects and can be purchased from theatrical and novelty shops.

Glitter gel
This comes in a range of colours and gives a sparkly finish. It can be purchased from costume shops.

Make-up brushes
These come in a range of sizes and shapes. It is a good idea to have different types to use for different effects. Wide brushes either have a flat or rounded edge and are used for large areas of modelling or for applying blusher, highlights or all-over powder. Medium brushes with a rounded edge are useful for modelling colour, while narrow brushes, either flat or pointed, are used for outlining and painting fine details and lips.

Make-up fixative
This is available from professional theatrical shops. It fixes the make-up, therefore making it last longer. Make sure the model's eyes are closed when spraying it.

Make-up palette
This provides a range of solid, vibrant colours that give very good effects. You can mix colours together if the set you have doesn't provide the range of colours you require.

Make-up (eye-liner) pencils
These are used for drawing fine details on the face. They can also be used for outlining your basic design, if necessary.

Make-up pots
These are purchased from specialist theatrical shops. They are more expensive but are excellent quality and come in a wonderful range of colours.

Plastic palette
Use as a surface for mixing face paints together to achieve more subtle colours.

Soft tissue
Use with a dab of cold cream cleanser to remove make-up or for wiping off excess make-up from your brush.

Sponges
Covered sponges such as powder puffs are used for applying dry powders. Cellulose or latex sponges can be used slightly damp to give an even colour. Stipple sponges are made from soft plastic and are used for creating textured effects such as beard growth, animal skins and other effects.

Temple white
This is available from theatrical shops and is applied to the hair to give an aged effect.

Wax make-up crayons
If you do not mind a less professional finish, these are a good, inexpensive option. They give a less solid colour and the result is less long-lasting but they are often formulated for young children to use themselves.

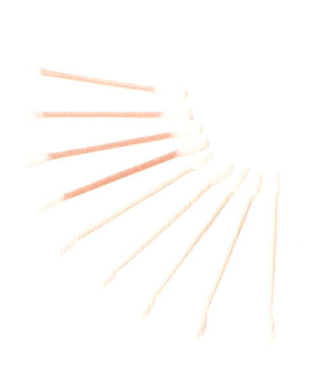

fine make-up brush

medium make-up brushes

make-up (eye-liner) pencils

eyebrow brush

- make-up fixative
- cleansing towels
- child's make-up kit
- cold cream cleanser
- make-up pots
- fake blood
- temple white
- make-up palette
- cotton buds
- sponges
- plastic palette
- soft tissue
- wax make-up crayons
- glitter gel
- wide make-up brushes

Applying a Base

An evenly applied, well-modelled base is the foundation for successful face-painting effects. Experiment with different colours, blended directly onto the face, to change the model's appearance.

YOU WILL NEED
make-up sponge
water-based face paints

1 Using a damp sponge, begin to apply the base colour over the face. To avoid streaks or patchiness, make sure the sponge is not too wet.

2 Make sure the base is applied evenly over the face and fill in any patchy areas.

3 Using a contrasting colour, sponge around the edge of the face.

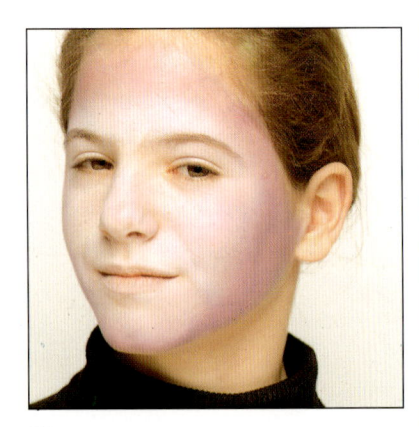

4 Blend the colours together for an even finish. Always make sure the base colours are dry before you start to decorate the face with other colours.

Shading

Shading can change the shape of your model's face dramatically.

YOU WILL NEED
powder face paints
soft make-up brush

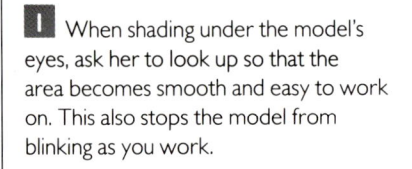

1 When shading under the model's eyes, ask her to look up so that the area becomes smooth and easy to work on. This also stops the model from blinking as you work.

2 To exaggerate the shape of the model's face, shade each cheekbone with blusher or dark powder face paint.

3 To shade the whole face, use a large soft brush.

DRESSING-UP FUN

Painting Lips

YOU WILL NEED
fine lipstick brush
water-based face paints

1 Using a fine lipstick brush, paint the lips. Ask the model to close her mouth as this makes the muscles firmer and easier to outline. Then ask the model to open her mouth to fill in the corners. You may need to wait a few seconds to allow the make-up to dry before going on to the next stage.

2 Rest your hand on the model's chin, on a piece of tissue or a powder puff. This will help you to paint an even outline around the lips. You might want to experiment with using a different colour for the outline, or extending the line beyond the natural curve of the model's mouth to create a different shape.

Ageing the Face

You can make even the young look very old with this technique.

YOU WILL NEED
water-based face paints
fine make-up brush
wide make-up brush

1 To find where wrinkles occur naturally, ask the model to frown. This will show where lines will occur with age. Apply fine lines of make-up in these areas. Ask the model to smile, and apply a fine line starting at either side of the nose, down the fold of the cheek.

2 Ask your model to purse her lips, and apply fine lines around the mouth, within the natural folds.

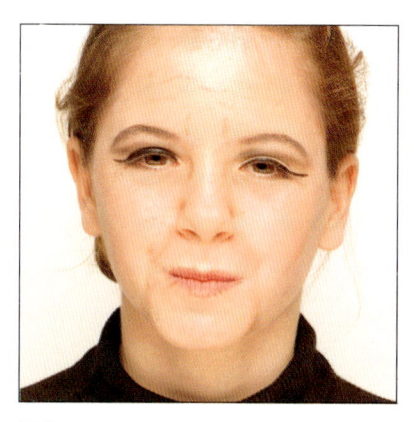

3 Finish by giving a light dusting of a lighter coloured base with a wide brush on the cheeks and temples.

Removing Make-up

Most face paints will come off with soap and water. If soap is too drying, or if some colours persist, you may want to remove make-up as follows.

YOU WILL NEED
cold cream cleanser
cotton wool ball or soft tissues

1 Pour the cream onto a damp cotton wool ball or tissue and gently rub the make-up off the face. Use a clean tissue or your fingers to apply more cold cream cleanser.

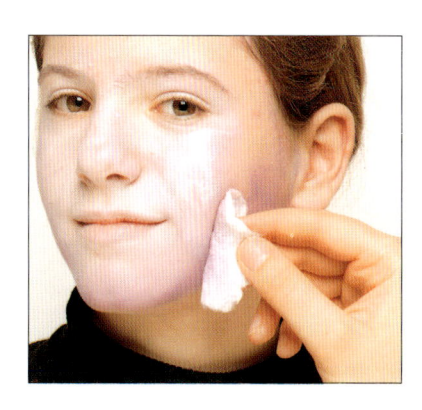

2 If desired, give a final cleanse with soap and water, and dry by patting the face with a soft towel.

Dressing-up Fun

Zombie

You could dress in black to make this character look even more creepy.

YOU WILL NEED
make-up sponge
water-based face paints
thick make-up brush
medium make-up brush
fine make-up brush
fake blood (optional)

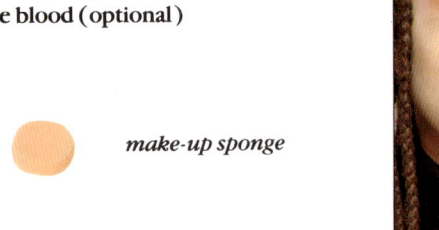

make-up sponge

water-based face paints

fine make-up brush

thick make-up brush

medium make-up brush

fake blood

1 Using a damp sponge, apply the base colour over the face, avoiding the area surrounding the eye. Use a thick brush to dust a darker colour on the forehead, around each eye and around the mouth, to create a bruised effect.

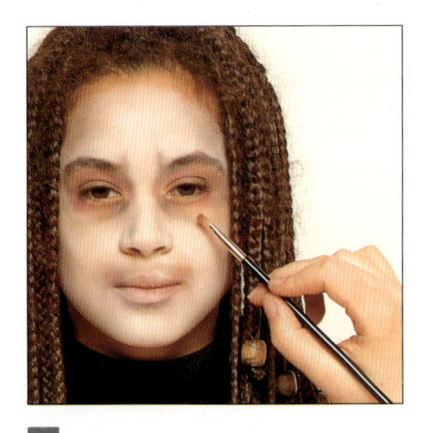

2 Using a medium brush, fill in the area surrounding the eye with a darker colour, then paint dark lines under the eyes and on the eyebrows.

3 Paint the lips a light colour and use a fine brush to paint on dark lines, making the lips look as if they are cracked. Using fake blood or red make-up, paint the corners of the mouth to look as if they are bleeding.

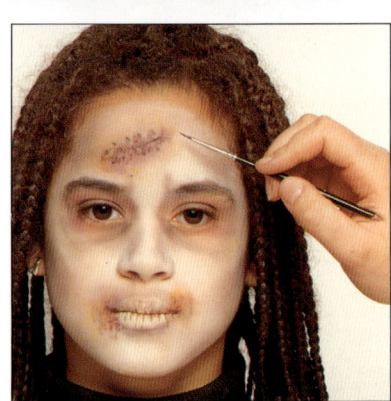

4 Use a fine brush to paint the scar on the forehead.

Gremlin

This mischievous creature is all dressed in green. Cover a green T-shirt with a piece of fur and wear a pair of green tights.

YOU WILL NEED
tape measure
hairband
fake fur
scissors
needle and thread
glue
felt
pencil

FOR THE FACE
water-based face paints
medium make-up brush

water-based face paints

medium make-up brush

1 Measure the length of the hairband and cut the fake fur to fit. Sew the fur onto the hairband, then sew or glue a strip of felt to the inside.

2 Cut out two pieces of fur for each ear, in the shape of softly rounded triangles. Make sure that the base of the triangles match the curve of the hairband. With right sides facing, sew the two ear pieces together. Turn right side out and stitch onto the hairband.

3 For the face, apply green areas with feathery brush strokes.

4 Paint a brown spot at the end of the nose and paint the lips the same colour, enlarging the top lip so that it meets the tip of the nose.

DRESSING-UP FUN

Spectacular Sea-face

Pretend you've just popped up from the ocean bed with this wonderful design of starfish and seaweed.

YOU WILL NEED
coloured face paints
tinsel wig (optional)

face paints

1. Paint the outlines of the sea-shapes such as fish, seaweed and starfish onto your face.

2. Colour in the starfish and seaweed.

3. Fill in the fish with bright colours. Add a mixture of details to them.

4. Carefully colour in around the shapes so that your whole face is covered with face paints. Put on the tinsel wig, if using.

88

Monkey

For the complete monkey outfit make a pair of furry ears and wear brown clothes. You could even make a brown tail.

YOU WILL NEED
make-up sponge
water-based face paints
fine make-up brush
medium make-up brush

water-based face paints

medium make-up brush

fine make-up brush

make-up sponge

1 Using a damp sponge, apply a yellow base colour over the face.

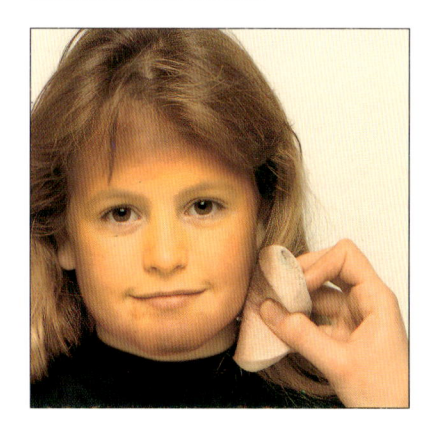

2 Rinse the sponge, then dab a few darker shades around the edge of the face, blending them in with the base.

3 Paint the outline of the monkey's mouth using a fine brush. Use a medium brush to fill in the marked area with black.

4 Paint the tip of the nose black and paint on a pair of eyebrows above the model's own. Using a fine brush, paint a few lines in between the eyebrows, under each eye and at each side of the mouth.

DRESSING-UP FUN

Owl

In this design, large yellow owl eyes are painted onto your eyelids, so when your eyes are closed, it looks as though they are wide open.

YOU WILL NEED
thick make-up brush
water-based face paints
medium make-up brush
fine make-up brush
hair spray
hair clips

medium make-up brush

thick make-up brush

water-based face paints

1 Using a thick brush, paint a white area around each eye, leaving bare the area immediately surrounding the eye.

2 Paint the rest of the face brown, except for the mouth, the upper lip and the tip of the nose.

3 Using a medium brush, apply red to the tip of the nose, the upper lip and the mouth.

4 Making sure the brush is not too wet, gently paint yellow on the eyelids and around the eye. Do not apply too close to the eyelashes. Using a fine brush, paint a black stripe across the top of each eyelid and a short stripe down the centre. Paint a black line around the red nose and mouth area and black streaks around the eye area.

5 Add feathery streaks around the eye area in yellow and white.

90

DRESSING-UP FUN

6 Brush the hair off the face into feathery tufts and secure it with hair spray and hair clips.

DRESSING-UP FUN

Frankenstein's Monster

Practise your monster's walk when you wear this costume. This will really scare your friends.

YOU WILL NEED
make-up sponge
water-based face paints
thick make-up brush
medium make-up brush
fine make-up brush
black swimming hat (bathing cap)

make-up sponge

water-based face paints

fine make-up brush

medium make-up brush

thick make-up brush

1 Using a damp sponge, apply the base colour over the face. Rinse the sponge, then apply a darker shade, avoiding the mouth and the nose area. Finally, shade the cheekbones with a third colour.

2 Using a medium brush, paint the eyebrows black and darken the eyelids and the area under each eye.

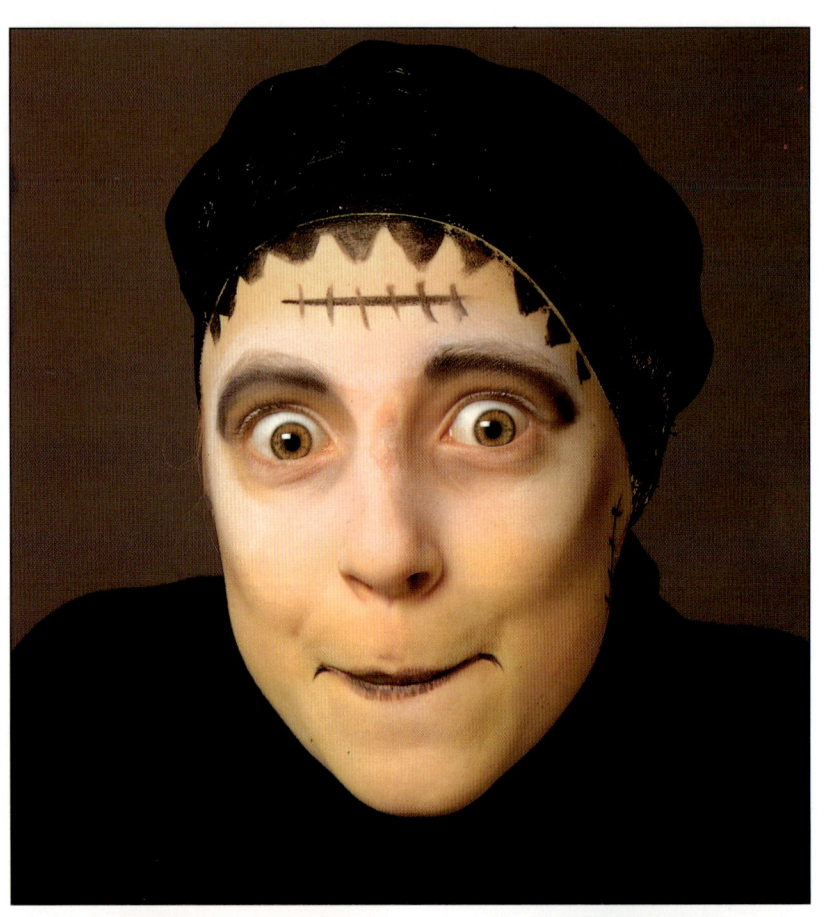

3 Paint the lips black and, using a fine brush, paint fine black lines at either side of the mouth.

4 Using a fine brush, paint a black scar on the forehead and on one side of the face. Put on a black swimming hat (bathing cap), making sure you hide most of the hair. Where the hat meets the forehead paint a jagged hair line.

DRESSING-UP FUN

Purple Monster

If you want to be a really gruesome monster, wear a set of rotten-looking plastic teeth. They can be bought from toy or joke shops.

YOU WILL NEED
make-up sponge
water-based face paints
fine make-up brush
medium make-up brush

water-based face paints

make-up sponge

fine make-up brush

medium make-up brush

1 Using a damp sponge, apply the base colour over the face. Dab a darker shade around the edge of the face and on the forehead, blending it with the base colour.

2 Using a fine brush, paint a pair of eyebrows slightly above the model's own. Paint the tip of the nose and paint on a droopy moustache just above the model's mouth. You might find it easier to sketch an outline for the shapes first and then fill them in.

3 Use a medium brush to paint on other shapes. Paint the shapes on one side of the face first and then paint the other side. This will help you to make sure the design is symmetrical. Paint the lips the same colour.

4 Decorate the face with silver and purple spots and other details.

Lion

The wilder your hair is the fiercer you will look. Try roaring and snarling in a mirror to see what different expressions you can make, but don't frighten your friends or family too much. Complete the look by making a pair of furry ears.

YOU WILL NEED
make-up sponge
water-based face paints
natural sea sponge
medium make-up brush
fine make-up brush or make-up (eye-liner) pencil
lipstick brush
thick make-up brush

make-up sponge

water-based face paints

medium make-up brush

fine make-up brush

thick make-up brush

lipstick brush

1 Using a damp sponge, apply the base colour over the face.

2 Using a natural sponge, dab a darker shade around the edge of the face as shown.

3 Using a medium brush, apply white make-up over each eyebrow to form an almost circular shape. Colour the area around the mouth and chin white.

4 Study the picture carefully so that you know where to paint the markings on the face. You might find it easier to outline some of them with a fine brush or make-up (eye-liner) pencil first and then fill them in. Only paint the top lip at this stage.

5 Paint the bottom lip red.

DRESSING-UP FUN

6 Using a thick brush, dust the nose and centre of the forehead with a shade of brown.

95

DRESSING-UP FUN

Butterfly

When you wear this pretty outfit, gently move your arms to make the wings flap.

YOU WILL NEED
2.5 m (2½ yd) milliner's wire
scissors
sticky tape
coloured netting
needle and embroidery thread
smaller pieces of different coloured netting
silver or gold elastic cord
hairband
2 paper baubles (balls)
paints
paintbrush
glue
glitter
felt

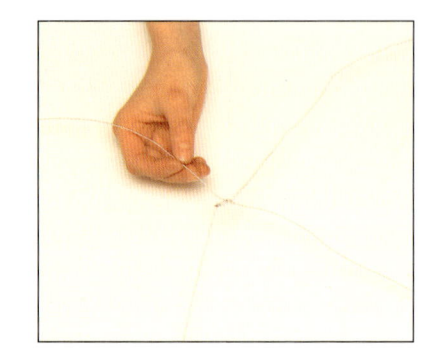

glue

hairband

paper bauble (ball)

glitter *netting*

1 Cut a piece of milliner's wire approximately 2 m/2 yd long. Bend the two ends together to make a big circle. For extra safety, secure the ends with a piece of sticky tape. Pinch the two sides of the wire circle together and twist. The wire should now resemble a figure-of-eight.

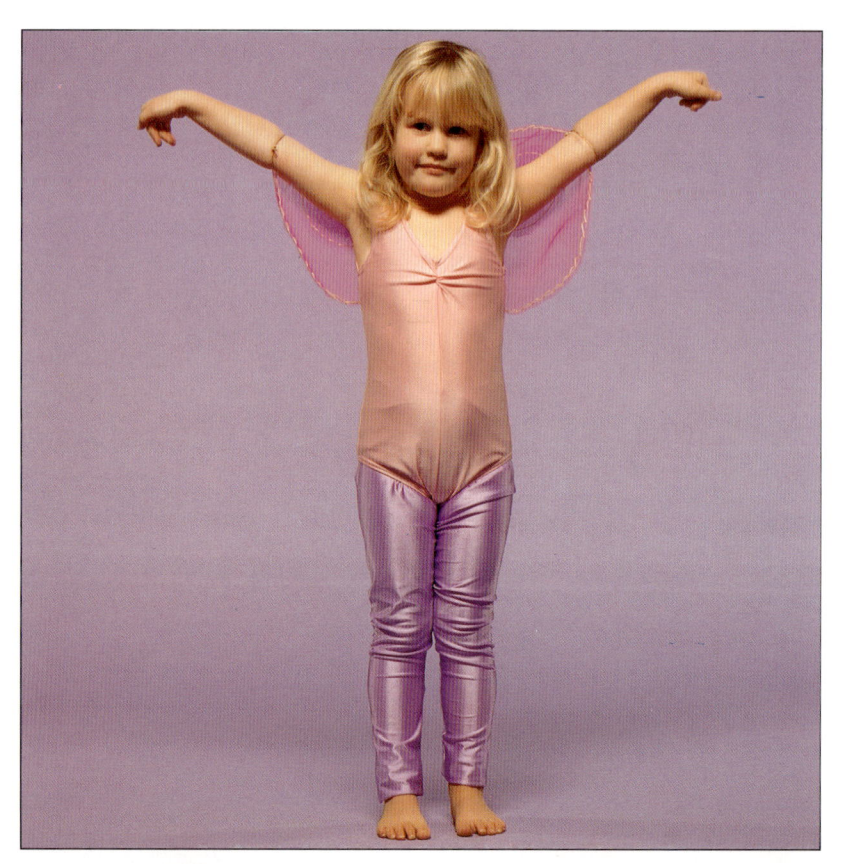

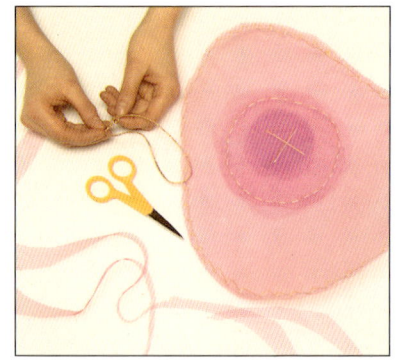

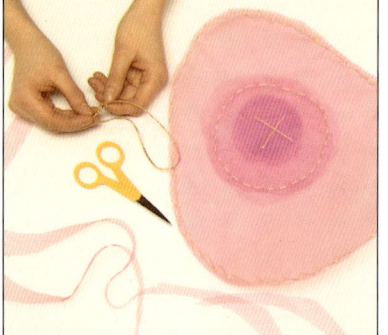

2 Place the wire frame between two pieces of coloured netting. Sew the netting onto the wire frame using a brightly coloured embroidery thread. Trim away any excess net. Cut out circles of different coloured netting and sew them onto each wing. To support the wings, thread a loop of elastic cord onto the outside of each wing for the arms to slip through.

3 Paint the hairband and each paper bauble (ball) a bright colour and leave them to dry thoroughly. Cut a short piece of wire and stick it into each bauble (ball). This will make covering it in glitter much easier. Paint the bauble (ball) with a coat of glue and dip it into the glitter. Leave the glue to dry.

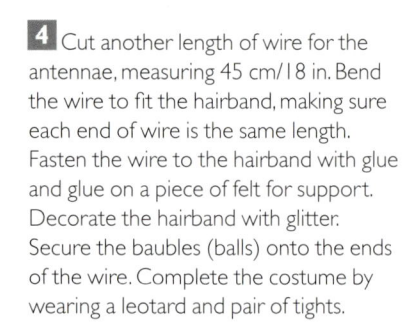

4 Cut another length of wire for the antennae, measuring 45 cm/18 in. Bend the wire to fit the hairband, making sure each end of wire is the same length. Fasten the wire to the hairband with glue and glue on a piece of felt for support. Decorate the hairband with glitter. Secure the baubles (balls) onto the ends of the wire. Complete the costume by wearing a leotard and pair of tights.

Tattoo

Wow your friends with this fake tattoo! A butterfly is shown below but you can make any design you like.

YOU WILL NEED
coloured face paints

face paints

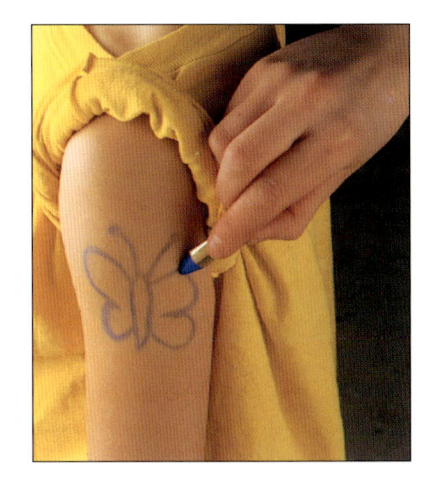

1 Paint the outline of a butterfly or your chosen design onto your arm.

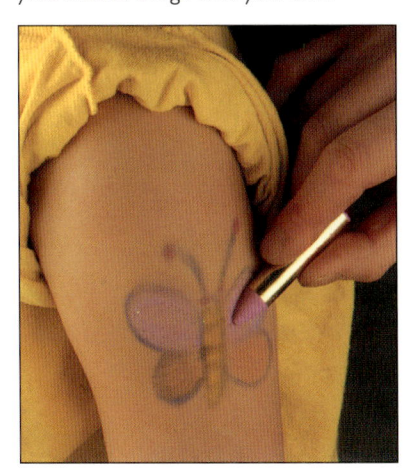

2 Carefully begin to colour it in.

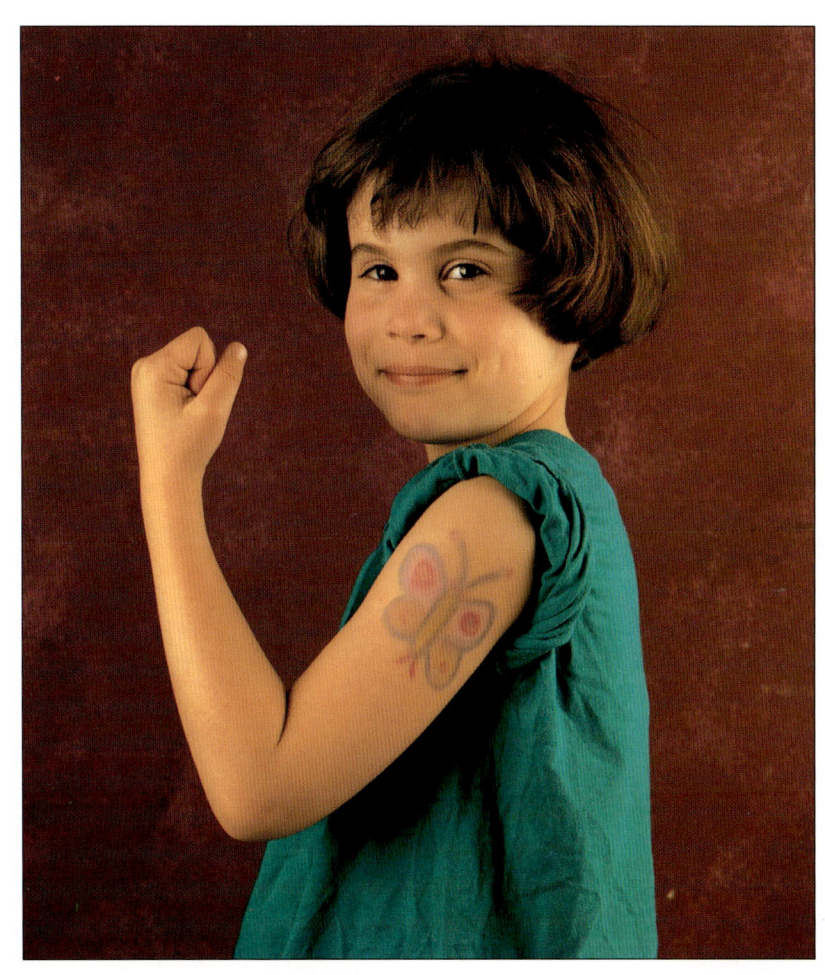

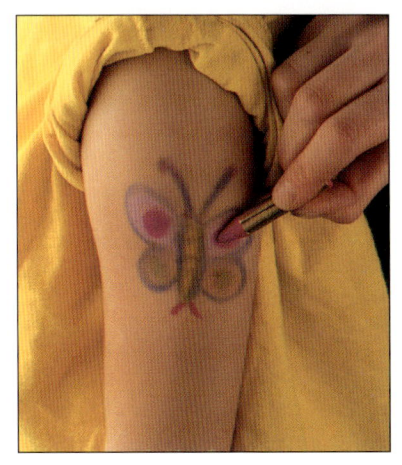

3 Try to make your design as beautiful as possible by drawing tiny patterns and other details.

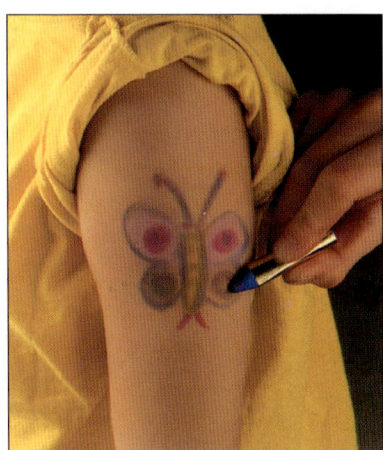

4 Complete your design. Face paints can smudge very easily, so look after your tattoo and don't let it rub against anything.

DRESSING-UP FUN

Ghost

Spook your friends in this fabulous disguise. See how long it takes before they guess who you are.

YOU WILL NEED
old white sheet
scissors
needle and thread or sewing machine
milliner's wire
black felt
fabric glue

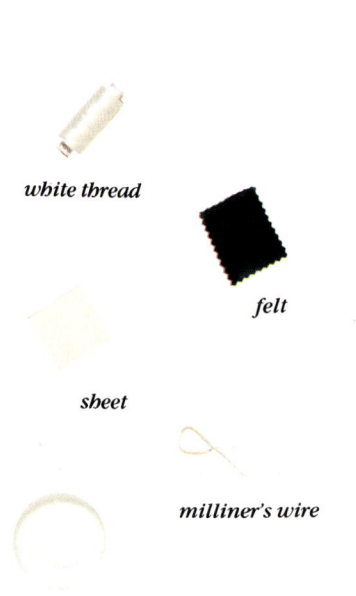

white thread

felt

sheet

milliner's wire

fabric glue

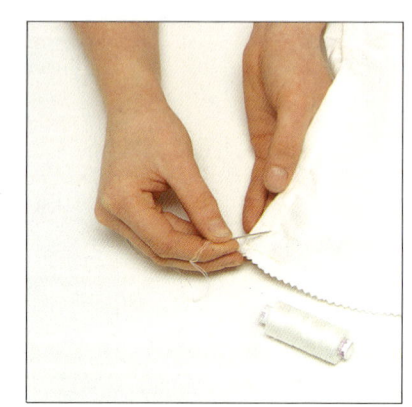

scissors

1 Cut two pieces of sheet in the shape of a dome, making sure the height of the dome is longer than your own height. Sew the two pieces together leaving an opening at the bottom. Sew another line of stitching parallel to the line you have sewn. This is to make a tube for the wire.

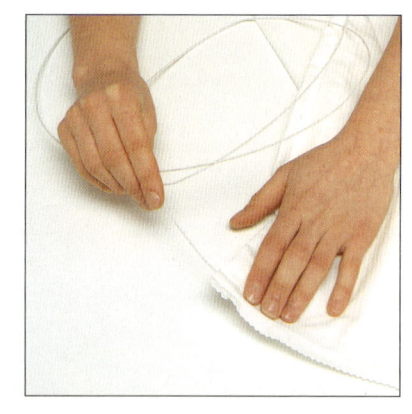

2 Thread the wire through the tube. Secure each end of the wire to the sheet with a few stitches.

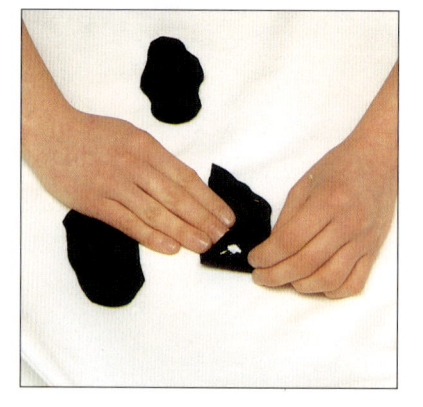

3 Cut out a mouth and pair of eyes from a piece of felt and glue them onto the sheet using fabric glue.

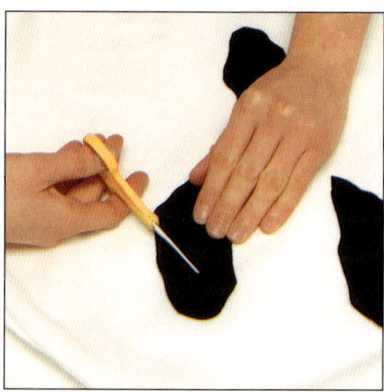

4 Cut small holes in the eyes and the mouth, so that you can see where you are going. Try the costume on and bend the wire to fit your body.

Egyptian Mummy

Make sure you wear a white T-shirt and a pair of white tights or leggings underneath the costume, just in case it starts to unravel!

YOU WILL NEED
old white sheet
scissors
needle and thread
white T-shirt and leggings or tights

FOR THE FACE
make-up sponge
water-based face paints

sheet

white thread

scissors

water-based face paints

make-up sponge

1 To make the costume, tear or cut strips of the sheet approximately 10 cm/4 in wide and as long as possible.

2 Sew the strips of fabric together to form one long strip.

3 For the face, use a damp sponge to apply a white base. Rinse the sponge, then dab light purple around the eye sockets to give a ghoulish appearance. Then wrap the fabric round the head first, leaving the face open. Gradually wrap the fabric down the body.

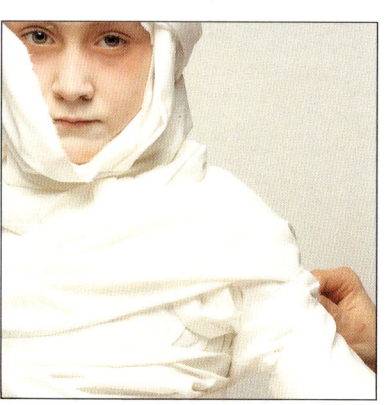

4 When you get to the hands, go back up the arm again, still wrapping the fabric around. Do the same with the legs. When you have wrapped the whole body, sew the end of the strip to part of the costume. To take the costume off, simply unravel the strip of fabric.

DRESSING-UP FUN

Astronaut

This space traveller looks all set for a journey to the stars and planets. Collect recycled containers to decorate the costume.

YOU WILL NEED
large balloon
newspaper
diluted PVA (white) glue
mixing bowl
pin
pencil
scissors
silver paint
paintbrush
foil pie dishes (pans)
tin foil
sticky tape
piece of foam rubber
plain T-shirt
cardboard containers, such as fruit cartons
old pair of gloves (optional)

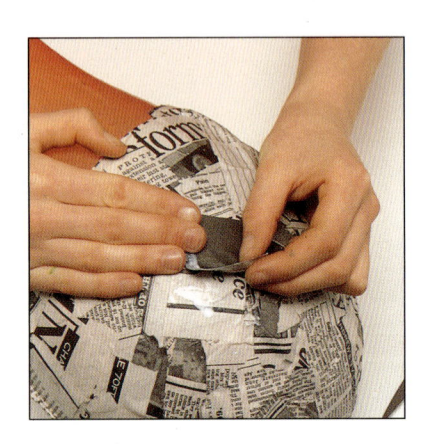

silver paint

tin foil

newspaper

scissors

PVA (white) glue

cardboard container

1 To make the helmet, blow up a large balloon and cover it with approximately 10 layers of papier-mâché. Leave to dry.

2 When the papier-mâché has dried, pop the balloon with a pin. Draw and cut out an opening for the face and remove the balloon.

3 Paint the helmet silver and decorate with shapes cut from pie dishes (pans).

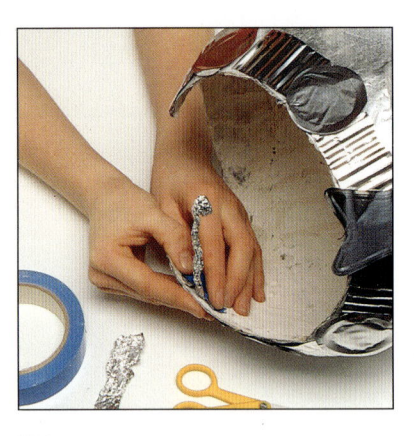

4 Make a microphone from a piece of rolled tin foil and tape it to the inside of the helmet. To make the helmet more comfortable to wear, glue a piece of foam rubber to the inside.

5 Decorate a plain T-shirt by gluing on containers and foil pie dishes (pans).

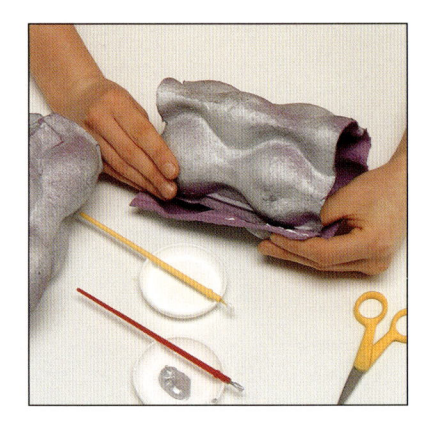

6 Make the arm and leg shields from cardboard containers. Fruit cartons have been used here. Paint the cartons silver and bend them to make a tube. Glue the edges together. If you have an old pair of gloves, paint them silver.

100

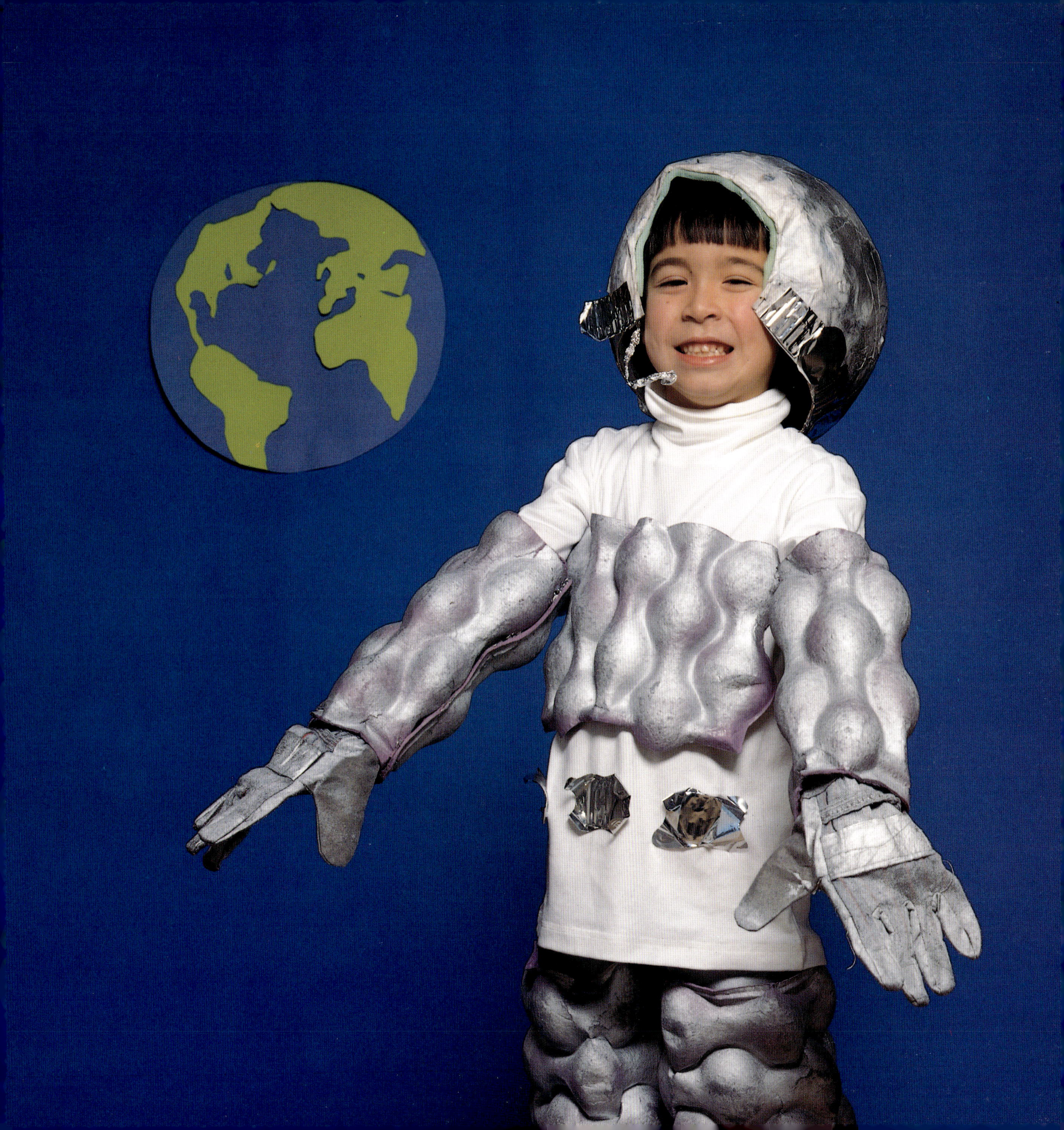

Sunflower

Dazzle your friends with this bright cheerful headdress. Wear yellow and green clothes to complete the costume.

YOU WILL NEED
pair of compasses
cardboard
scissors
ribbon
sticky tape
pencil
yellow paper
glue
black paint
paintbrush

FOR THE FACE
make-up sponge
water-based face paints
medium make-up brush

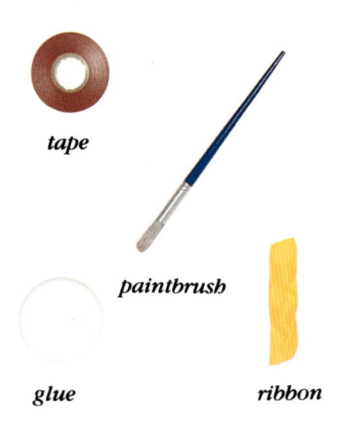

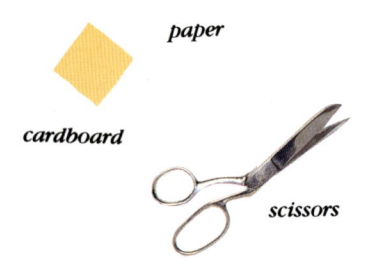

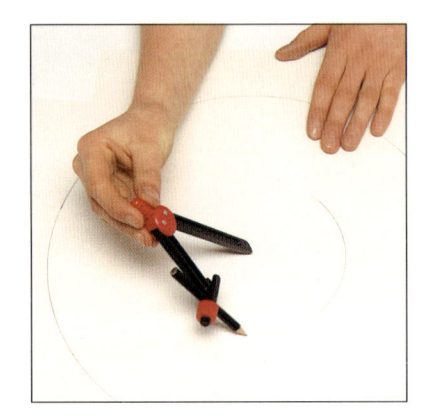

1 To make the costume, use a pair of compasses to draw and cut out a circle from a piece of cardboard. Draw and cut out a circle in the middle big enough for your face to show through.

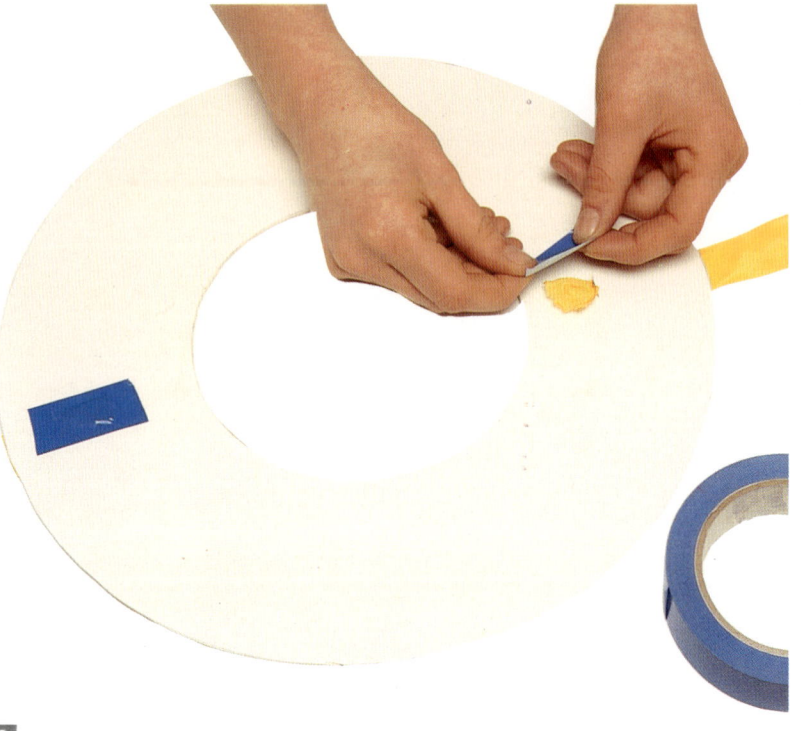

2 Make a slit either side of the circle and thread a piece of ribbon through. Secure the ribbon with a knot and a piece of sticky tape.

3 Draw a petal shape onto yellow paper, and use it as a template for the others. You will need about 42 petals for a full sunflower. Cut out the petals.

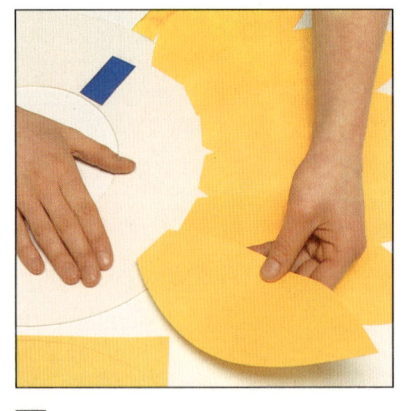

4 Starting at the edge of the cardboard circle, glue on the petals so that they overlap each other. When you have covered the outer edge start on the second row and finish off in the centre of the circle.

5 Paint black marks around the centre of the sunflower and leave the paint to dry. When you are ready to wear the flower, tie the ribbon around your head in a bow.

Dressing-up Fun

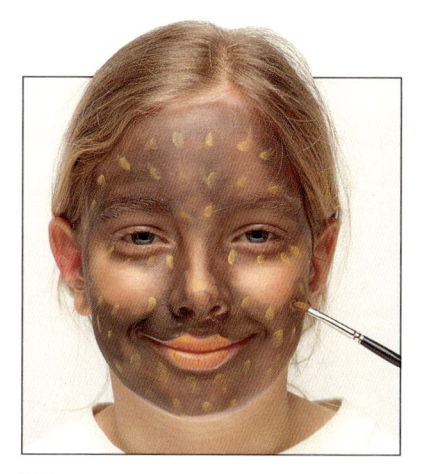

6 For the face, use a damp sponge to apply a brown base colour. Use a medium brush to paint yellow spots on the base colour. Paint the lips the same colour.

7 Paint yellow highlights under each eye and on the nose.

Pumpkin

You will certainly win the biggest pumpkin competition if you wear this outfit.

YOU WILL NEED
hairband
green paint
paintbrush
scissors
green fabric
needle and matching thread or sewing machine
stuffing (batting)
3 m (3 yd) orange fabric
fabric tape
milliner's wire
safety pin
elastic

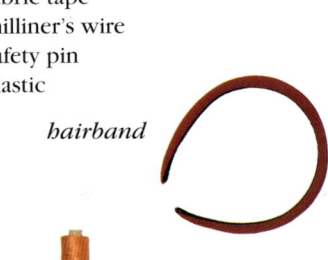

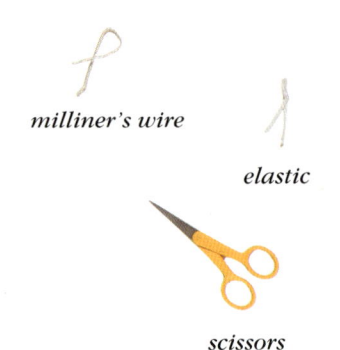

hairband

thread

fabric

milliner's wire

elastic

scissors

1 To make the pumpkin stalk, first paint the hairband green and leave it to dry. Cut out two pieces of green fabric and sew them together with the right sides facing. Leave a gap and turn right sides out. Fill the stalk with stuffing (batting) and sew up the end. Sew the stalk onto the centre of the hairband.

2 To make the pumpkin body, first fold over the two long sides of the orange fabric and sew a line of stitches on each long side to make a 1.5 cm (⅝ in) tube for the elastic.

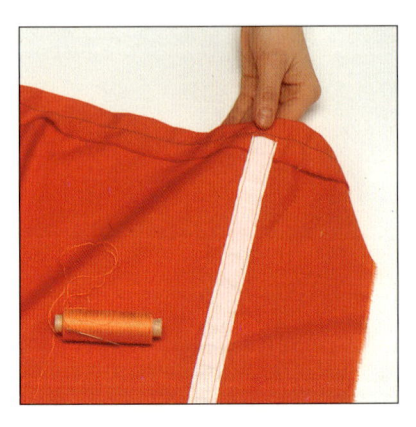

3 Sew lengths of fabric tape widthwise on the reverse side of the fabric. You will need to sew on approximately five lengths of tape, positioned equal distances apart.

4 Thread a length of milliner's wire through each fabric tape tube. Bend the ends over and sew them onto the tape.

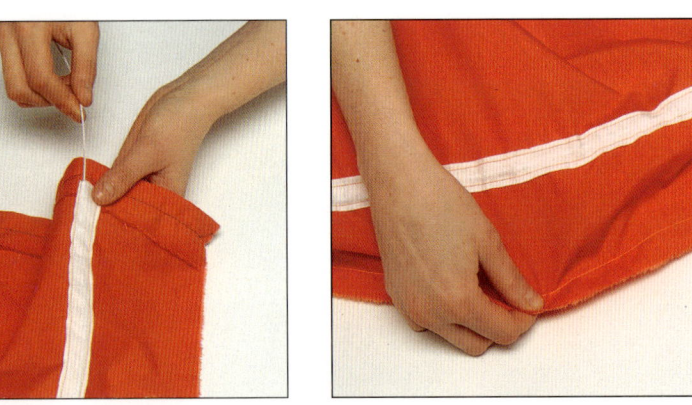

5 With the right sides facing fold the fabric in half widthwise, and turn so that the tubes for the elastic are at the top and bottom. Sew the shorter sides together.

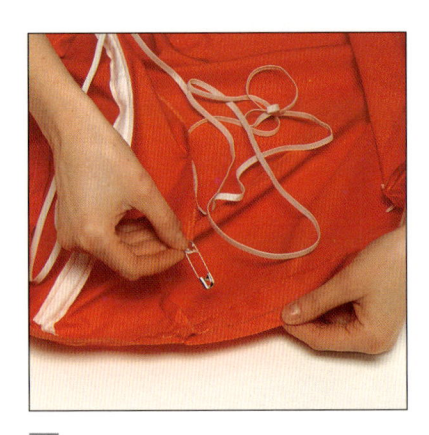

6 Attach a safety pin to the elastic and thread through the top and bottom tubes. Pull the end of the elastic to gather the fabric and tie a double knot. Before you try on the pumpkin costume, bend the wires so that they are curved, to make a full, round shape.

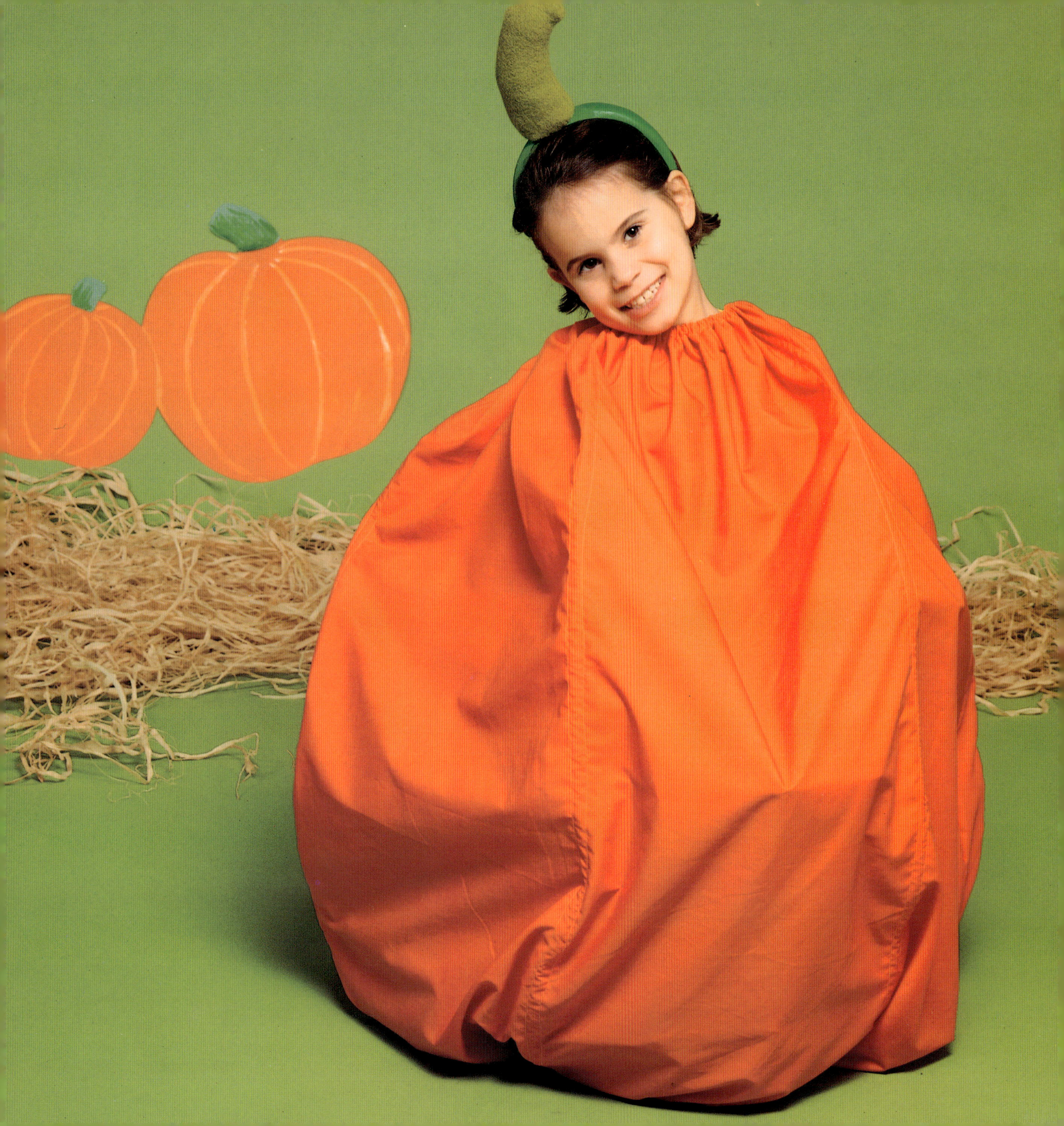

Skeleton

This is the perfect outfit for spooking your friends and family on Hallowe'en.

YOU WILL NEED
black leotard
white fabric paints
paintbrush
black leggings

FOR THE FACE
black make-up (eye-liner) pencil
water-based face paints
medium make-up brush

water-based face paints

medium make-up brush

fabric paint

paintbrush

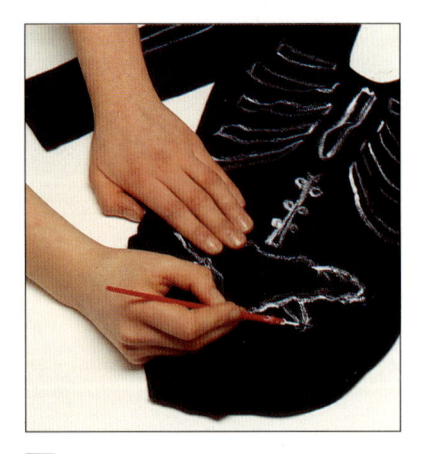

1 To make the costume, use white fabric paint to draw on the outline of the skeleton's body, making sure that the leotard is lying flat.

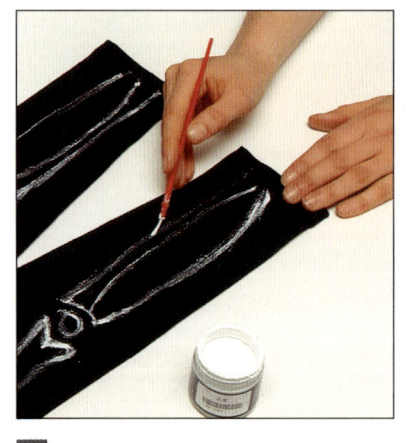

2 Paint the outline of the skeleton's legs on the front of the leggings.

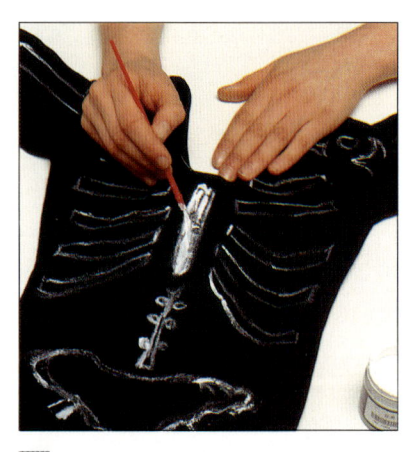

3 Fill in the outlined areas with white on both the leotard and leggings.

4 Using a black make-up (eye-liner) pencil, draw a circular outline around each eye, a small triangle above each nostril, and a large mouth shape around the model's own mouth. Draw an outline around the edge of the face.

5 Using a medium brush, paint the face white, avoiding the shapes you have just drawn in pencil.

6 Paint the eyes, the triangles above the nostrils and the sides of the face black. Paint a thick black outline around the mouth and fill the mouth area in white. Divide the mouth into a set of ghostly teeth with black lines.

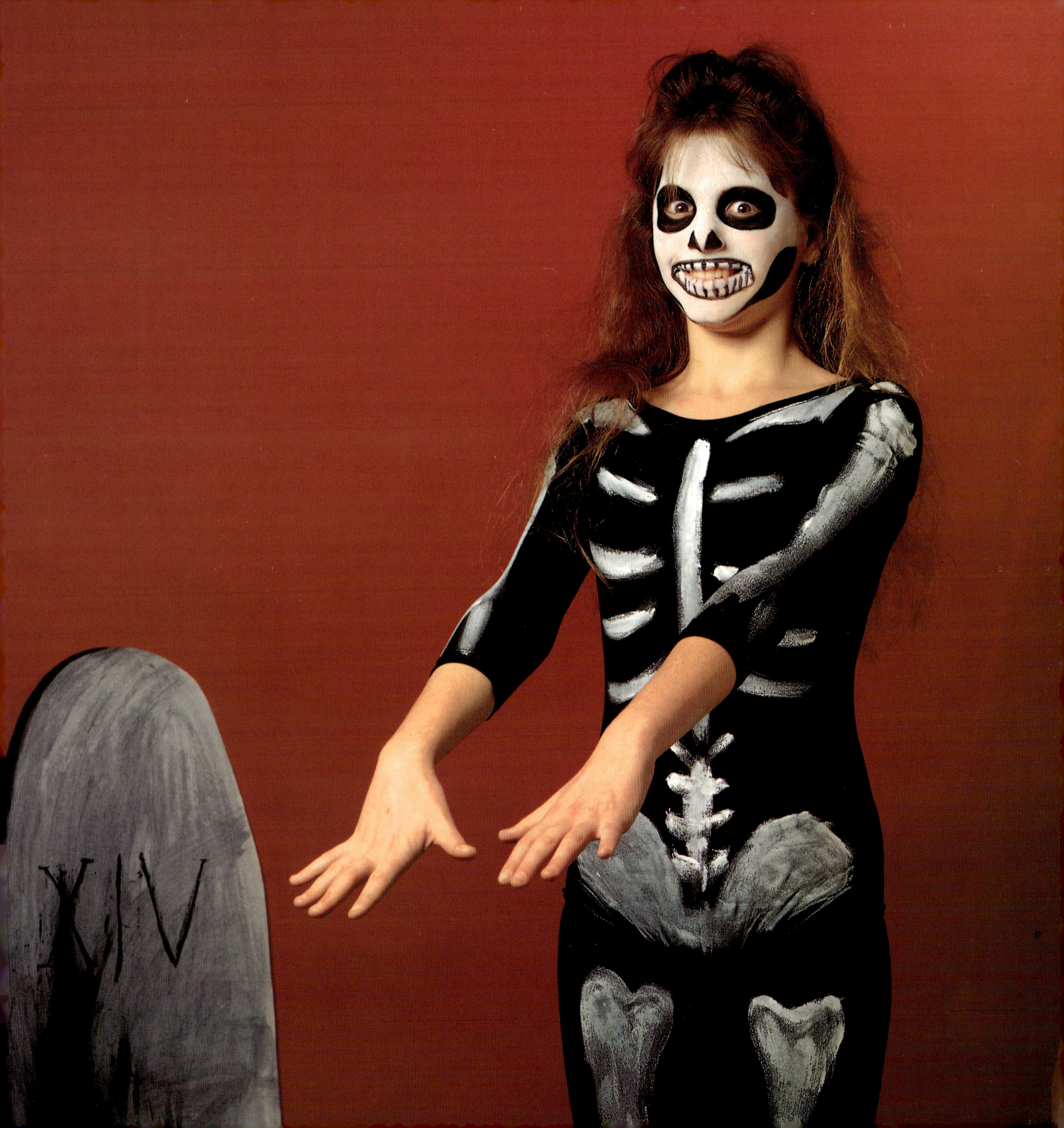
XIV

DRESSING-UP FUN

Carrot

For the complete outfit, dress up in an orange T-shirt and leggings and, if you have an old pair of shoes, paint them orange.

YOU WILL NEED
pencil
cardboard, in 2 shades of green
scissors
glue

FOR THE FACE
make-up sponge
water-based face paints

cardboard

glue

scissors

1 Draw lots of differently shaped leaves on green cardboard and cut them out.

2 Cut two strips of green cardboard 5 cm/2 in wide and long enough to fit around your head. Glue the leaves along one of the strips.

3 Glue the other strip on top of the first, sandwiching the base of the leaves between the two. Leave the glue to dry.

4 Curve the card to fit around your head and glue the two ends of the strip together. Leave the glue to dry before trying the headdress on.

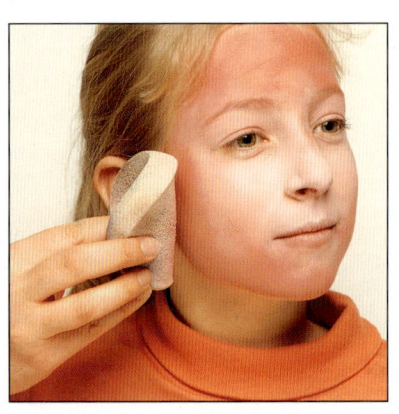

5 For the face, use a make-up sponge to apply an orange base all over.

108

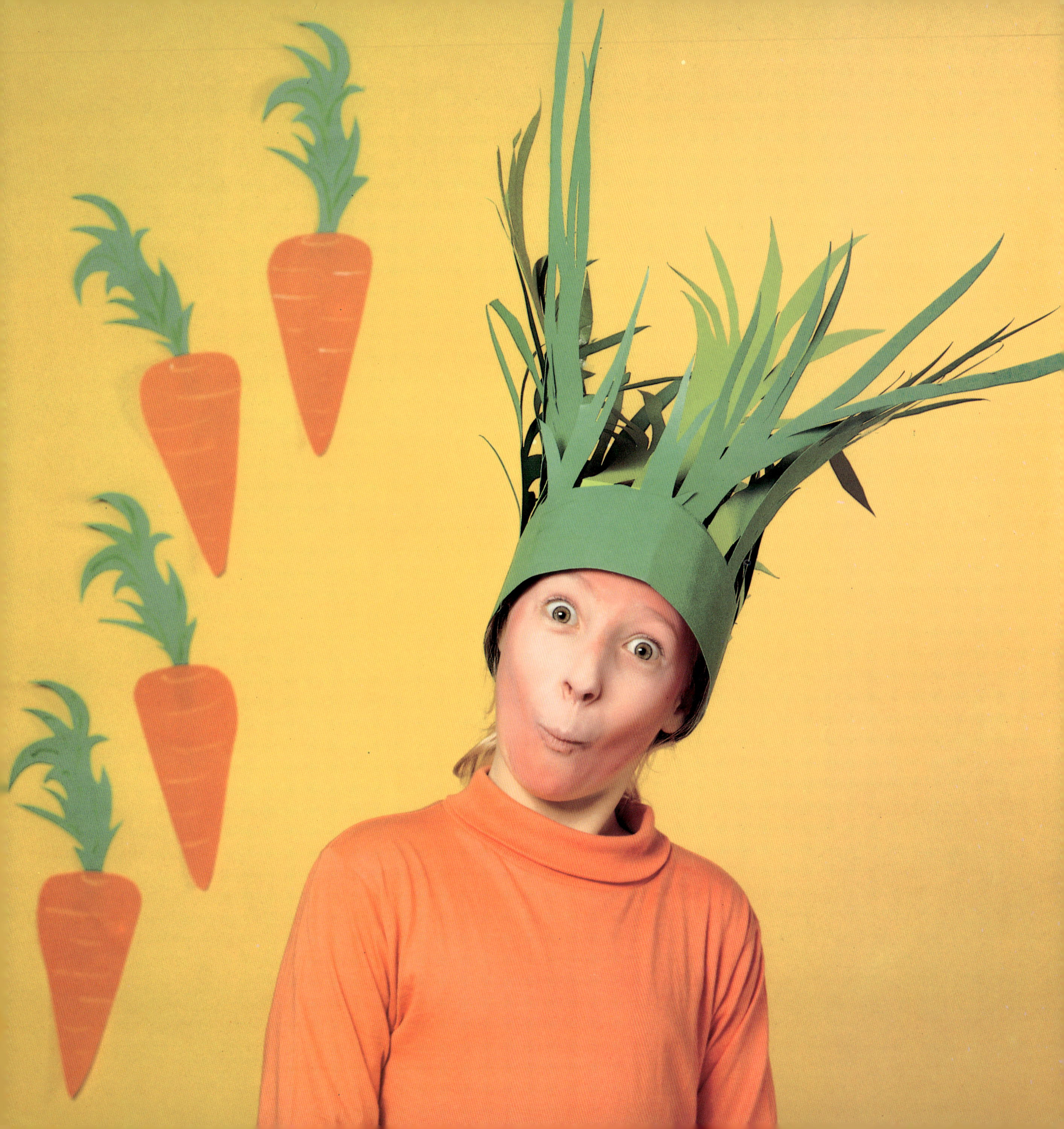

Super Hero

Be a hero for a day and make your very own costume.

YOU WILL NEED
cardboard
scissors
tin foil
coloured foil papers
glue
silver cardboard
ribbon
sticky tape

FOR THE CAPE
leotard or catsuit
2 m (2 yd) fabric
needle and matching thread

silver cardboard

coloured foil papers

scissors

glue

1 To make a wristband, first cut out a cardboard triangle and cover it in tin foil. Cut a smaller triangle in coloured foil paper and glue it onto the silver triangle. Cut out the letter 'S' in silver cardboard and glue it onto the coloured triangle. Cut a strip of silver cardboard 5 cm/2 in wide and long enough to fit around your wrist. Glue the two ends together to make a band and glue on the triangle. Make another wristband the same way.

2 To make the waistband, cut a piece of cardboard to fit around your waist. Cut a circle from cardboard and cover it in tin foil. Cut a star from coloured foil paper and glue it onto the silver circle. Cut out the letter 'S' in cardboard and glue it onto the star. Glue the circle onto the waistband.

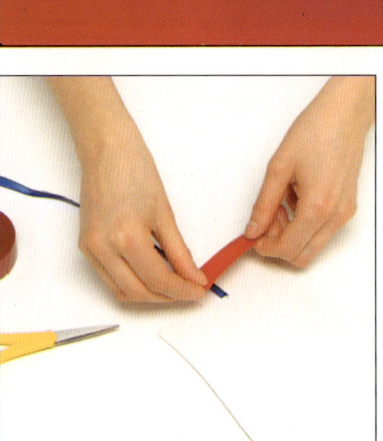

3 At each end of the waistband, attach a piece of ribbon with sticky tape. To make the headband, cut a strip of silver cardboard to fit around your head. Glue it and leave to dry. You can decorate this in a similar way to the wristbands or cape.

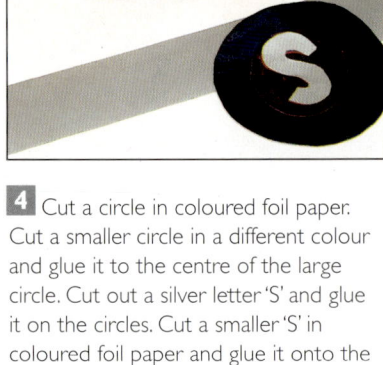

4 Cut a circle in coloured foil paper. Cut a smaller circle in a different colour and glue it to the centre of the large circle. Cut out a silver letter 'S' and glue it on the circles. Cut a smaller 'S' in coloured foil paper and glue it onto the silver 'S'. Make a cape as opposite.

DRESSING-UP FUN

Super Heroine

Impress your friends and family with your heroic powers and dress up in this futuristic costume.

YOU WILL NEED
cardboard
scissors
tin foil
coloured foil papers
glue
silver cardboard
ribbon
sticky tape
coloured cardboard (optional)

FOR THE CAPE
leotard or catsuit
2 m (2 yd) fabric
needle and matching thread

scissors

coloured foil papers

glue

1 Make the wristbands, waistband and headband as for the Super Hero's outfit, varying the decorations, if you like.

2 To make the pendant, cut out a star in silver cardboard and glue the letter 'S' onto it. On the back of the star, attach a piece of ribbon in a loop with strong sticky tape.

3 To make the cloak you will need a leotard or catsuit. Sew one end of the fabric onto the shoulder straps.

4 Where the fabric joins the straps, glue on silver cardboard triangles.

DRESSING-UP FUN

Regal Crown

Crown yourself King or Queen of the castle!

YOU WILL NEED
tape measure
card (cardboard)
pencil
ruler
scissors
shiny coloured paper
ribbon
glue
paintbrush
silver and gold paper
glitter

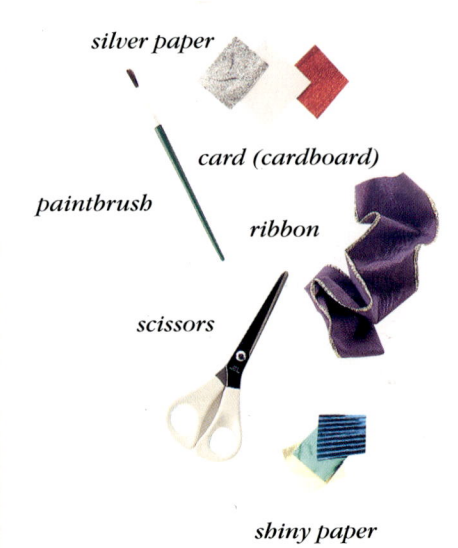

ruler
pencil
glitter
glue
silver paper
paintbrush
card (cardboard)
ribbon
scissors
shiny paper

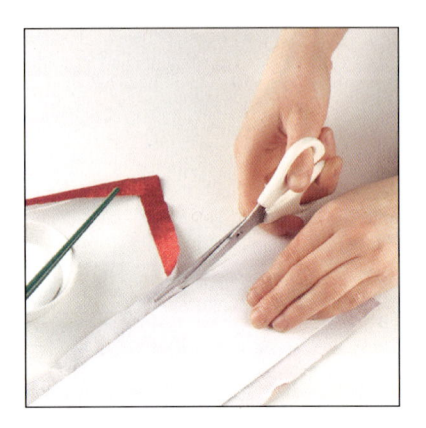

1 Measure around your head with a tape measure so that you know how long to cut the card (cardboard) band. Remember to allow a few centimetres (inches) for gluing the band together. Cut a strip of card 8 cm/3 in deep with a pair of scissors. Cover the card in shiny paper and stick on a piece of ribbon with glue.

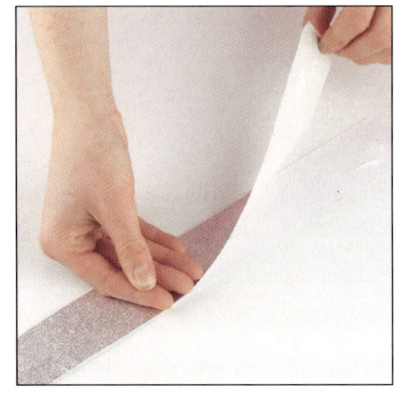

2 Cut out two strips of card (cardboard) measuring 4 x 30 cm (1½ x 12 in). Cover them in silver paper.

3 Make six jewel circles from shiny paper and glitter and glue them onto the ribbon.

4 Attach the silver strips to the inside of the crown band using glue and leave to dry.

5 Trace out five more jewel shapes from card (cardboard) and cut them out. Cover each one in gold paper and decorate with circles of shiny paper and glitter.

DRESSING-UP FUN

6 When the jewels are dry, glue them onto the silver bands.

113

GARDENING FUN

Equipment

You don't need lots of fancy equipment and you don't need all these tools to start gardening. For many projects just a trowel and hand fork will do, but as you get more enthusiastic, some of these tools will be very useful.

Bamboo canes
Canes are for staking plants, making a compost bin and a wigwam for climbing plants.

Broom
Gardening can be rather like housework because there is always a lot of tidying up to do.

Buckets
Good for collecting weeds and carrying soil, hand tools or even water.

Potting compost (soil)
This is used for potting house plants. It will feed your plants the nutrients they need.

Fork
For loosening the soil, and adding compost and manure.

Gardening gloves
Use these to protect your hands from thorns and stinging nettles, and to keep them clean. Try to find a pair that fits properly, if they are too big they can be difficult to work in.

Hand fork
For carefully loosening the soil between plants in small flower beds and for window boxes.

Hoe
For weeding. It slices like a knife under the roots of weeds which then shrivel up and die.

Penknife
Often useful instead of scissors.

Rake
For making a level surface.

Scissors
Used mainly for cutting garden twine, but useful for snipping off all sorts of things.

Secateurs (clippers)
For cutting off plant stems and small branches.

Seed tray
Seed trays are used for sowing seeds and growing seedlings.

Spade
For turning over the soil by digging and for making holes for planting trees and shrubs.

Trowel
A mini spade for making small holes and digging up big weeds.

Twine
This is gardening string for tying plants, and for marking out a straight line.

Watering can
A very important piece of equipment as without water plants die quickly. Immediately after planting always water thoroughly with the sprinkler for a gentle rain-like shower.

Wheelbarrow
For carting all sorts of things round the garden.

Wire
Useful for holding plants against walls and fences. Little pieces are used for pegging down.

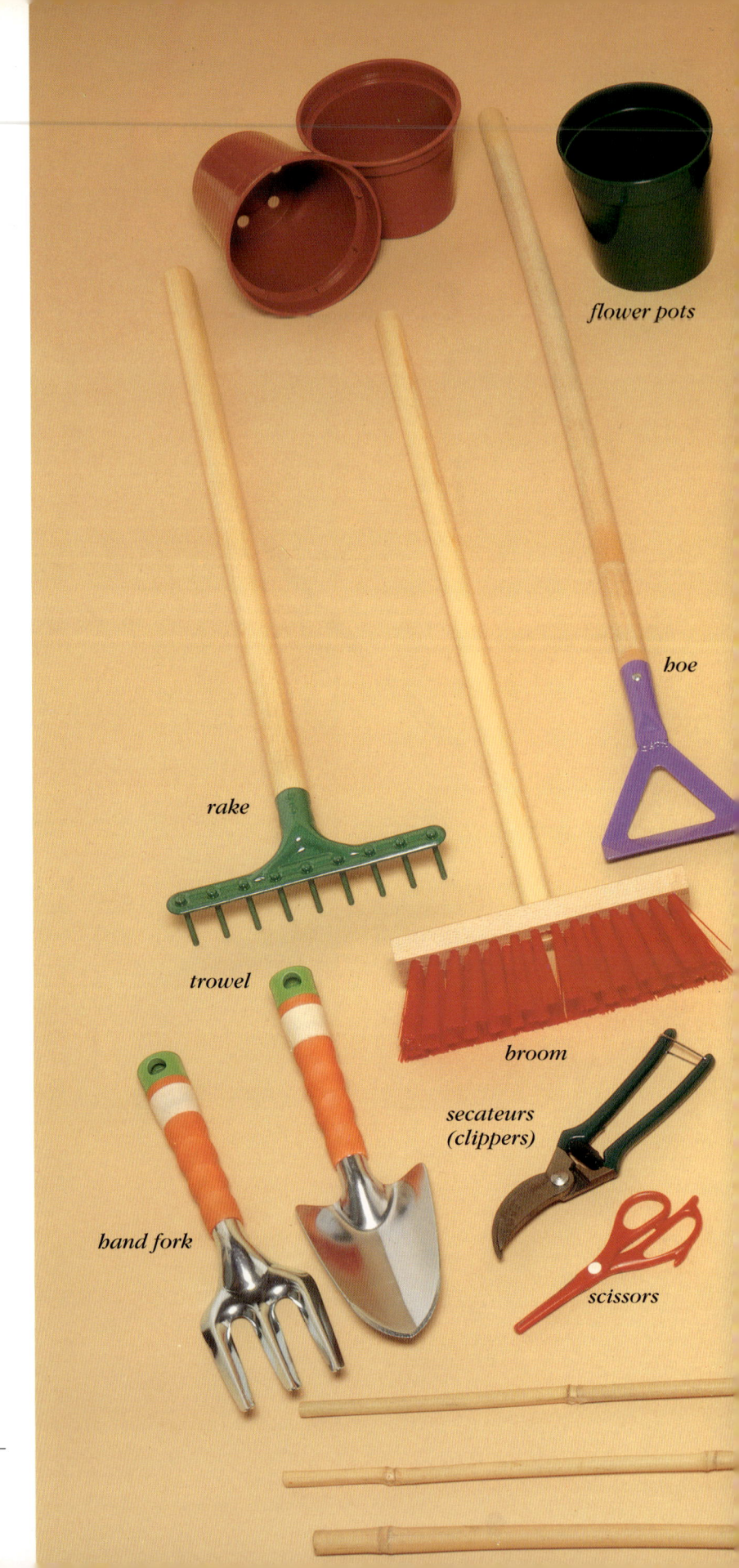

- seed tray
- spade
- wheelbarrow
- fork
- wire
- gloves
- buckets
- compost
- twine
- penknife
- watering can
- bamboo canes

GARDENING FUN

Glossary

Bulb
Some plants have an underground part that is specially adapted for storing food and protecting the start of a shoot. A dry bulb is a resting plant, as soon as it has some water and something to grow in, roots will grow from the bottom and a shoot from the top.

Cloche (bell jar)
This is a cover that is put over tender plants to protect them from the weather. The simplest one is the top half of a plastic bottle (with the top removed so that air can get in).

Compost
There are different sorts of compost. Potting compost (soil) is used to grow plants in, and also for seed sowing. It is better than soil because it is carefully made to a recipe that makes sure it holds air, water and plant food. Buy peat-free compost if you can, to protect threatened peat bogs. Garden compost is made from recycled vegetable and fruit peelings and tea leaves and garden clippings. All the ingredients are heaped together in a compost bin where after a few months they turn into rich compost that is full of goodness, perfect for digging into beds.

Cutting
A cutting is a piece of a plant stem, usually the tip, that when planted will make its own roots and grow into another plant.

Drainage
Water, whether it is rain or from a watering can, is used by plants as it passes through the soil. The water that doesn't get used must be able to escape from the soil, or drain away, otherwise the plant's roots become waterlogged and the plant dies. Flower pots must always have holes in the bottom, and garden soil should be forked over occasionally to help any excess water drain away.

Earthing up
When you are growing potatoes you need to cover up the first shoots with soil or potting compost. This is called earthing up and it encourages the stems to make more potatoes and stops light getting to them. Light turns potatoes green which is slightly poisonous.

Fertile
A fertile soil is one that is in good condition and holds lots of food for plants.

Fertilizer
Fertilizer is food for plants. There are many different sorts in granules, powders or liquids. It will say on the packet which type of plant it is for. Buy organic fertilizer whenever you can, chemical ones can be toxic.

Flower
The flower is the part of a plant from which the fruit or seed will develop. They are usually brightly-coloured to attract the insects which pollinate them.

Germination
When a seed starts to grow, it germinates by growing leaves and stems.

Leaf
Leaves are used by plants to catch food. Green leaves trap sunlight and carbon dioxide from the air and turn it into sugars for energy to grow. In return, they give back oxygen to the air which all animals need.

Manure
Manure is made from the straw bedding of horses or cattle, it has all their droppings mixed in with it. It isn't smelly at all, because the animals only eat grass which decomposes naturally and is full of goodness. Manure is forked into flower beds and put in the bottom of planting holes and is an excellent fertilizer.

Pinching out
Pinching out is removing the top pair of leaves from the stem tip; this makes a plant grow bushy rather than tall and thin.

Pollen
The fine, yellow dust which you see inside a flower is called pollen. It is usually collected by bees from the stamens – which are the male part of the flower – and carried to the female part of another flower (the stigma), this is called pollination.

116

GARDENING FUN

Pricking out (thinning)
When seeds germinate they are usually growing close together and need to be moved into a bigger pot where they have more room to grow. This is normally done when they have three or four leaves, it is called pricking out (thinning).

Rootball
This is the area immediately around the base of the plant where there are lots of feeding roots. It gets bigger as the plant grows.

Runner
Some plants, like strawberries, make long stems that creep over the soil. When they find an empty spot, the stem will make roots and eventually grow into a new plant.

Secateurs (clippers)
Tough gardeners' scissors that can be used for cutting thick plant stems.

Seed
Seeds are like tiny time-capsules, they can rest for years, carrying a minute package of information and energy which will grow into a new plant when water and soil are added.

Seed bed
A seed bed is a piece of soil that has been prepared for planting seeds, with a firm, level surface.

Seed drill
A seed drill is a groove in the soil into which seeds are sown.

Shrub
A shrub is a bush that will live for many years.

Soil
The soil is the top layer of earth in which plants grow. It is made from tiny particles of rocks, which have been worn down over millions of years, mixed with minute bits of dead plants.

Sowing
When you put seeds into the soil to grow you are sowing them. You can sow seeds directly into the soil, or into seed trays to keep on your windowsill. Remember to water thoroughly whenever you sow some seeds.

Stake
A stake is a stout, strong stick that is used to support a plant and stop it falling over or growing the wrong way.

Stem
The part of the plant that is above the ground and carries the leaves and flowers is called the stem.

Weed
A weed is any plant that is growing somewhere you don't want it to be. They are usually plants that grow very fast and if you leave them, they take over.

117

Bugs: the good, the bad and the ugly

Bugs can be gardeners' friends as well as enemies, so it is important to recognize the good guys like ladybird and lacewing larvae, as well as the baddies.

Here are some of the most common and important bugs which you will find in your garden. Encourage the insects which are on your side to stay by creating the right environment for them. Don't be frightened of them! They're much smaller than you and each one has an important role to play in the life of a garden.

Examine your garden for these insects and find out who lives where.

THE GOOD

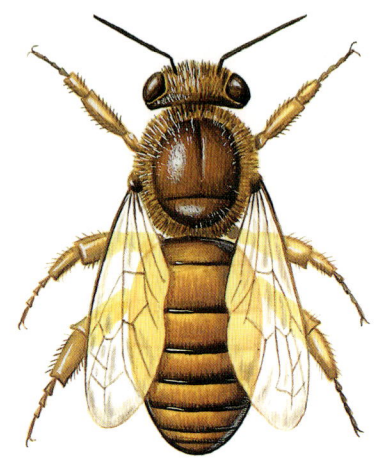

Butterfly and bee tub.

Bees
Without bees we would have hardly any fruit or vegetables because they play the vital role of pollinating the flowers.

Beetles
Beetles scurry around at night feeding on the small insects and slugs that feed on your plants.

Lacewings
These pretty insects have see-through lacy wings, and the larvae feed on plant-eating greenflies (aphids).

GARDENING FUN

Ladybirds
Both the ladybird itself and its larvae feed greedily on greenfly (aphids) and help to keep them under control.

Encourage lacewings to stay in your garden by making them somewhere to live.

THE BAD

Caterpillars
Caterpillars feed hungrily on all sorts of plants. If they are on your cabbages, you might want to get rid of them. However, many caterpillars are fascinating to watch and they do turn into beautiful moths and butterflies.

Greenflies (aphids)
Greenflies (aphids) have pointed mouths with which they pierce the leaves and stems of plants and suck out the sap. The plants then become misshapen and weak.
   A blast of water will help to reduce the numbers – soapy water is best. The trouble with a lot of chemical sprays is that they kill all the good guys too, who would normally help to keep the greenflies (aphids) under control.

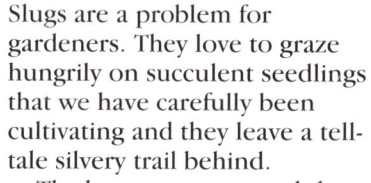

Slugs
Slugs are a problem for gardeners. They love to graze hungrily on succulent seedlings that we have carefully been cultivating and they leave a tell-tale silvery trail behind.
   The best way to control them is to go out at night when they are feeding, pick them off and drop them in a pot of salty water. Or buy some slug pellets.

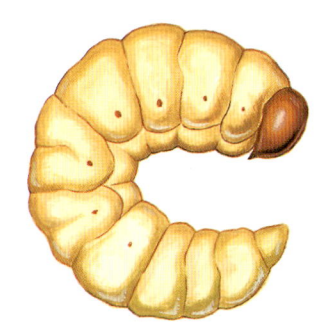

Vine weevil
This is a baddie, no doubt about it! The adult weevil lives a secretive life feeding on the leaves of plants, but it is their larvae that do the real damage. They feed off the roots of plants, usually of those growing in pots and containers although they can sometimes be found in flower beds too.
   Plants being attacked start to wilt, then topple over as soon as you touch them because they have no roots left. If you find any, immediately throw away all the compost or soil that the affected plant was growing in.

THE UGLY

Lily beetle
Lily beetles are often left alone because they are a pretty bright red colour. Their larvae, however, are one of the ugliest things around. They are covered in a horrible jelly-like mucus which protects them.
   Both the adult beetles and the larvae feed on lily leaves and stems and can quickly strip a plant so watch out for them!

A Bag of Potatoes

Home-grown potatoes taste ten times better than bought ones, and nothing could be easier to grow. Start them off early in the year using potatoes either from your vegetable rack at home, or, better still, using special seed potatoes from a garden centre. When the plant starts flowering the potatoes are ready for harvesting. This is about 10-12 weeks after planting.

You will need
seed potatoes
egg box
strong, dark coloured plastic bag
potting compost (soil)
sharp object to make holes in bag

potting compost (soil)

screwdriver

egg box

seed potatoes

plastic bag

watering can

bucket

1 To help your potatoes get off to a speedy start, put them in an egg box with the end that has the most eyes pointing upwards. This is where the baby shoots will grow from. Place the box on a cool but light windowsill and leave for a few weeks until the first signs of life appear – little fat green leaves.

2 Fill the plastic bag one-third full of potting compost (soil), and make a few holes with a screwdriver in the bottom so that excess water can drain through.

3 Plant 2 or 3 potatoes in the bag, with their shoots pointing upwards.

4 Cover them over with potting compost (soil) so you end up with the bag half full. Give the bag a good water and put it outside, in a sheltered place where it will not get caught by a frost.

5 After several weeks when the shoots are between 15 and 30 cm (6 and 12 in) tall, add more compost (soil) so the bag is completely full. This is called earthing up and it encourages the stems to make more potatoes as well as stopping light getting to them.

! Safety Note
Always take great care when using any sharp objects.

Did you know?
Sunlight makes potatoes go green and green potatoes are poisonous to eat – enough to give you an upset tummy.

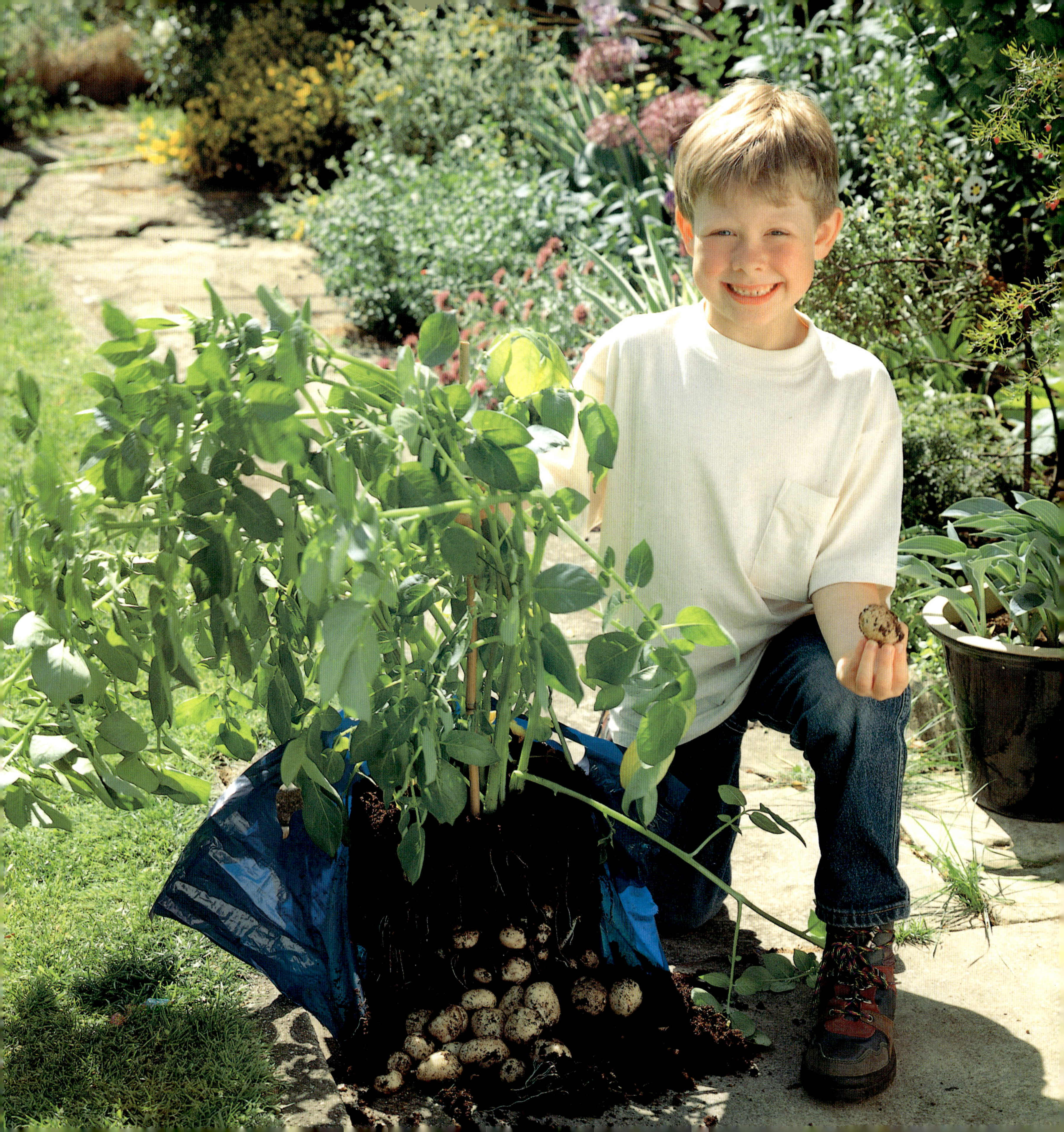

GARDENING FUN (SPRING)

Good Enough to Eat!

You don't need a large garden to grow fruit and vegetables – it is possible to grow some in just a window box. Strawberries and bush or trailing types of tomatoes are small enough, so are radishes and lettuces.

GARDENER'S TIP
To get a plant out of a pot, turn it upside down with the stem between your fingers. With the other hand, firmly squeeze the bottom of the pot to loosen it.

YOU WILL NEED
window box
potting compost (soil)
tomato plants
strawberry plants
radish seeds
lettuce seeds
nasturtium seeds

DID YOU KNOW?
Nasturtium leaves and flowers are edible, with a hot, peppery taste. They look lovely on a plate of salad.

window box

strawberry plants

potting compost (soil)

tomato plants

nasturtium seeds

lettuce seeds

radish seeds

1 Fill the window box with potting compost (soil) to just below the rim.

2 Plant the tomatoes in the back corners of the window box.

3 Plant the strawberries about 30 cm (12 in) away from the tomatoes.

4 Sow radish and lettuce seeds 1 cm (½ in) apart The radishes will come first, then the lettuces can have the space.

5 Sow some nasturtium seeds in the corners so that they can grow up and trail over the edge. Water thoroughly.

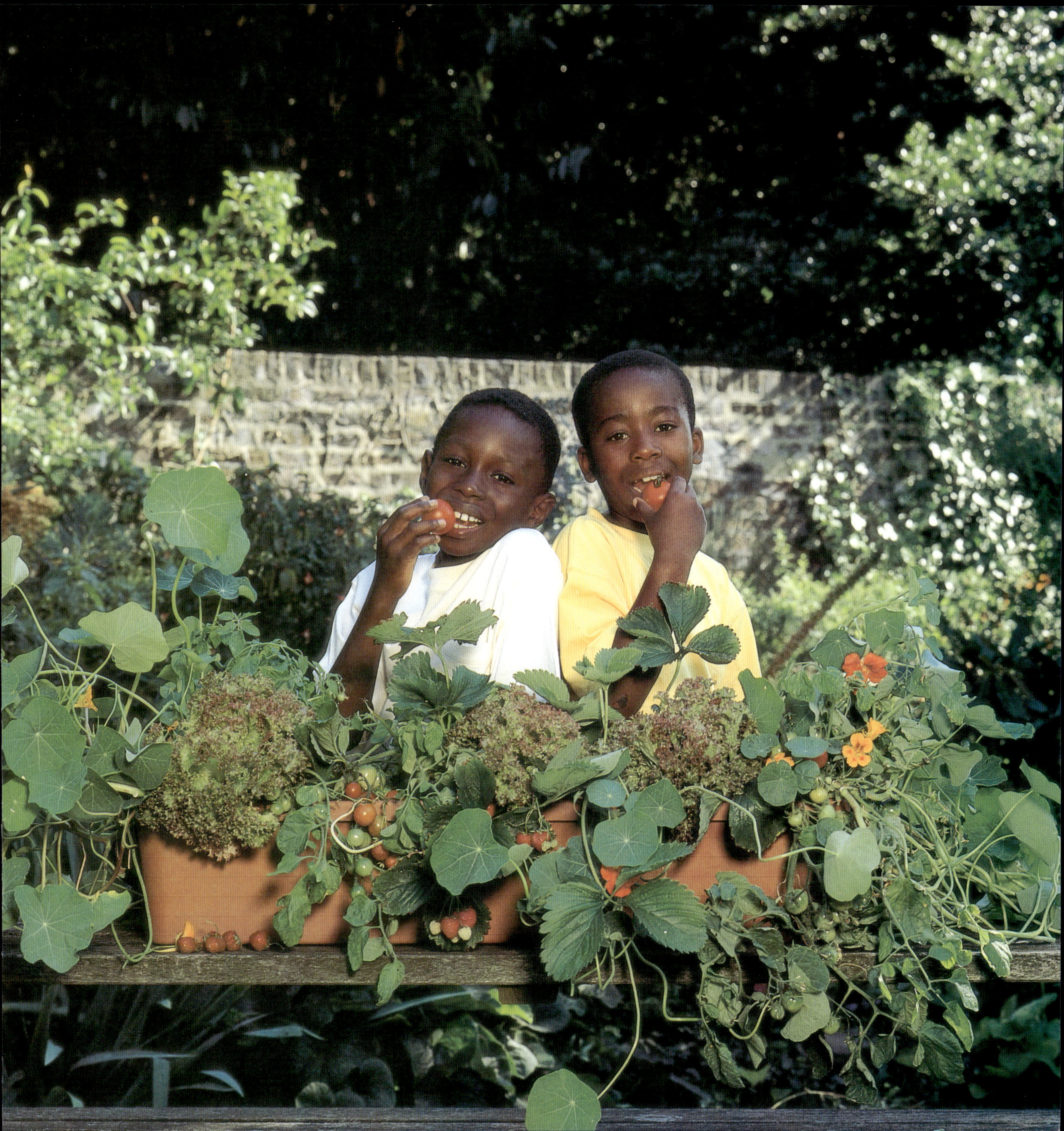

The Tallest Sunflower

Sunflowers are one of the speediest plants to grow in your garden. In just 6 months they outstrip everything else and can easily grow up to 3 metres (10 ft) tall.

They need some sort of support to stop them blowing over in windy weather. Plant them against a wall or fence that you can tie them to, or use a tall bamboo cane.

You will need
small flower pot
potting compost (soil)
sunflower seeds
watering can
a very tall bamboo cane – at least 2 m (6 ft)
string

flower pots

sunflower seeds

potting compost (soil)

bamboo canes

string

1 Fill the flower pots with compost (soil) and sow 2 or 3 seeds about 1 cm (1/2 in) deep. Water them in using a watering can with a sprinkler on the end.

2 When the seeds have germinated, pull out all but the strongest seedling in each pot.

3 Keep the pots on a sunny window sill until the seedlings have grown and the weather is warm, then plant outside.

4 Put the cane in the soil and tie it loosely to the plant. Measure the height of the plant when the flower appears.

GARDENING FUN (SPRING)

Lovely Lilies

Few flowers have as much going for them as lilies. They are exotic, colourful and often heavily scented. They are also easy to grow and are perfect for planting in pots. Be sure to buy only fat, healthy bulbs with thick, fleshy roots.

YOU WILL NEED
pebbles
large flower pot
potting compost (soil)
3 lily bulbs

potting compost (soil)

flower pot

pebbles

lily bulbs

1 Put a layer of pebbles in the bottom of a large flower pot so that water can drain away easily.

2 Fill the pot half full with potting compost (soil).

3 Plant the lily bulbs, taking great care of the roots, and spacing the bulbs evenly in the pot.

4 Cover with compost (soil), finishing a little way below the rim of the pot, then water them well.

GARDENER'S TIP
When the flowers die cut them off. Let the leaves die and in autumn (fall) replant the bulbs into fresh compost and they will grow all over again!

125

GARDENING FUN (SPRING)

Blooming Old Boots

Don't these look great? It is a blooming wonderful way to recycle an old pair of boots, the bigger the better. It just goes to show that almost anything can be used to grow plants in as long as it has a few holes in the bottom for drainage. Try an old football, a sports bag, or even an old hat, for plant containers with lots of character.

! SAFETY NOTE
Always take great care when using any sharp objects.

YOU WILL NEED
knife
old pair of working boots
potting compost (soil)
selection of bedding plants
watering can

knife

bedding plants

watering can

potting compost (soil)

old boot

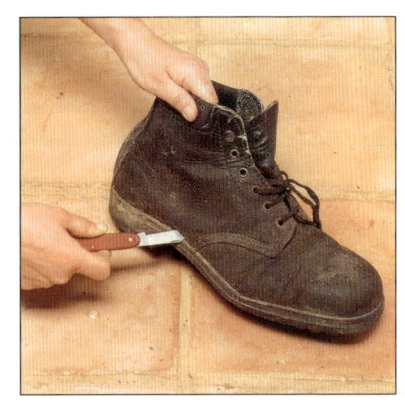

1 Using a knife very carefully (in fact you will probably need help), make some holes in between the stitching of the sole for drainage. Even better if there are holes there naturally!

2 Fill the boots with potting compost (soil), pushing it down right into the toe.

3 Plant flowers that can cope with hot, dry places like geraniums and verbenas which will trail over the edge.

4 Squeeze in a pansy with a contrasting flower colour, and a trailing lobelia plant. Lobelia grows in the smallest of spaces and will delicately tumble over the edge.

5 The boot needs watering every day in the summer, and blooms even better if you mix some plant food in to the water once a week.

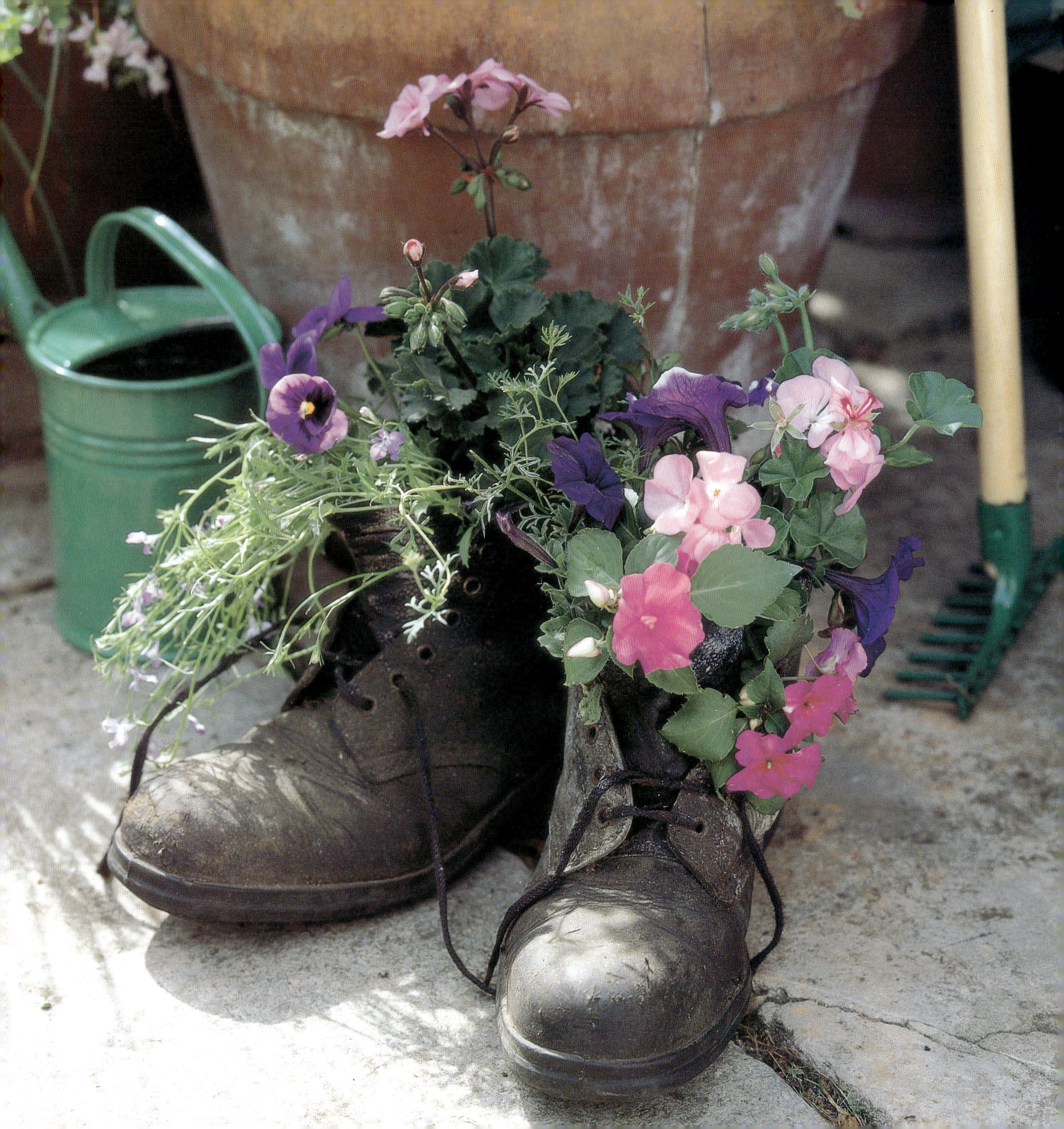

GARDENING FUN (SPRING)

Sprouting Seeds

How do you grow fresh vegetables at any time of the year without having a garden? Sprouting seeds. They grow quickly, are very good for you and taste delicious too, so who could ask for more? These bean sprouts are grown from mung beans, but other dried seeds like chickpeas (garbanzo beans) and whole lentils work well too. For the quickest results try tiny alfalfa seeds. All these are easy to buy from any health food shop and many supermarkets.

YOU WILL NEED
flat-bottomed dish
cotton wool or kitchen paper towel
mung beans
newspaper

newspaper

mung beans

flat-bottomed dish

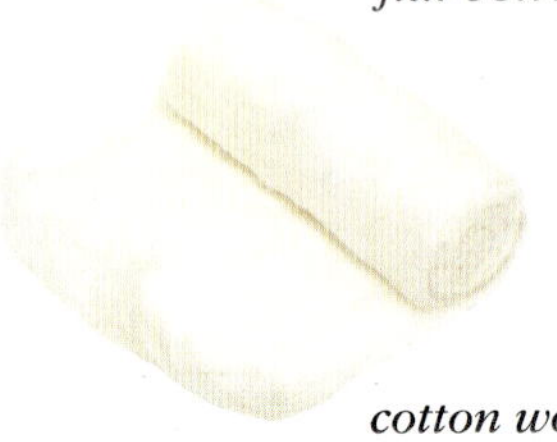

cotton wool

1 Wash the beans and soak them overnight in cold water.

2 Next morning, cover a flat-bottomed dish with a layer of cotton wool, or several sheets of kitchen paper towels, and water.

3 Wash the beans again and spread them evenly over the damp bottom of the dish.

4 Cover the dish with newspaper to keep out light and put it in a warm place. The beans will soon sprout and be ready to eat in 6-9 days. Don't let them grow too long, they should be plump and about 2.5 cm (1 in) long for the best taste.

VARIATION

Another way of sprouting larger seeds is to put a large spoonful of dry seeds such as chickpeas (garbanzo beans) into a wide-necked jar and cover with a small piece of muslin (cheesecloth), secured by an elastic band. Fill the jar with water and swish the seeds around a bit, then pour the water out. Do this at least once every day (twice if you can) to stop them going bad. They will take between 2-7 days to sprout, depending on what type you are growing.

DID YOU KNOW?

To cook bean sprouts, wash them, then boil in a pan of salted water for 2 minutes. Drain, and serve with butter and a few drops of soy sauce.

GARDENING FUN (SPRING)

GARDENING FUN (SPRING)

Grow Spaghetti

Yes, it's true! This type of marrow (summer squash) is packed with vegetable spaghetti. It only needs cooking to spill out its treasures. Bake it in the oven, or boil it until soft, add some butter and give it a twirl.

GARDENER'S TIP
If more than one seedling germinates, leave the strongest looking one in the pot and pull out the others.

YOU WILL NEED
small flower pot
potting compost (soil)
spaghetti marrow seeds
hand fork
manure or garden compost
trowel
hand fork

flower pots

spaghetti marrow seeds

potting compost (soil)

1 Fill a small flower pot with potting compost (soil) and make it level. Plant 3 seeds, pushing them in about 1 cm (½ in) deep.

2 Prepare the soil well, by forking over and adding some manure or garden compost.

3 When the young plant has 3 or 4 fully grown leaves and the weather is nice and warm, plant it outside in the prepared spot.

DID YOU KNOW?
All marrows (squashes) have separate male and female flowers and to get fruit they need to be pollinated. It is easy to tell which flower is which because the female one always has a swelling at the bottom beneath the petals.

4 When the plant flowers, play the part of a bee by picking off a male flower and dusting the yellow pollen onto the middle of the female one to pollinate it.

5 They are very greedy plants for both water and food. When the first flowers appear, start to add some fertilizer to its water once a week. Choose a fertilizer made especially for flowers and fruit and you will be rewarded with plates piled with vegetable spaghetti.

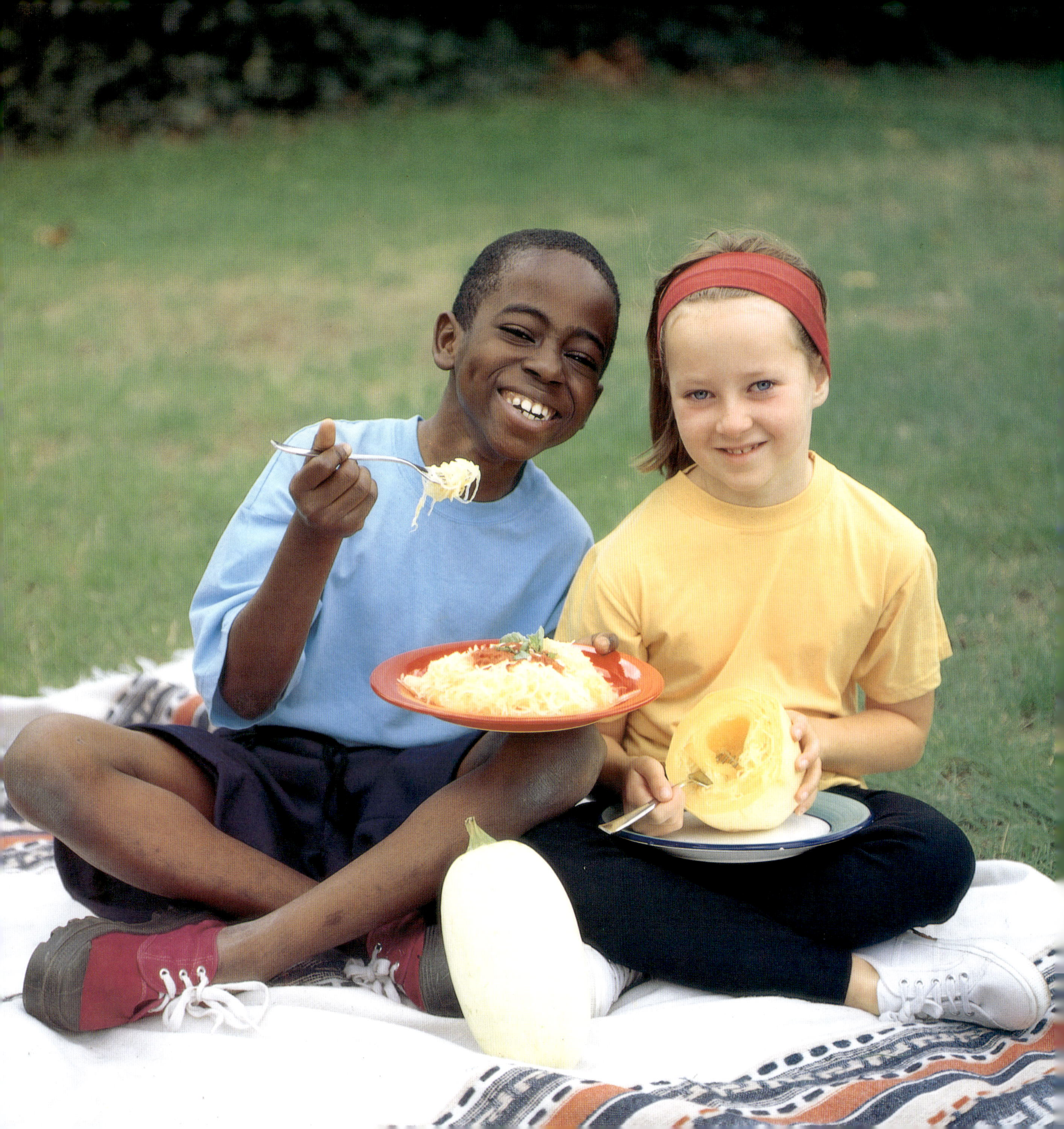

GARDENING FUN (SPRING)

Wigwam Runners

Runner beans are climbing plants and need something to run up, so a wigwam is just the thing. This looks just as good in a flower bed as in a vegetable garden. The flowers are pretty and are followed by long, tasty beans which, if you pick them every few days, will grow all summer.

YOU WILL NEED
fork
manure or garden compost
5 x 2 m (6 ft) bamboo canes
garden string
runner bean seeds

garden string

runner bean seeds

bamboo canes

compost

DID YOU KNOW?
Runner beans came from the tropical parts of America, so it is no surprise that they like their roots to be in warm soil. They also grow fast – you could have a plate of beans in just 7 weeks!

1 At the end of spring, when the days are warm and there are no more frosts, fork over a patch of soil. Add a bucketful of manure or well-rotted garden compost and mix it in well.

2 Push 5 long bamboo canes into the ground, in a circle measuring roughly 1 m (3 ft) across the middle.

3 Gather the canes together at the top and tie with a piece of string to make a wigwam shape.

4 Plant a seed about 3 cm (1¼ in) deep on both sides of each cane. Water thoroughly. They will soon germinate and start to run up the canes. When they reach the top, pinch out the top few centimetres (inches) of the stem.

GARDENING FUN (SUMMER)

Turn Detective

Watch out! Be careful where you step. There is a fascinating, hidden world going on unnoticed right beneath your feet. Take time to look and you will be amazed what there is to discover on a mini safari in a garden.

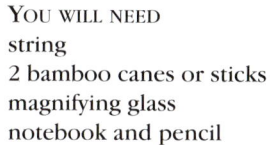

YOU WILL NEED
string
2 bamboo canes or sticks
magnifying glass
notebook and pencil

string

bamboo canes

pencil

magnifying glass

notebook

1 Tie a piece of string about 1.5 m (5 ft) long to 2 bamboo canes or sticks.

2 Peg this down across some long grass or a woodland edge.

3 Creep along the line of string very slowly, centimetre by centimetre, (inch by inch) with your nose to the ground looking through a magnifying glass.

4 Try to identify what you find with the help of nature books, or start a nature diary to make notes in.

GARDENING FUN (SUMMER)

Desert Garden

If you like dreaming of hot, sunny places and plants that are not too much trouble, then cacti and succulents are the plants for you. Keep this desert garden on a sunny windowsill and water it well during the summer but hardly at all in the winter. With this winter rest, a cactus might surprise you with a dazzling display of flowers.

YOU WILL NEED
clay flower pot
pebbles
special cacti compost (soil) or potting compost (soil), grit and sand
rocks
cacti and succulent plants
strips of folded newspaper
gravel

potting compost (soil)

cacti and succulent plants

newspaper

grit and sand

rocks

flower pot

pebbles

1 Find a container that is not too deep but quite wide at the top – it must have holes for drainage. Put a handful of pebbles in the bottom. Fill the pot with special cacti compost (soil) or mix your own, using equal quantities of potting compost (soil), grit and sand.

2 Position one or two large rocks in the container.

3 Pick the cacti up with strips of folded newspaper to protect yourself from getting pricked, and plant them around the rocks.

4 Cover the surface with gravel. During the spring and summer water like ordinary houseplants, but during the winter water about once a month when the compost (soil) is very dry.

134

GARDENING FUN (SUMMER)

Pot of Herbs

A handful of herbs adds the finishing touch to all sorts of dishes. You can keep this pot anywhere in the garden, on a balcony or even on a window sill, to give you lovely, fresh snippets just when you want them. Put in a silver and a golden thyme because thyme is one of the best herbs for pots, not growing too large and great for soups and sauces.

YOU WILL NEED
large pot
pebbles
potting compost (soil)
selection of herbs such as curry plant, marjoram, parsley, chives and thyme

herbs

large pot

potting compost (soil)

pebbles

1 Put a good handful of pebbles in the bottom of the pot so water can drain out easily (herbs don't like soggy feet).

2 Fill the pot almost full with potting compost (soil). The curry plant is the tallest, so plant that in the middle.

3 Plant the marjoram towards the back because it is the next biggest.

4 Work around the pot planting chives, parsley and thyme. You can start using the herbs as soon as you like!

GARDENER'S TIP
Larger herbs like mint, rosemary and fennel, are great for the first year, but in the second they will outgrow the pot and swamp anything else in it, so it is really best to give them a pot each. Remember to keep all your herbs well watered but not too soggy.

GARDENING FUN (SUMMER)

Minty Tea

Sprigs of mint look and taste great in cool summer drinks and mint tea is delicious either hot or cold at any time of the year.

YOU WILL NEED
mint leaves
teapot
boiling water
sugar or honey to taste

mint leaves

teapot

! SAFETY NOTE
Always take great care when pouring boiling water.

1 Pick a large handful of mint leaves.

2 Tear the leaves into little pieces.

3 Put the leaves into the teapot.

4 Pour on boiling water and leave to steep for 5 minutes before pouring out to drink immediately, or leave until cool and then chill in the refrigerator. Add a little sugar or honey for a special treat.

GARDENER'S TIP
Mint grows very quickly by long running stems that creep through the soil making new plants along their length. Cut one of these off and plant it in a large pot.

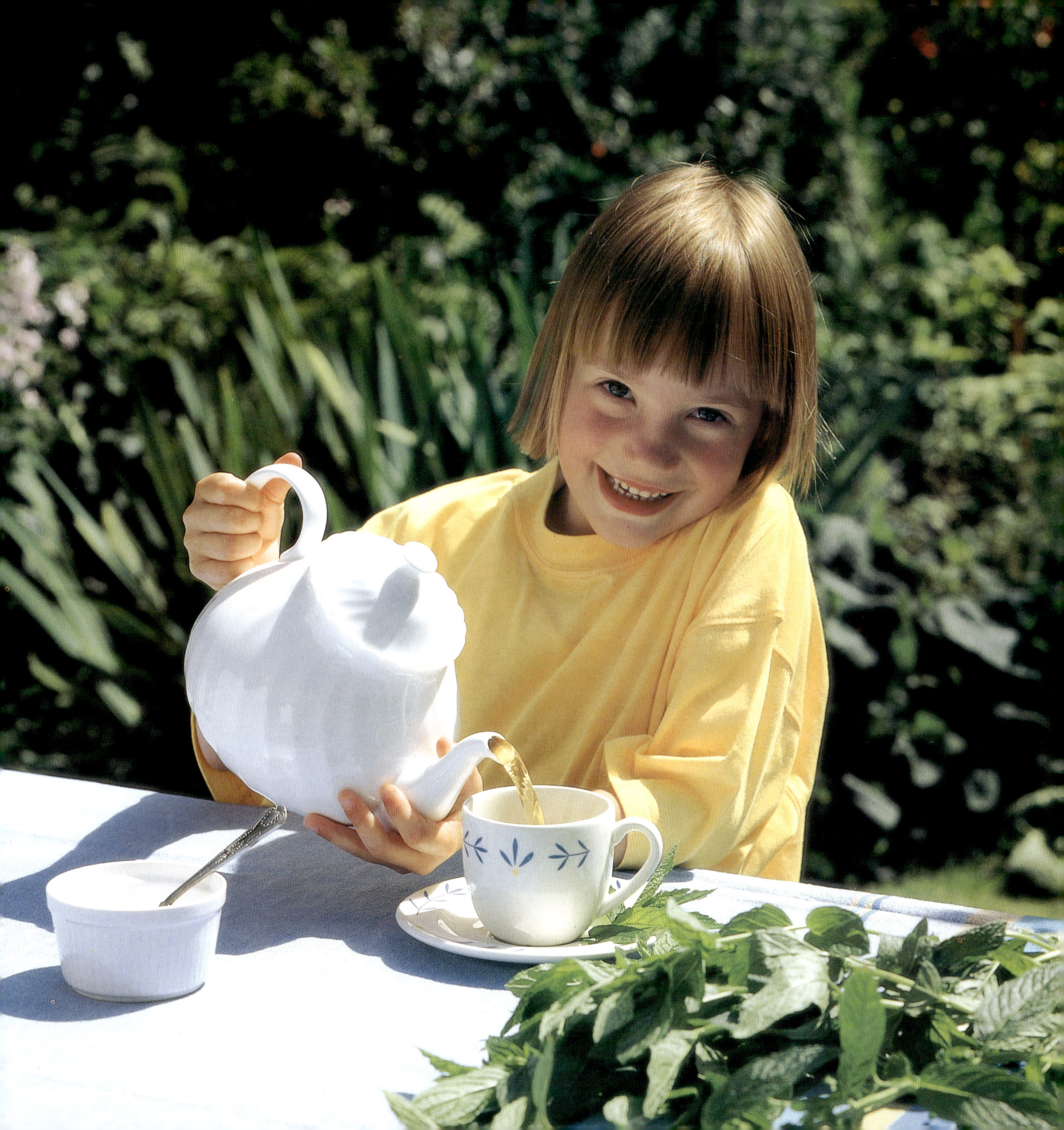

GARDENING FUN (SUMMER)

Long-lasting Lavender

Need something to make your room smell nice? Here is just the thing – some good old-fashioned English lavender. Fill bowls with dried lavender or make muslin (cheesecloth) bags to put among your clothes.

YOU WILL NEED
scissors
fresh lavender
raffia
sheet of paper
small bowl

scissors

raffia

paper

bowl

lavender

1 Cut whole stalks of lavender when the flowers are showing colour, but are not fully opened.

2 Tie them in small, loose bundles with a bit of raffia.

3 Hang them upside down in a warm, dry place for a few days.

4 When the flowers are completely dry, rub them free of the stalks onto a sheet of paper. Tip the lavender flowers into a small bowl.

! SAFETY NOTE
Always take great care when using any sharp objects.

GARDENING FUN (SUMMER)

Press Them Pretty

With a flower press you can keep colourful, summer flowers to cheer you up on a winter's day. A flower press is very easy to make out of things you might just throw away.

YOU WILL NEED
card (cardboard)
scissors
pretty gift wrap
sticky tape
corrugated cardboard
newspaper
flowers
ribbon

ribbon

gift wrap

card (cardboard)

newspaper

corrugated cardboard

sticky tape

1 Cut out two matching pieces of card (cardboard) any size you like, and cover them with pretty gift wrap, using sticky tape.

2 Cut out two matching pieces of corrugated cardboard to fit. Because it is crinkled, it lets in the air which slowly dries the flowers.

! SAFETY NOTE
Always take great care when using any sharp objects.

3 Build the press in layers starting with a piece of card (cardboard), then a piece of corrugated cardboard and finally some thick layers of newspaper cut to fit. Lay the flowers on top. Cover with more newspaper and the second sheet of corrugated cardboard.

4 Put the remaining piece of card (cardboard) on top, then tie two pieces of ribbon tightly around, finishing them off with a bow. Keep the press in a warm, airy place for about a week. Your pressed flowers can then be made into birthday cards or pretty pictures.

139

GARDENING FUN (SUMMER)

Scare Them Off!

Fed up with those pesky pigeons stealing your precious plants? Give them a fright by making a scarecrow out of odds and ends that you find lying around. Model it on someone you know and give them a shock too!

YOU WILL NEED
2 sticks - one 1.85 m (6ft) long, the other 1.25 m (4 ft) long
nails
hammer
spade
old pillowcase
permanent marker pen
straw for stuffing
thick string
safety pins
old clothes

pillowcase *hat*
scarf
shirt *straw*

! SAFETY NOTE
Always take great care when using a hammer.

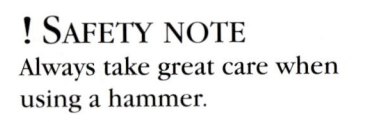

1 Put the longer stick on the ground and lay the shorter one across it about 30 cm (12 in) from the top. Nail them together with a couple of nails so that the frame is good and strong. Dig a 30 cm (12 in) hole, plant the frame and fill up the hole with soil.

2 Using a marker pen, draw a face on the pillowcase with the open end down. Then bring the top corners together and tie. Fill the pillowcase with straw.

3 Put the head over the top of the frame so that the stick goes up into the straw. Tie the open end of the pillowcase tightly around the stick with a piece of string. Pin the hat to the head with safety pins.

4 Tie the trouser bottoms up and fill them with straw.

5 Attach the trousers to the frame by running string through the back belt loop and around the stick.

6 Put the shirt on so the ends of the short stick go through the armholes and fill it with straw. Now you have a permanent guest in your garden!

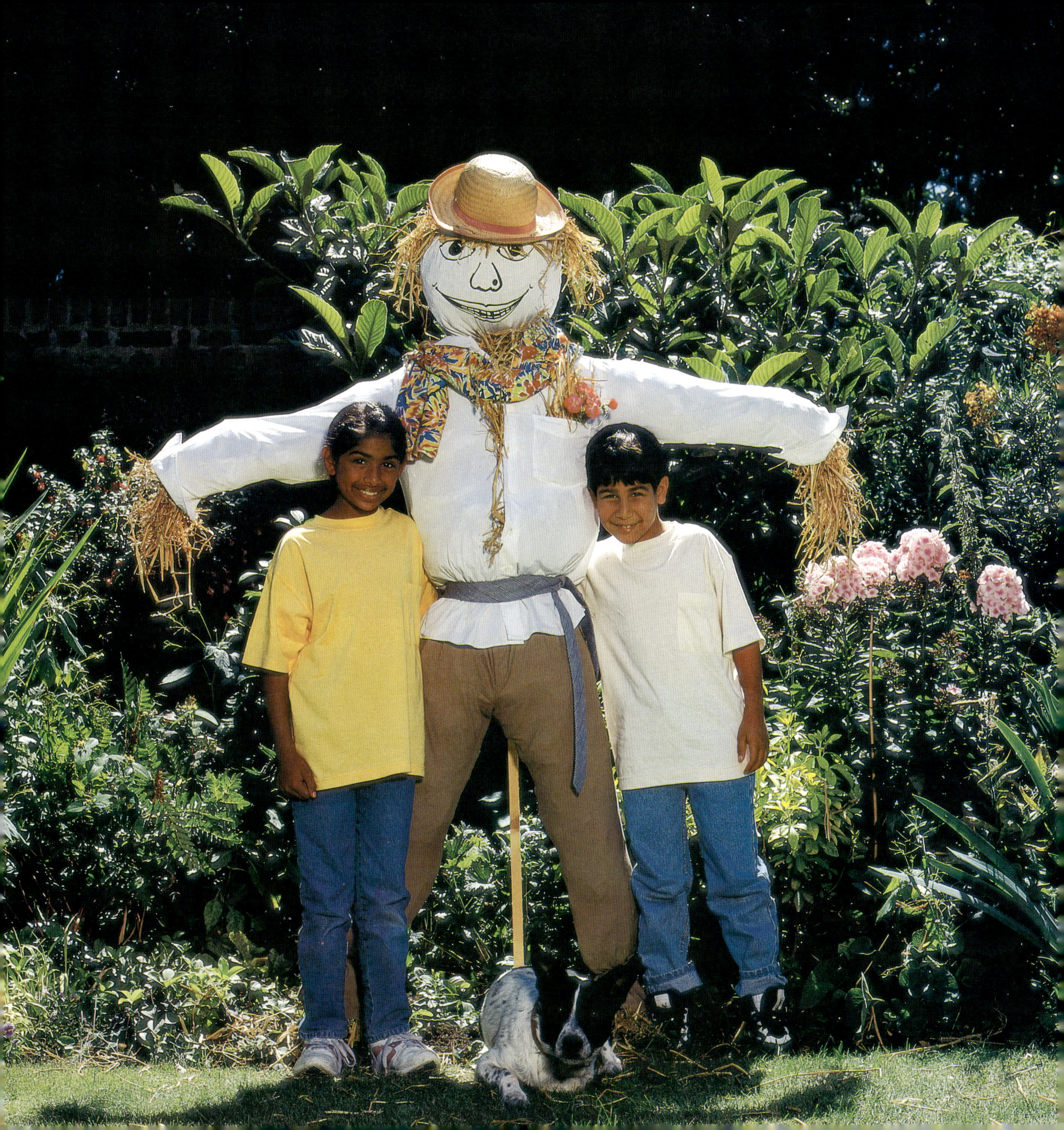

GARDENING FUN (AUTUMN/FALL)

Monkey Nuts

Most of us like eating peanuts, but it is surprising how little most people know about the plant that they come from. In fact peanuts are not really nuts at all, but are related to peas and beans. The plant is quite small and lives for just one season. Its flowers bend down to the ground after they have been pollinated, and plant themselves in the soil where the fruit or "nuts" develop.

YOU WILL NEED
large flower pot – at least 12 cm (5 in) in diameter
potting compost (soil)
peanuts in their shells (unsalted)
cling film (plastic wrap)

potting compost (soil)

peanuts

flower pot

cling film (plastic wrap)

1 Fill a large pot with potting compost (soil) and press down lightly to make the surface level. Crack the peanuts across the middle with your fingers.

2 Plant the peanuts on their sides, putting in about 7-8 spaced evenly apart.

3 Cover them with about 2 cm (¾ in) of potting compost (soil) and water them well.

4 Cover the whole pot with cling film (plastic wrap) to keep them warm and moist and encourage them to grow. Remove the cling film (plastic wrap) when they have germinated, which should take about 2 weeks.

GARDENER'S TIP
Peanuts which have been roasted will not grow. Peanut plants will only produce fruit in very hot countries.

142

GARDENING FUN (AUTUMN/FALL)

Name It

Every time you sow some seeds, don't forget to stick a label in the pot. Many seedlings look the same, so if you don't label them you could end up with monster sunflowers in a window box!

YOU WILL NEED
large plastic yogurt pot
scissors
ruler
ballpoint pen

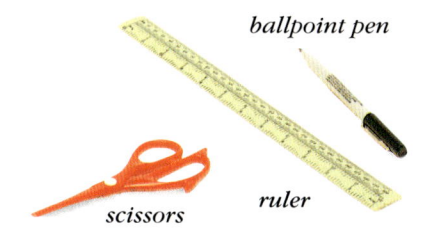

yogurt pot

ballpoint pen

ruler

scissors

1 Cut lengthways down the side of a large yogurt pot, then carefully cut out the bottom.

2 Open the side out flat and cut off the rim. Using a ruler and ballpoint pen, draw lines about 2 cm (³/₄ in) apart.

! **SAFETY NOTE**
Always take great care when using any sharp objects.

3 Cut along the lines with the scissors.

4 Cut a tapered point at one end to stick into the pot or soil. Now your labels are ready to write on.

143

GARDENING FUN (AUTUMN/FALL)

Glass Gardening

Welcome to the world of glass gardens, plants that live within a jar. This is a mini tropical rainforest, it does not need much watering because the water is recycled. Jars and bowls of almost all shapes and sizes can be transformed into a glass garden, so see what you can find. A large sweet (candy) jar does a first class job but I bet you don't get a chance to empty one of those very often!

YOU WILL NEED
gravel
glass bowl
charcoal
potting compost (soil)
selection of small houseplants
spoon and fork attached to pieces of cane to make long-handled tools for planting
plate or lid

potting compost (soil)
plate
glass bowl
charcoal
houseplants
fork
spoon
gravel

1 Put a generous layer of gravel in the bottom of the container.

2 Mix two handfuls of charcoal into the potting compost (soil), then fill the container one-third full.

3 Start to plant delicate plants that are normally quite difficult to grow indoors. This is a silver fern.

4 Then add an aluminium plant and a small African violet.

5 A polka-dot plant and some creeping moss completes the planting. Now give it a thoroughly good drink to start the water cycle off.

6 Put a plate or lid on top to close the glass garden.

GARDENER'S TIP
By moving the top on and off, you can control the atmosphere inside. If water is running continuously down the sides, it is probably too wet, so take off the lid for a few days to let it dry out. Slight fogging collecting on the glass means the conditions are perfect – if there is no fogging, the conditions could be too dry and you will need to do some hand watering.

DID YOU KNOW?
Water in a glass jar is recycled in much the same way as it is in the earth's atmosphere. Inside the jar water evaporates from the surface of the soil and from the plants themselves, but rather than rising to form high clouds in the atmosphere, it collects on the inside of the glass and runs down the sides (like rain), and as the plants are watered the cycle is complete.

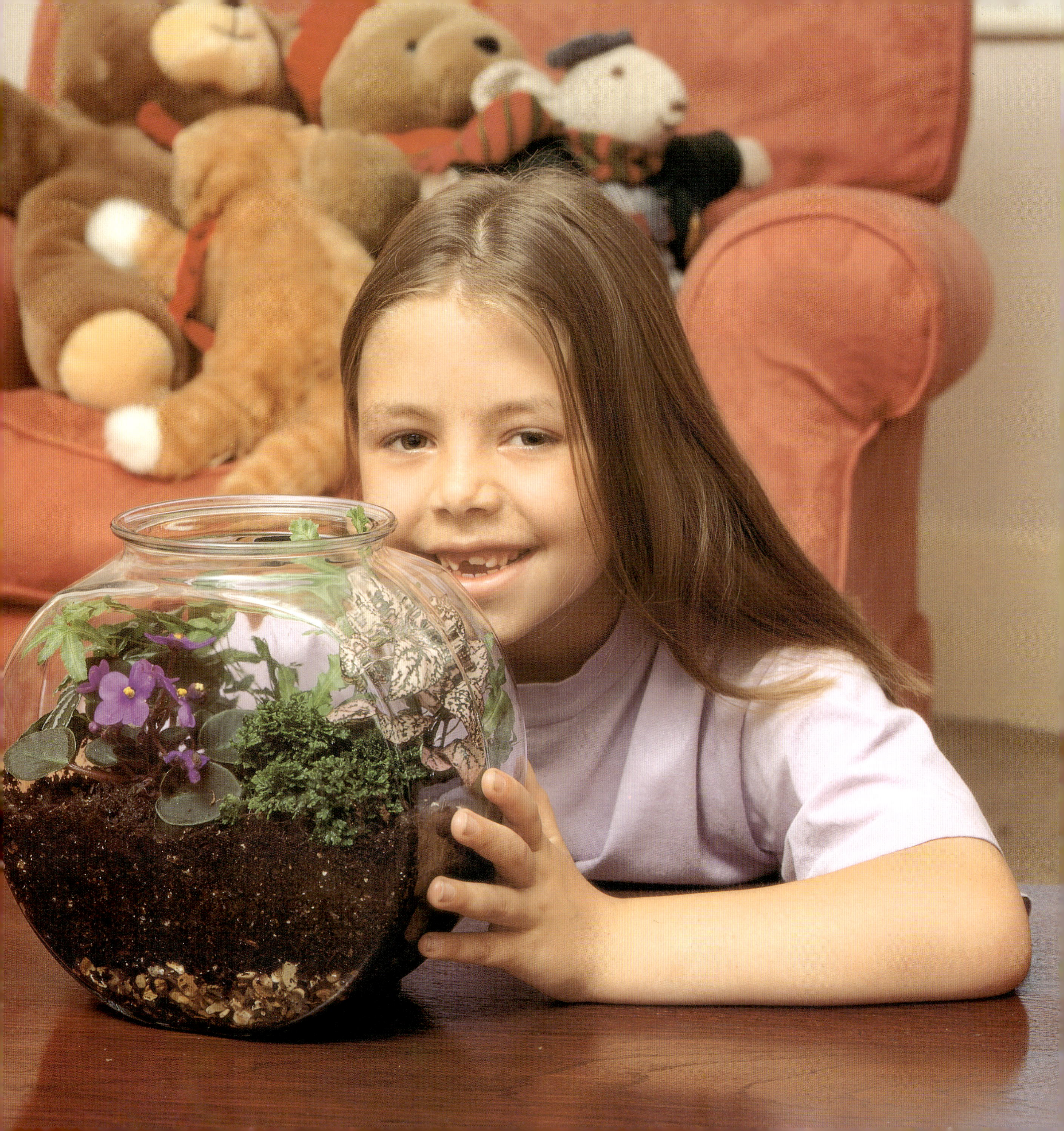

GARDENING FUN (WINTER)

Rock It

Part of the fascination of rock gardens is that it is possible to create a small piece of hillside or mountain in your own garden. Play around with the rocks until you are happy with their position and keep standing back a few paces to get a proper picture of the overall effect.

GARDENER'S TIP
There are many alpine plants to choose from. Most will be quite small and slow-growing which is just what you want for a rockery.

YOU WILL NEED
spade
gardening gloves
rocks
garden soil
trowel
alpine plants
grit

rocks

garden soil

grit

trowel

gardening gloves

alpine plants

1 Wearing gardening gloves, put the biggest rock in a hole that is deep enough to bury the bottom third. Lean the rock back slightly and press in firmly.

2 Arrange the next two biggest rocks either side of the first. Fill in the gaps with some garden soil. Use lots of soil so that a mound begins to form.

3 Put two or three more rocks on the next level, making sure they are secure. Then fill in with more soil.

4 Place a final rock on the top, making sure it is still one-third buried.

5 Plant a collection of alpine plants among the rocks, putting a small handful of grit in the bottom of each planting hole – the soil on a hillside is much quicker draining than most garden soils and alpine plants don't like wet feet.

6 Cover the soil around the plants with a layer of grit, which gives it a natural finish and stops any water sitting in puddles around the plants.

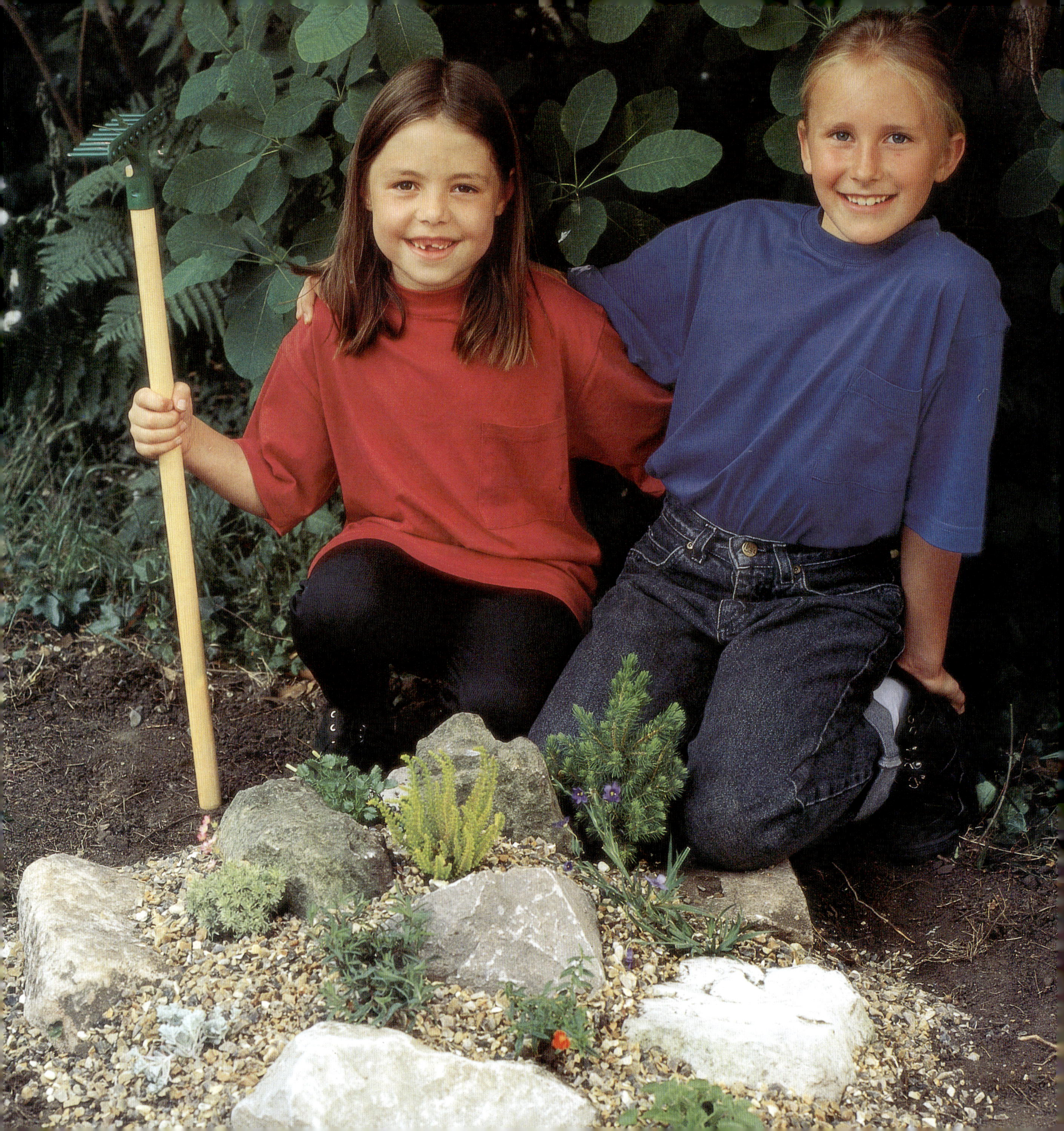

GARDENING FUN (WINTER)

Crazy Grass-head

Crazy grass-heads make great mates to have lounging around on your windowsill. Grow a head of long, wild green hair for a cool dude, or keep it trimmed regularly and looking neat and tidy. They cost practically nothing to make and are very original presents for your friends, if you can bear to give them away.

GARDENER'S TIP
The bottom of the sock sucks up water from the paper cup. Never let it go thirsty or the hair will wilt! Keep it on a windowsill that gets plenty of daylight.

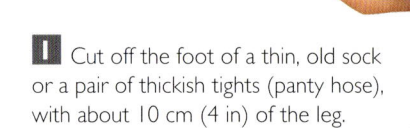

YOU WILL NEED
old sock or pair of tights (panty hose)
scissors
grass seed
potting compost (soil)
cotton thread
elastic band
pieces of felt
fabric glue
paper cup

1 Cut off the foot of a thin, old sock or a pair of thickish tights (panty hose), with about 10 cm (4 in) of the leg.

2 Put a generous handful of grass seed in the end of the toe and press it down in a thick layer.

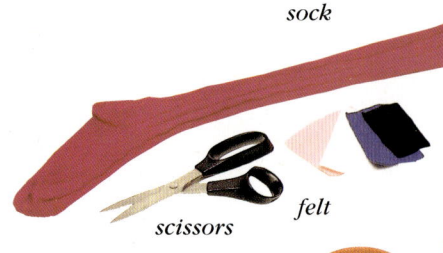

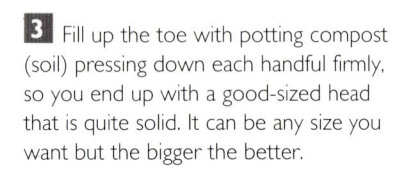

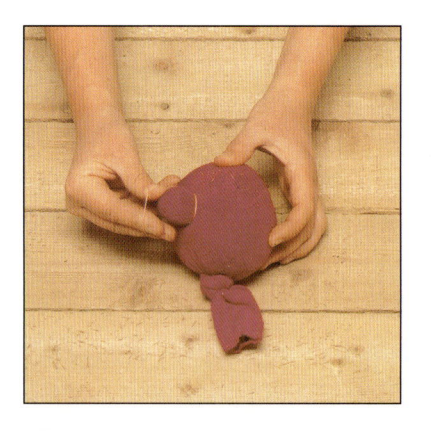

3 Fill up the toe with potting compost (soil) pressing down each handful firmly, so you end up with a good-sized head that is quite solid. It can be any size you want but the bigger the better.

4 Knot the end like a balloon, or tie it firmly with string or strong cotton thread. Make the nose by pulling out a wodge in the middle and fixing an elastic band around the bottom.

5 Cut out the eyes, mouth and even a beard or moustache from the felt. Stick them in place using fabric glue. Leave to dry overnight. Next morning sit the head on top of a paper cup filled with water.

! SAFETY NOTE
Always take great care when using any sharp objects.

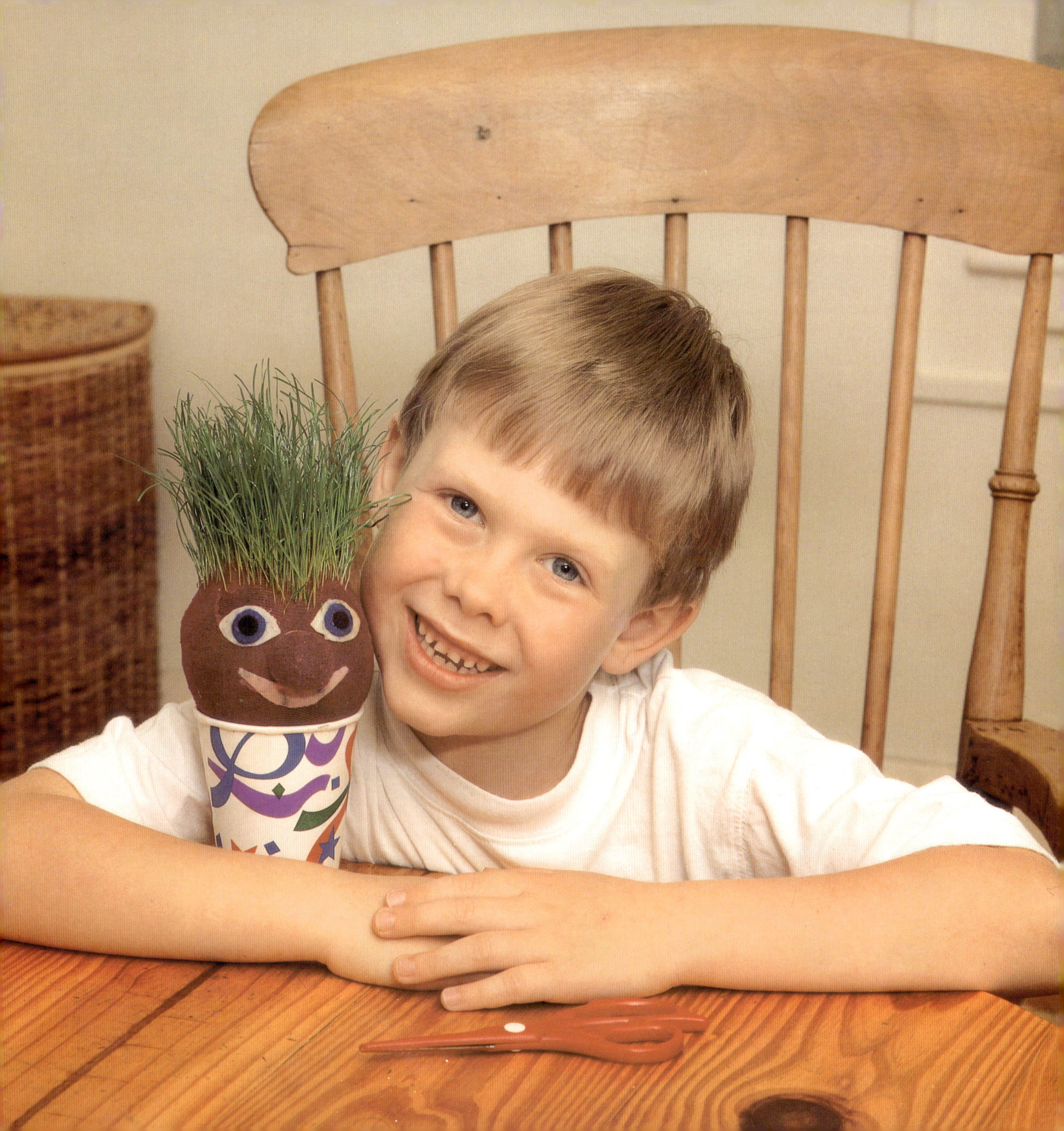

GARDENING FUN (WINTER)

Wonderful Worms

Worms are truly wonderful creatures that we often take for granted. They keep the soil healthy by making channels for air and water and by eating plant remains. A wormery is an excellent way of making potting compost from kitchen scraps. It is on a smaller scale than a compost bin and provides a richer material which can be used for potting up plants. The type of worms that live most happily in a wormery are not earthworms which you find in the soil, but tiger worms which you can buy from most fishing tackle shops.

YOU WILL NEED
hand drill
small dustbin (trash can)
gravel
newspaper
potting compost (soil)
tiger worms
vegetable peelings

dustbin (trash can)
gravel
potting compost (soil)
vegetable peelings
tiger worms
hand drill
newspaper

1 Drill two rows of drainage holes 2.5 cm (1 in) up from the bottom of a small dustbin (trash can), plus a row of air holes around the top.

! SAFETY NOTE
Always take great care when using any type of drill.

3 Cover with a layer of wet newspaper, which stops the compost (soil) falling through onto the gravel.

2 Put a 10 cm (4 in) layer of gravel in the bottom.

4 Then add a 10 cm (4 in) layer of potting compost (soil).

5 Now add a good handful of tiger worms, use gloves if you like!

150

GARDENING FUN (WINTER)

6 Add a thin layer of vegetable peelings and cover everything with a thick layer of newspaper. It will take a couple of weeks for the worms to settle into their new home. Don't add more vegetable peelings until the worms have started to work on the previous batch and only add a thin layer at a time.

DID YOU KNOW?
Worms' favourite foods are banana skins, tea-bags, carrot and potato peelings, and all greens. They are not very keen on orange or lemon skins so it is best to leave them out.

151

Equipment

There are probably lots of weird and wonderful things in the kitchen cupboards and drawers. Here's a guide to help you find out what they do.

Blenders
Also called liquidizers, these are usually attached to an electric whisk motor or a food processor and are tall and deep, with blades at the base. Ideal for turning things into liquid such as fruit for sauces and milk shakes. Hand-held blenders can be used in a small bowl or mug.

Bowls
Mixing bowls come in all sorts of sizes and the most useful are made from heatproof glass. Use large ones for pastry and whisking egg whites; smaller ones are better for smaller quantities, such as mixing dips.

Chopping boards
Lots of people use the same board for all their preparation, but it's much more hygienic to use a different one for each type of job. It is possible to buy boards with coloured handles, so the same one is always used for the same job. A wooden board is best for cutting bread. Scrub boards well after use.

Electric whisk
A whisk's main function is to beat in air and make the mixture bigger and thicker, as in, for example, cream and cake mixtures. But a whisk can also blend things together and make them smooth, such as sauces.

Food processor
This is actually a giant blender, with a large bowl and, usually, lots of attachments. The metal chopping blade is the one we use most, it's best with dry ingredients like vegetables and pastry. The plastic blade is for batters and cakes. Some processors also have grating blades and slicing plates.

Graters
A pyramid-shaped or box-shaped grater is the most useful type. Each side has a different grating surface, made up of small, curved, raised blades. Use the coarsest one for vegetables and cheese and the finer sides for grating orange and lemon rind. Stand the grater on a flat surface while you use it and grated food collects inside the pyramid. Scrub well with a brush after use. There are also very small graters, for whole nutmegs.

Measuring equipment
Most homes have some sort of measuring equipment, whether this is scales, spoons or cups.
Recipes seem to have lots of weights listed; this is because different countries use different ways to measure things. As long as you stick to the same ones for each recipe, you shouldn't have any problems.

The metric quantity is mentioned first, such as 115 g, followed by the imperial measurement – 4 oz – and these are ways to measure dry ingredients, such as flour, vegetables and chocolate.
When you measure liquids, there are three measurements to choose from. The metric measurement, such as 300 ml, followed by ½ pint – the imperial one; and, finally, 1¼ cups, which is the American measure. Most measuring jugs have all these measurements written on the side for easy measuring.
Small amounts of both dry and wet ingredients are often measured in millilitres (ml) and tablespoons (tbsp). 15 ml is the same as 1 tbsp and 5 ml is the same as 1 teaspoon (1 tsp). The spoon should be level.

Pans
Saucepans and frying pans can be made from different metals; some are even glass! The most popular are aluminium pans and stainless steel ones. Pans need to have a thick base to stop food from sticking.

Safety first for whisks, blenders and processors
Never put your hand in the processor to move something while it is plugged in. And keep your fingers away from whisks while they are whizzing round. Treat all electrical equipment very carefully and unplug everything before you fiddle around with blades.

- bun tin (pan)
- saucepans
- saucepan
- springform cake tins (pans)
- frying pan
- wire cooling rack
- measuring cups
- grater
- muffin tin (pan)
- whisks
- food processor
- weighing scales
- mixing bowls
- electric blender
- measuring spoons
- measuring jug
- chopping boards

COOKING FUN

Preparing Onions

Keeping the onions a similar size means they all cook at the same time, but we don't want any sliced fingertips, so take care. Keep a tissue nearby in case the onions make you cry!

1 Cut the onion in half with the skin still on. Lie the cut side flat on a board. Trim off both ends. Peel off the skin.

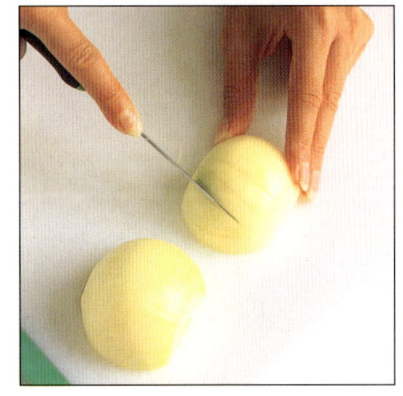

2 Make several parallel cuts lengthways (from trimmed end to end), but not cutting right to one end.

3 Make cuts at right angles to the first ones, at the same distance apart. The onion will be finely chopped. Finally, chop the end.

COOK'S TIP
To slice an onion, cut down through each half to make lots of vertical slices.

Preparing Carrots

Although they are often just sliced in circles, carrots can look much more attractive cut in a different way. The fresher the carrot, the easier it is to cut and the nicer it looks!

1 Peel the carrot, using this quick method with a swivel peeler, and trim the ends.

2 Cut the carrot into short lengths and then into thin slices, lengthways. You will need a sharp knife for this job, so be very careful.

3 Cut each thin slice into fine strips, about the size of matchsticks.

COOK'S TIP
Use tiny cutters to stamp out shapes from the thin carrot slices, to garnish soups or salads.

154

Cooking Fun

Separating Eggs

Meringues and some sauces call for just egg whites, so they must be separated from the yolk.

1 Break the egg onto a saucer.

2 Stand an egg cup over the yolk and hold it firmly in place, taking care not to puncture the yolk.

3 Hold the saucer over the mixing bowl and let the egg white slide in, holding onto the egg cup. The yolk will be left on the saucer.

Cook's Tip
The yolk may be needed for glazing, so check the recipe before you throw it away.

Grating

The most popular grater is the pyramid or box type, which offers different-sized blades.

1 The very fine side is for grating whole nutmeg. Hold the nutmeg in one hand and rub it up and down the grater. Sometimes, it is easier to do this directly over the food.

2 The finer blades are best for citrus fruits. The blades only work downwards and you might need to brush out some of the rind from the inside with a dry pastry brush.

3 The coarsest side is best for cheese, fruit and vegetables. The blades work when you press downwards and the food will collect inside the grater.

Cook's Tip
The jagged punched holes down one side of the grater are ideal for making breadcrumbs.

Pizza Faces

These funny faces are very easy to make. The base is a crispy crumpet (English muffin) topped with tomato sauce and melted cheese. The toppings are just suggestions – you can use whatever you like to create the shapes for the smiley faces.

Makes 9

INGREDIENTS
30 ml/2 tbsp vegetable oil
1 onion, finely shredded
200 g/7 oz can chopped tomatoes
25 g/2 tbsp tomato purée (paste)
9 crumpets (English muffins)
220 g/7.5 oz packet of processed cheese slices
1 green bell pepper, seeded and chopped
4–5 sliced cherry tomatoes
salt and pepper

crumpet (English muffin)

onion

cheese slices

tomato purée (paste)

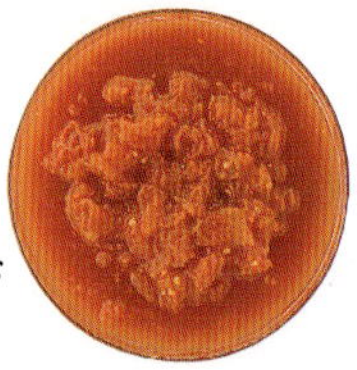

chopped tomatoes

! IMPORTANT SAFETY NOTE
Make sure an adult helps make the sauce. Stand away from the frying pan so the hot oil doesn't splash out.

1 With the help of an adult, preheat the oven to 220°C/425°F/Gas 7. Heat the oil in a large pan, add the onion and cook for about 2–3 minutes.

2 Add the can of tomatoes, tomato purée (paste) and salt and pepper. Bring to a boil and cook for 5–6 minutes until the mixture becomes thick and pulpy. Leave to cool.

3 Lightly toast the crumpets (English muffins) under the grill (broiler). Lay them on a baking sheet. Put a heaped teaspoonful of the tomato mixture on the top and spread it out evenly. Bake in the preheated oven for 25 minutes.

4 Cut the cheese slices into strips and arrange them with the green pepper and the cherry tomatoes on top of the pizzas to make smiley faces. Return to the oven for about 5 minutes until the cheese melts. Serve the pizzas while still warm.

COOKING FUN

Roly Poly Porcupines

A meal in itself! Everyone loves frankfurter sausages (hot dogs) and they're especially good if skewered into hot baked potatoes. Always serve with a big bowl of tomato ketchup nearby.

Serves 4

INGREDIENTS
4 large baking potatoes
6–8 frankfurter sausages (hot dogs)
50 g/2 oz cherry tomatoes
50 g/2 oz mild Cheddar cheese
2 sticks (stalks) celery

TO SERVE
iceberg lettuce, shredded
small pieces of red bell pepper and black olive
1 carrot

celery

potatoes

cherry tomatoes

frankfurter sausages (hot dogs)

Cheddar cheese

IMPORTANT SAFETY NOTE

You may need an adult to help chop the vegetables. Make sure an adult takes the potatoes from the oven, and leave them to cool for a while before touching.

1 With the help of an adult, preheat the oven to 200°C/400°F/Gas 6. Scrub the potatoes and prick them all over. Bake in the oven for 1–1¼ hours until soft.

2 Meanwhile, prepare the frankfurters (hot dogs). Heat the frankfurter sausages in a large pan of boiling water for 8–10 minutes until they are warmed through. Drain and leave to cool slightly.

3 Cut the cherry tomatoes in half and when cool enough to handle, chop the sausages into 2.5 cm (1 in) pieces. Cut the cheese into cubes and slice the celery. Arrange them onto toothpicks.

4 When the potatoes are cooked, remove them from the oven. Pierce the skin all over with the toothpicks topped with the frankfurters, cheese cubes, cherry tomatoes and celery slices. Serve on shredded lettuce and decorate the porcupine's head with pieces of red pepper and olive, and a carrot snout.

157

Tasty Toasts

Next time friends come over to watch a video, surprise them with these delicious treats.

Serves 4

INGREDIENTS
2 red bell peppers, halved lengthways and seeded
30 ml/2 tbsp oil
1 garlic clove, peeled and crushed
1 French baton (short French stick)
45 ml/3 tbsp pesto
50 g/2 oz/⅓ cup soft goat's cheese

garlic

French baton (stick)

soft goat's cheese

red bell peppers

oil

pesto

1 Put the pepper halves, cut-side down, under a hot grill (broiler) and let the skins blacken. Carefully put the halves in a plastic bag, tie the top and leave them until they are cool enough to handle. Peel off the skins and cut the peppers into strips.

2 Put the oil in a small bowl and stir in the garlic. Cut the bread into slanting slices and brush one side with the garlic-flavoured oil. Arrange the slices on a grill (broiler) pan and brown under a hot grill (broiler).

3 Turn the slices over and brush the untoasted sides with the garlic-flavoured oil and then with the pesto.

4 Arrange pepper strips over each slice and put small wedges of goat's cheese on top. Put back under the grill (broiler) and toast until the cheese has browned and melted slightly.

Chilli Cheese Nachos

Viva Mexico! Silence that hungry tummy with a truly spicy snack. Make it as cool or as hot as you like, by adjusting the amount of sliced jalapeno peppers. Olé!

Serves 4

INGREDIENTS
115 g/4 oz bag chilli tortilla chips
50 g/2 oz Cheddar cheese, grated
50 g/2 oz Red Leicester cheese, grated
50 g/2 oz pickled green jalapeno chillies, sliced

FOR THE DIP
30 ml/2 tbsp lemon juice
1 avocado, roughly chopped
1 beefsteak tomato, roughly chopped
salt and pepper

1 Arrange the tortilla chips in an even layer on a flameproof plate which can be used under the grill (broiler). Sprinkle all the grated cheese over and then scatter as many jalapeno chillies as you like over the top.

beefsteak tomato
pickled green jalapeno chillies
avocado
grated Cheddar cheese
lemon juice
chilli tortilla chips
grated Red Leicester cheese

2 Put the plate under a hot grill (broiler) and toast until the cheese has melted and browned – keep an eye on the chips to make sure they don't burn.

3 Mix the lemon juice, avocado and tomato together in a bowl. Add salt and pepper to taste and serve with the chips.

Pancake Parcels

Be adventurous with your pancakes! Don't just stick to lemon and sugar – try this savoury version for a real change.

Serves 4

INGREDIENTS
FOR THE PANCAKES
115 g/4 oz/1 cup plain (all-purpose) flour
1 egg
300 ml/½ pint/1¼ cups milk
2.5 ml/½ tsp salt
25 g/1 oz/2 tbsp butter, for frying
spring onions (scallions)

FOR THE FILLING
200 g/7 oz/scant 1 cup cream cheese with chives
90 ml/6 tbsp double (heavy) cream
115 g/4 oz ham, cut in strips
115 g/4 oz cheese, grated
salt and pepper
15 g/½ oz/¼ cup fresh breadcrumbs

1 To make the pancakes, put the flour, egg, a little milk and the salt in a bowl and beat together with a wooden spoon. Gradually beat in the rest of the milk until the batter looks like double (heavy) cream. (The milk must be added slowly or the batter will be lumpy.)

2 Melt a little butter in a medium-size frying pan and pour in just enough batter to cover the base in a thin layer. Tilt and turn the pan to spread the batter out. Cook gently until set, then turn over with a palette knife and cook the second side. If you feel brave enough, try tossing the pancakes!

3 Slide the pancake out of the pan. Stack the pancakes in a pile, with a piece of greaseproof (wax) paper between each one to stop them sticking to each other. There should be enough batter to make four large pancakes. Preheat the oven to 190°C/375°F/Gas 5.

4 Make the filling. Beat the cream cheese and cream in a bowl. Add the ham and half the cheese; season well with salt and pepper. Put a spoonful of the mixture in the centre of a pancake.

5 Fold one side over the mixture and then the other. Fold both ends up as well to make a small parcel. Arrange the parcels on a baking sheet, with the joins underneath. Make three more parcels in the same way.

6 Sprinkle the remaining cheese and the breadcrumbs over the parcels and cover with foil. Cook for 20 minutes. Remove the foil. Cook for 10 minutes more, until browned. Tie green spring onion (scallion) leaves neatly around the parcels.

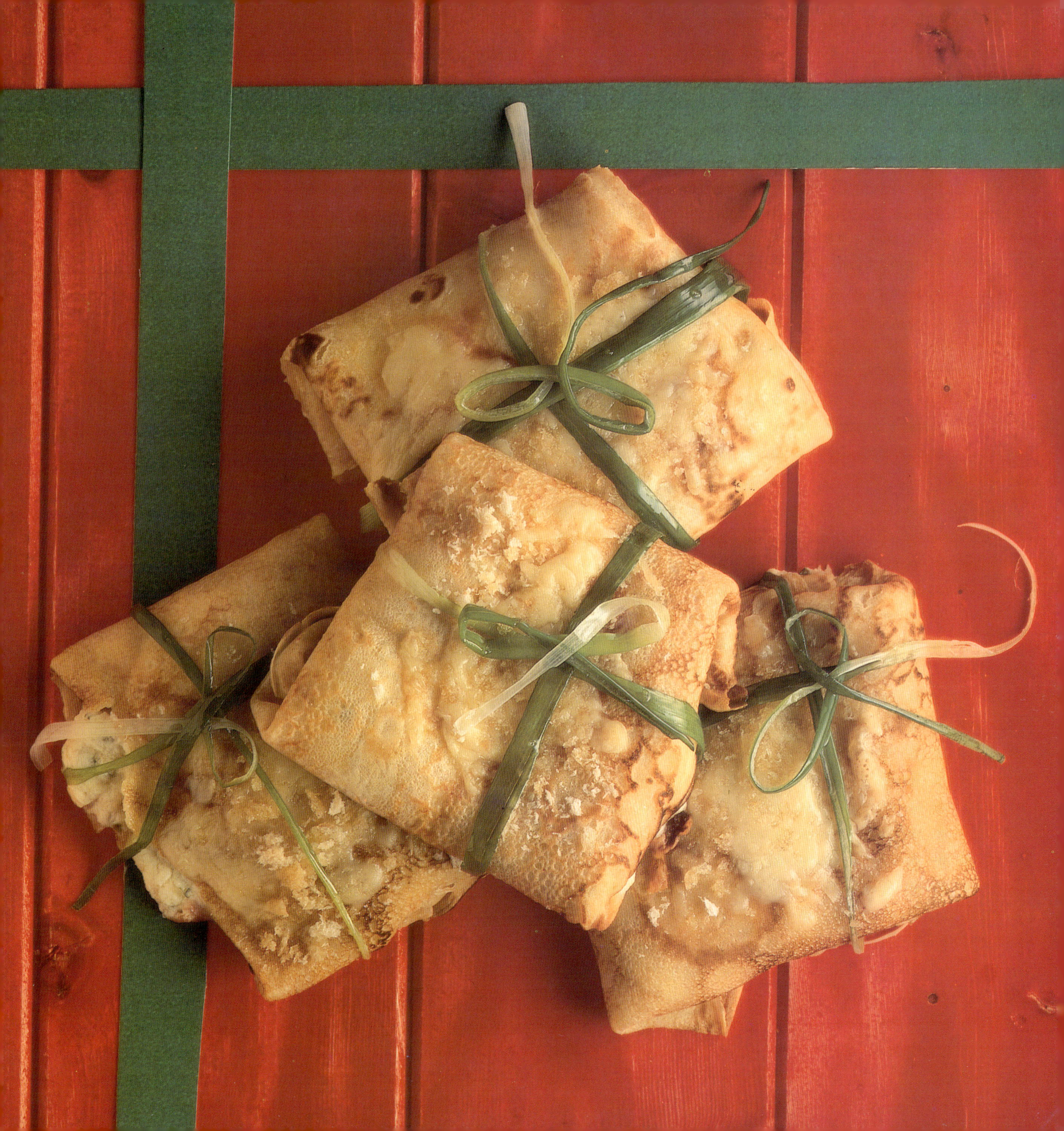

Chunky Cheesy Salad

Something to really sink your teeth into – this salad is chock-a-bloc with vitamins and energy. Serve on large slices of crusty bread.

Serves 4

INGREDIENTS
¼ small white cabbage, finely chopped
¼ small red cabbage, finely chopped
8 baby carrots, thinly sliced
50 g/2 oz small mushrooms, quartered
115 g/4 oz cauliflower, cut in small florets
1 small courgette (zucchini), grated
10 cm/4 in piece of cucumber, cubed
2 tomatoes, roughly chopped
50 g/2 oz sprouted seeds
50 g/2 oz/½ cup salted peanuts
30 ml/2 tbsp sunflower oil
15 ml/1 tbsp lemon juice
salt and pepper
50 g/2 oz cheese, grated
crusty bread, to serve

1 Put all the prepared vegetables and the sprouted seeds in a bowl and mix together well.

2 Stir in the peanuts. Drizzle the oil and lemon juice over. Season well with salt and pepper and leave to stand for about 30 minutes to allow the flavour to develop.

3 Sprinkle grated cheese over just before serving on large slices of crusty bread. Have extra dressing ready, in case anybody wants more.

COOKING FUN

Yellow Chicken

An all-time Chinese favourite that you can stir-fry in a few minutes. Serve with boiled rice.

Serves 4

INGREDIENTS
30 ml/2 tbsp oil
75 g/3 oz/¾ cup salted cashew nuts
4 spring onions (scallions), roughly chopped
450 g/1 lb boneless, skinless chicken breasts, cut in strips
165 g/5½ oz jar Chinese yellow bean sauce

Chinese yellow bean sauce

spring onions (scallions)

chicken

cashew nuts

oil

1 Heat 15 ml/1 tbsp of the oil in a frying pan and fry the cashew nuts until browned. This does not take long, so keep an eye on them. Lift them out with a slotted spoon and put them to one side.

2 Heat the remaining oil and fry the spring onions (scallions) and chicken for 5–8 minutes, until the meat is browned all over and cooked.

3 Return the nuts to the pan and pour the jar of sauce over. Stir well and cook gently until hot. Serve at once.

COOK'S TIP

Cashew nuts are quite expensive, but you can buy broken cashews, which are cheaper and perfectly good for this dish. You could also use almonds, if you prefer.

Tiny Toads

Serve these mini-sized portions of toad-in-the-hole with peas.

Serves 4

INGREDIENTS
115 g/4 oz/1 cup plain (all-purpose) flour
1 egg
300 ml/½ pint/1¼ cups milk
45 ml/3 tbsp fresh mixed herbs, e.g. parsley, thyme and chives, roughly chopped
24 cocktail sausages
salt and pepper

FOR THE ONION GRAVY
15 ml/1 tbsp oil
2 onions, sliced
600 ml/1 pint/2½ cups stock
15 ml/1 tbsp soy sauce
15 ml/1 tbsp whole-grain mustard
25 g/1 oz/2 tbsp cornflour (cornstarch)
30 ml/2 tbsp water

1 Preheat the oven to 200°C/400°F/Gas 6. Put the flour, egg and a little milk in a bowl and mix well with a wooden spoon. Gradually mix in the rest of the milk to make a batter. Season well with salt and pepper and stir in the herbs.

2 Lightly oil eight 10 cm/4 in non-stick Yorkshire pudding tins and arrange three sausages in each. Cook in the hot oven for 10 minutes.

COOK'S TIP
Use vegetarian sausages for friends who don't eat meat.

3 Carefully take the tins out of the oven and use a ladle to pour batter into each tin. Put them back in the oven and cook for 30–40 minutes more, until the batter is risen and browned.

4 Meanwhile, heat the oil in a pan. Fry the onions for 15 minutes until browned. Add the stock, mustard and soy. Bring to the boil. Mix the cornflour (cornstarch) and water together in a cup and pour into the gravy. Bring to the boil, stirring. Serve with the toads.

Honey Chops

These tasty, sticky chops are very quick and easy to prepare and grill (broil), but they would be just as good barbecued. Serve with herby mashed potatoes or chips (fries).

Serves 4

INGREDIENTS
450 g/1 lb carrots
15 ml/1 tbsp butter
15 ml/1 tbsp soft brown sugar
15 ml/1 tbsp sesame seeds

FOR THE CHOPS
4 pork loin chops
50 g/2 oz/¼ cup butter
30 ml/2 tbsp clear honey
15 ml/1 tbsp tomato purée (paste)

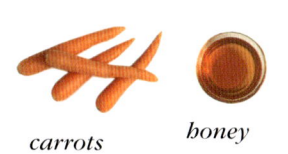

carrots
honey
butter
tomato purée (paste)
pork loin chops
soft brown sugar
sesame seeds

1 Cut the carrots into matchstick shapes, put them in a saucepan and just cover them with cold water. Add the butter and brown sugar and bring to the boil. Turn down the heat and leave to simmer for 15–20 minutes, until most of the liquid has boiled away.

2 Line the grill (broiler) pan with foil and arrange the pork chops on the rack. Beat the butter and honey together and gradually beat in the tomato purée (paste), to make a smooth paste. Preheat the grill (broiler) to high.

3 Spread half the honey paste over the chops and grill (broil) them for 5 minutes, until browned.

4 Turn the chops over, spread them with the remaining honey paste and return to the grill (broiler). Grill the second side for a further 5 minutes, or until the meat is cooked through. Sprinkle the sesame seeds over the top of the carrots and serve with the chops.

COOK'S TIP
If the chops are very thick, put under a medium-hot grill (broiler) for longer to make sure they are cooked in the middle.

Peanut Cookies

Packing up a picnic? Got a birthday party to go to? Make sure some of these nutty biscuits are on the menu.

Makes 25

INGREDIENTS
225 g/8 oz/1 cup butter
30 ml/2 tbsp smooth peanut butter
115 g/4 oz/1 cup icing (confectioners') sugar
50 g/2 oz/scant ½ cup cornflour (cornstarch)
225 g/8 oz/2 cups plain (all-purpose) flour
115 g/4 oz/1 cup unsalted peanuts

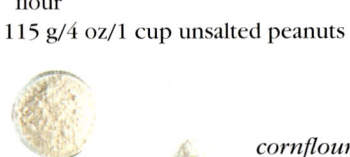

plain (all-purpose) flour

cornflour (cornstarch)

peanut butter

butter

unsalted peanuts

icing (confectioners') sugar

1 Put the butter and peanut butter in a bowl and beat together. Add the icing (confectioners') sugar, cornflour (cornstarch) and flour and mix together with your hands, to make a soft dough.

2 Preheat the oven to 180°C/350°F/Gas 4 and lightly oil two baking sheets. Roll the mixture into 25 small balls, using floured hands, and place the balls on the two sheets. Leave plenty of room for the cookies to spread.

3 Press the tops of the balls of dough flat, using either the back of a fork or your fingertips.

4 Press some of the peanuts into each of the cookies. Cook for about 15–20 minutes, until lightly browned. Leave to cool for a few minutes before lifting them carefully onto a wire rack with a palette knife (metal spatula). When they are cool, pack them in a tin.

COOK'S TIP
Make really monster cookies by making bigger balls of dough. Leave plenty of room on the baking sheets for them to spread, though.

COOKING FUN

Five-Spice Fingers

Light, crumbly biscuits (cookies) with an unusual Chinese five-spice flavouring.

Makes 28

INGREDIENTS
115 g/4 oz/½ cup margarine
50 g/2 oz/½ cup icing (confectioners') sugar
115 g/4 oz/1 cup plain (all-purpose) flour
10 ml/2 tsp five-spice powder
oil, for greasing
grated rind and juice of ½ orange

icing (confectioners') sugar

orange

five-spice powder

margarine

plain (all-purpose) flour

1 Put the margarine and half the icing (confectioners') sugar in a bowl and beat with a wooden spoon, until the mixture is smooth, creamy and soft.

2 Add the flour and five-spice powder and beat again. Put the mixture in a large piping bag fitted with a large star nozzle.

3 Preheat the oven to 180°C/350°F/Gas 4. Lightly grease two baking sheets and pipe short lines of mixture, about 7.5 cm/3 in long, on them. Leave enough room for them to spread. Cook for about 15 minutes, until lightly browned. Leave to cool slightly, before lifting them onto a wire rack with a palette knife (metal spatula).

4 Sift the remaining amount of icing (confectioners') sugar into a small bowl and stir in the orange rind. Add enough juice to make a thin icing and brush it over the fingers while they are still warm. Leave to cool a little and serve.

COOK'S TIP
Delicious served with ice cream or creamy desserts.

Monster Meringues

A mouth-watering dessert made from meringue, whipped cream and tangy summer fruits.

Serves 4

INGREDIENTS
3 egg whites
175 g/6 oz/¾ cup caster (superfine) sugar
15 ml/1 tbsp cornflour (cornstarch)
5 ml/1 tsp white wine vinegar
few drops vanilla essence (extract)
225 g/8 oz assorted red summer fruits
300 ml/½ pint/1¼ cups double (heavy) cream
1 passion fruit

double (heavy) cream
caster (superfine) sugar
strawberries
cornflour (cornstarch)
passion fruit
redcurrants
vanilla essence (extract)
eggs
white wine vinegar
raspberries

COOK'S TIP
Draw six 7.5 cm (3 in) circles and pipe smaller meringues, if you aren't hungry enough for a monster dessert.

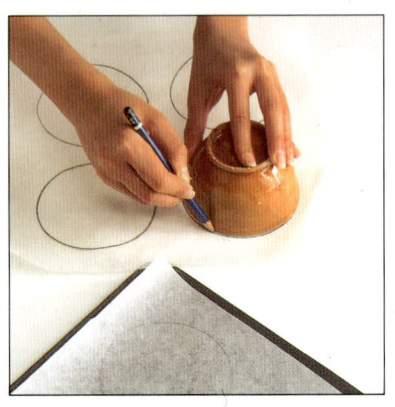

1 Preheat the oven to 140°C/275°F/Gas 1. In pencil, draw eight 10 cm/4 in circles on two separate sheets of baking parchment (parchment paper) that will fit on two flat baking sheets.

2 Put the egg whites into a very clean, dry bowl and whisk until stiff. This will take about 2 minutes with an electric whisk; peaks made in the meringue should keep their shape when it's ready. Add the sugar gradually and whisk well each time. The mixture should now be very stiff.

3 Use a metal spoon to gently stir in the cornflour (cornstarch), white wine vinegar and vanilla essence (extract). Put the meringue into a large piping bag, fitted with a large star nozzle.

4 Pipe a solid layer of meringue in four of the drawn circles and then pipe a lattice pattern in the other four. Put the meringues in the oven and cook for 1¼–1½ hours, swapping shelf positions after 30 minutes, until lightly browned. The paper will peel off the back easily when the meringues are cooked.

5 Roughly chop most of the summer fruits, reserving a few for decoration. Whip the cream and spread it over the solid meringue shapes. Scatter the fruit over. Halve the passion fruit, scoop out the seeds with a teaspoon and scatter them over the fruit. Put a lattice lid on top of each and serve with the reserved fruits.

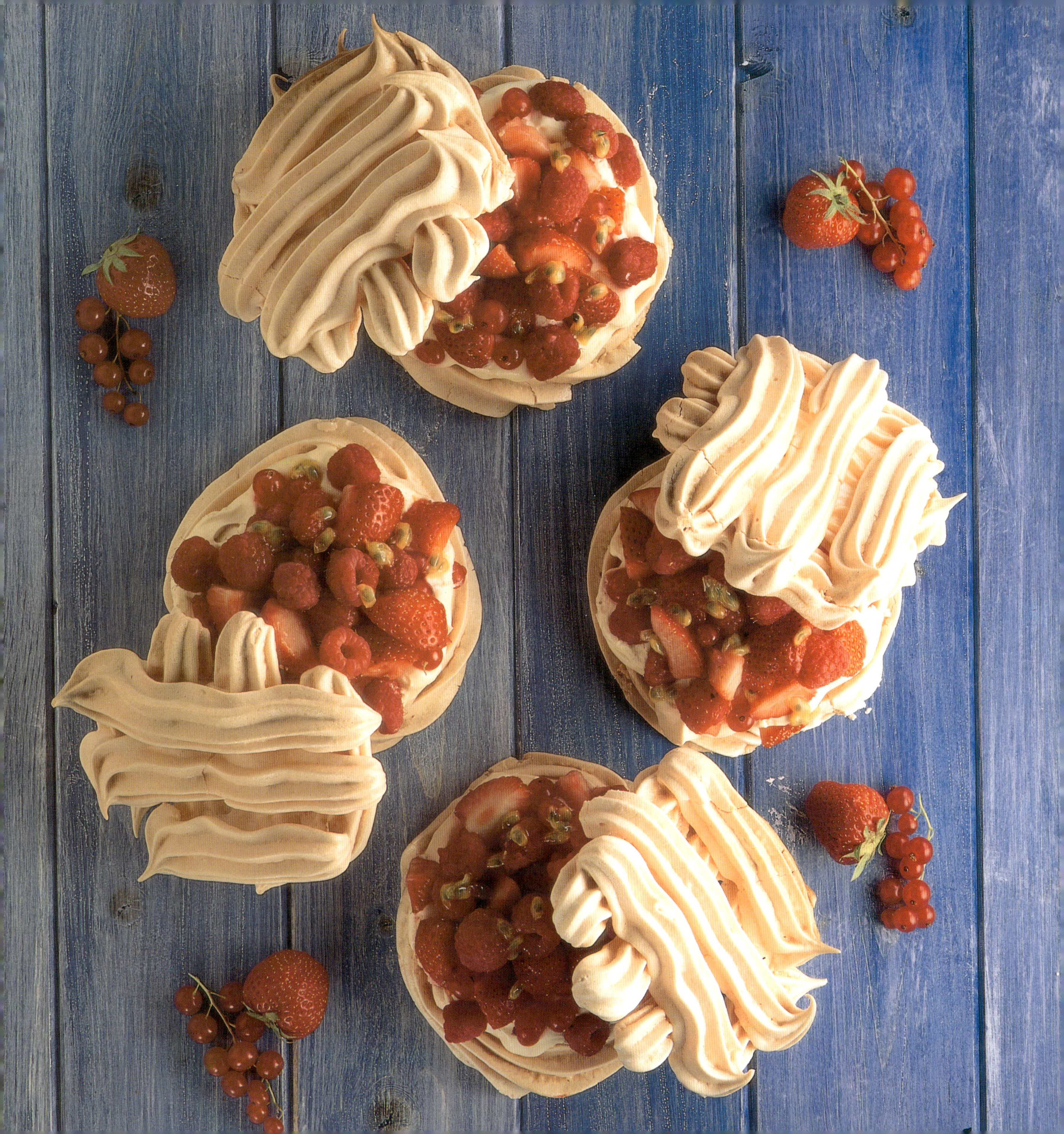

Chocolate Puffs

These are always a firm favourite and so easy and cheap to make.

Serves 4–6

INGREDIENTS
150 ml/¼ pint/⅔ cup water
50 g/2 oz/¼ cup butter
65 g/2½ oz/generous ½ cup plain (all-purpose) flour, sifted
2 eggs, beaten

FOR THE FILLING AND ICING
150 ml/¼ pint/⅔ cup double (heavy) cream
225 g/8 oz/1½ cups icing (confectioners') sugar
15 ml/1 tbsp cocoa powder
30–60 ml/2–4 tbsp water

1 Put the water in a saucepan, add the butter and heat gently until it melts. Bring to the boil and remove from the heat. Tip in all the flour at once and beat quickly until the mixture sticks together, leaving the side of the pan clean. Leave to cool slightly.

2 Add the eggs, a little at a time, to the mixture and beat well each time, by hand with a wooden spoon or with an electric whisk, until the mixture is thick and glossy and drops reluctantly from a spoon (you may not need to use all of the egg). Preheat the oven to 220°C/425°F/Gas 7.

3 Dampen two baking sheets with cold water and put walnut-sized spoonfuls of the mixture on them. Leave some space for them to rise. Cook for 25–30 minutes, until golden brown and well risen. Use a palette knife (metal spatula) to lift them onto a wire rack and make a small hole in each one with the handle of a wooden spoon to allow the steam to escape. Leave to cool.

4 To make the filling and icing, whip the cream until thick. Put it into a piping bag fitted with a plain or star nozzle. Push the nozzle into the hole in each puff and squirt a little cream inside. Put the icing (confectioners') sugar and cocoa in a small bowl and stir together. Add enough water to make a thick glossy icing. Spread a spoonful of icing on each puff and serve.

COOK'S TIP

If the unfilled puffs go soggy, put them back into a hot oven for a few minutes and they will crisp up again.

170

Cooking Fun

Let's Get Tropical

Supermarkets are full of weird and wonderful fruits that make a really tangy salad when mixed together. Serve with cream or yogurt.

Serves 4

INGREDIENTS
1 small pineapple
2 kiwi fruit
1 ripe mango
1 watermelon slice
2 peaches
2 bananas
60 ml/4 tbsp tropical fruit juice

tropical fruit juice
watermelon
mango
pineapple
peaches
kiwi fruit
bananas

1 Cut the pineapple into 1 cm/½ in slices. Work round the edge of each slice, cutting off the skin and any spiky bits. Cut each slice into wedges and put them in a bowl.

2 Use a potato peeler to remove the skin from the kiwi fruit. Cut them in half lengthways and then into wedges. Add to the fruit bowl.

3 Cut the mango lengthways into quarters and cut round the large flat stone. Peel the flesh and cut it into chunks or slices.

4 Cut the watermelon into slices, cut off the skin and cut the flesh into chunks. Remove the seeds. Cut the peaches in half, remove the stones and cut the flesh into wedges. Slice the bananas. Add all the fruit to the bowl and gently stir in the fruit juice.

COOKING FUN

Chocolate Brownies

Scout out these delicious, moist and chewy cakes, and guide yourself to a chocolate treat!

Makes 9

INGREDIENTS
65 g/2½ oz/⅓ cup butter
50 g/2 oz plain (semi-sweet) chocolate
150 g/5 oz/scant 1 cup soft brown sugar
2 eggs, beaten
65 g/2½ oz/generous ½ cup plain (all-purpose) flour
50 g/2 oz/½ cup roughly chopped pecans or walnuts
25 g/1 oz/¼ cup icing (confectioners') sugar

icing (confectioners') sugar

soft brown sugar

butter

plain (all-purpose) flour

eggs

plain (semi-sweet) chocolate

pecans

1 Put the butter and chocolate in a bowl and stand it over a saucepan of hot, but not boiling water. Make sure the water doesn't touch the bowl. Leave until they have both melted and then stir them together.

2 Stir the sugar into the butter and chocolate mixture and leave for a while to cool slightly.

3 Cut a piece of baking parchment or greaseproof (wax) paper to fit the base of an 18 cm/7 in square cake tin (pan).

4 Preheat the oven to 180°C/350°F/Gas 4. Beat the eggs into the chocolate mixture, then stir in the flour and nuts.

5 Pour the mixture into the lined cake tin (pan) and level the top. Cook for 25–35 minutes, until firm around the edges but still slightly soft in the middle.

6 Cut into nine squares and leave to cool in the tin (pan). Dredge with a little icing (confectioners') sugar and serve hot or cold, whichever you prefer.

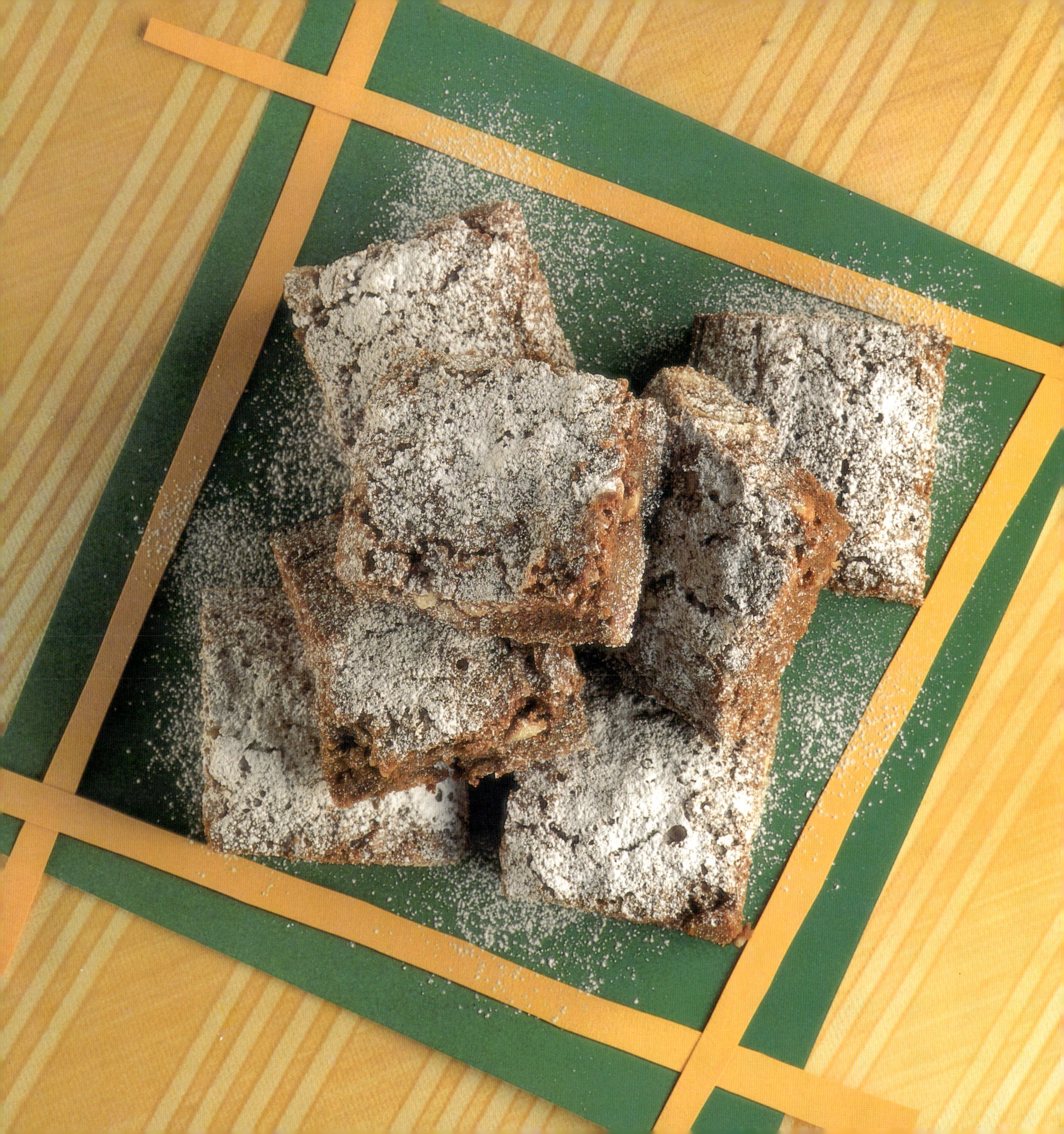

Blueberry Muffins

These monster muffins contain whole fresh blueberries that burst in the mouth when bitten.

Makes 9

INGREDIENTS

375 g/13 oz/3¼ cups plain (all-purpose) flour
200 g/7 oz/scant 1 cup caster (superfine) sugar
25 ml/1½ tbsp baking powder
175 g/6 oz/¾ cup butter, roughly chopped
1 egg, beaten
1 egg yolk
150 ml/¼ pint/⅔ cup milk
grated rind of 1 lemon
175 g/6 oz/1½ cups fresh blueberries

1 Preheat the oven to 200°/400°F/Gas 6. Line a muffin tin (pan) with nine large paper muffin cases (cups).

2 Put the flour, sugar, baking powder and butter in a bowl. Use your fingertips to rub the butter into the flour, until the mixture looks like breadcrumbs.

3 In a separate bowl, beat the egg, egg yolk, milk and lemon rind together.

4 Pour the egg and milk mixture into the flour mixture, add the blueberries and mix gently together.

5 Share the mixture among the paper cases and cook for 30–40 minutes, until they are risen and brown.

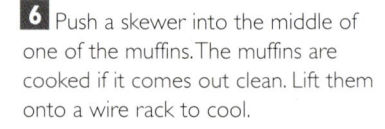

6 Push a skewer into the middle of one of the muffins. The muffins are cooked if it comes out clean. Lift them onto a wire rack to cool.

COOK'S TIP

As the muffins have fresh fruit in them, they will not keep for longer than four days, so best eat them immediately!

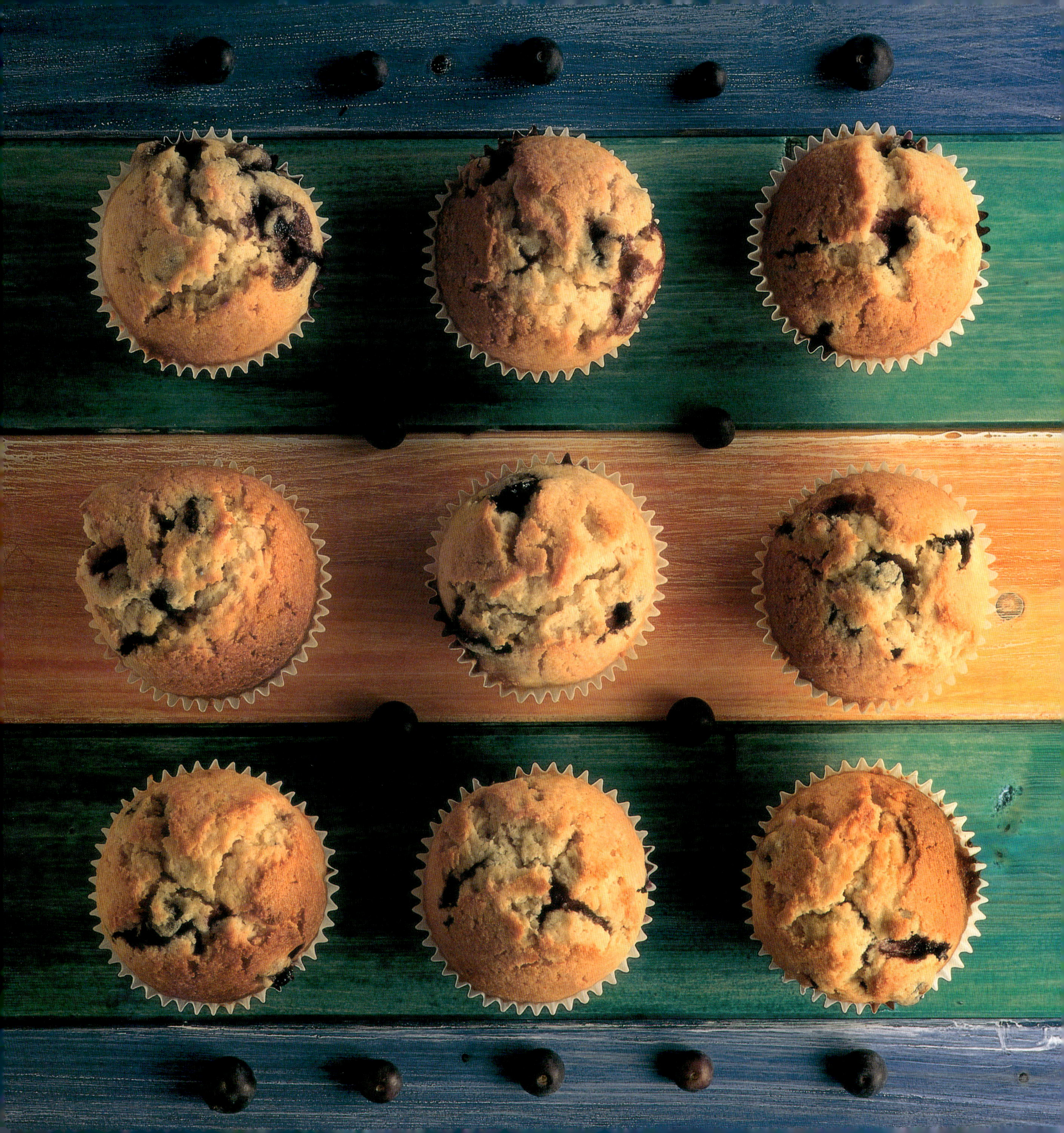

Chunky Choc Bars

This no-cook cake is a smash hit with everyone.

Makes 12

INGREDIENTS
350 g/12 oz plain (semi-sweet) chocolate
115 g/4 oz/½ cup butter
400 g/14 oz can condensed milk
225 g/8 oz digestive biscuits, (graham crackers) broken
50 g/2 oz/⅓ cup raisins
115 g/4 oz ready-to-eat dried peaches, roughly chopped
50 g/2 oz hazelnuts or pecans, roughly chopped

1 Line an 18 x 28 cm/7 x 11 in cake tin (pan) with clear film (plastic wrap).

2 Put the chocolate and butter in a large bowl over a pan of hot but not boiling water (the bowl must not touch the water) and leave to melt. Stir until well mixed.

3 Beat the condensed milk into the chocolate and butter mixture.

4 Add the biscuits (crackers), raisins, peaches and nuts and mix well, until all the ingredients are coated in chocolate.

5 Tip the mixture into the prepared tin, making sure it is pressed well into the corners. Leave the top craggy. Put in the fridge and leave to set.

6 Lift the cake out of the tin using the clear film (plastic wrap) and then peel it off. Cut into 12 bars and keep chilled – until you are ready to eat them.

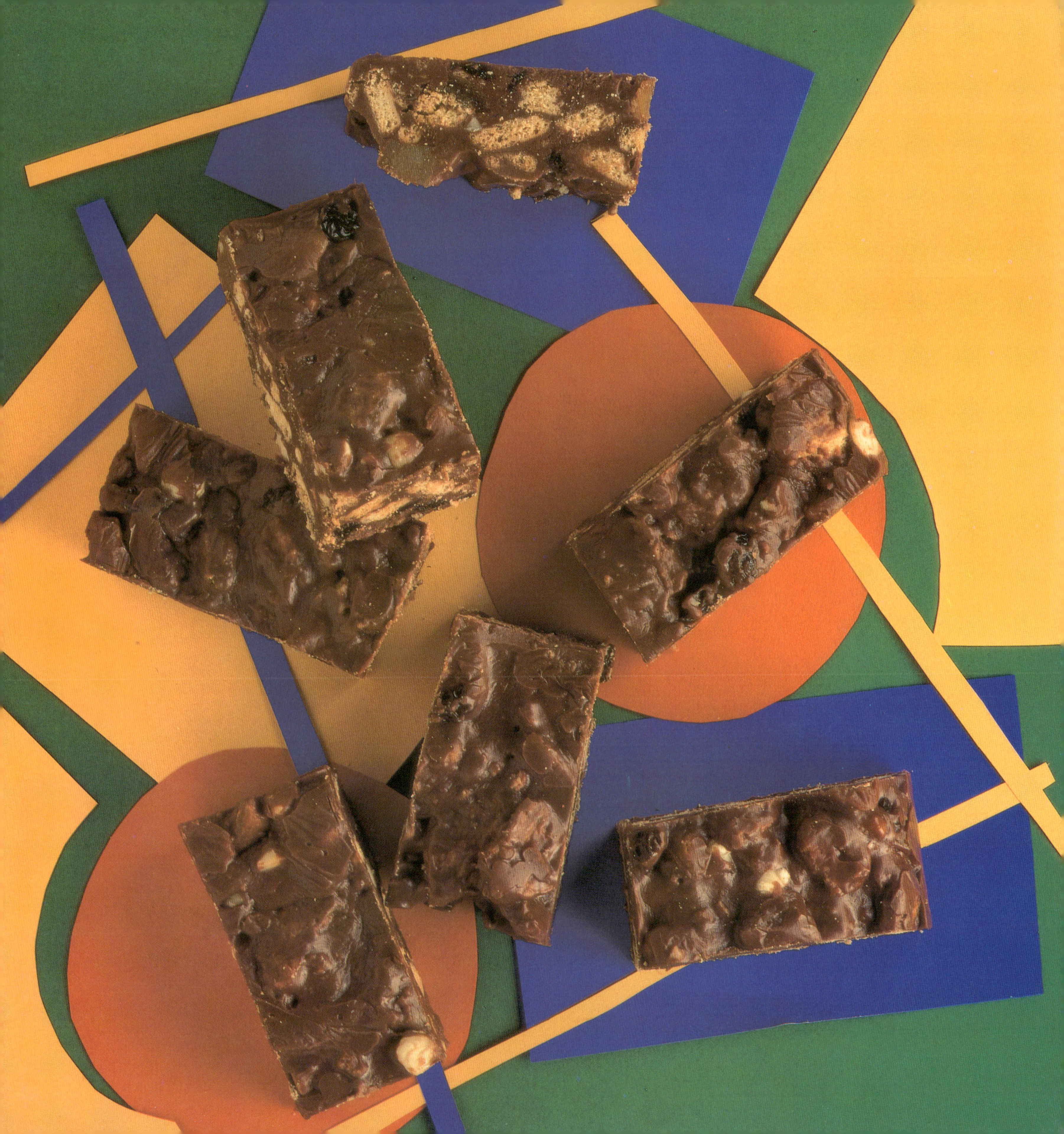

Lemon Meringue Cakes

This is a variation on cupcakes – soft lemon sponge topped with crisp meringue.

Makes 18

INGREDIENTS
115 g/4 oz/½ cup margarine
200 g/7 oz/scant 1 cup caster (superfine) sugar
2 eggs
115 g/4 oz/1 cup self-raising (rising) flour
5 ml/1 tsp baking powder
grated rind of 2 lemons
30 ml/2 tbsp lemon juice
2 egg whites

self-raising (rising) flour
caster (superfine) sugar
lemon juice
baking powder
eggs
lemons
margarine

COOK'S TIP
Make sure that you whisk the egg whites enough before adding the sugar – when you lift out the whisk they should stand in peaks that just flop over slightly at the top. Use a mixture of oranges and lemons, for a sweeter taste.

1 Preheat the oven to 190°C/375°F/Gas 5. Put the margarine in a bowl and beat until soft. Add 115 g/4 oz/½ cup of the sugar and continue to beat until the mixture is smooth and creamy.

2 Beat in the eggs, flour, baking powder, half the lemon rind and all the lemon juice.

3 Stand 18 small paper cases (cups) in two bun tins (muffin pans), and share the mixture between them all.

4 Whisk the egg whites in a clean bowl, until they stand in soft peaks.

5 Stir in the remaining sugar and lemon rind.

6 Put a spoonful of the meringue mixture on each cake. Cook for about 20–25 minutes, until the meringue is crisp and brown. Serve hot or cold.

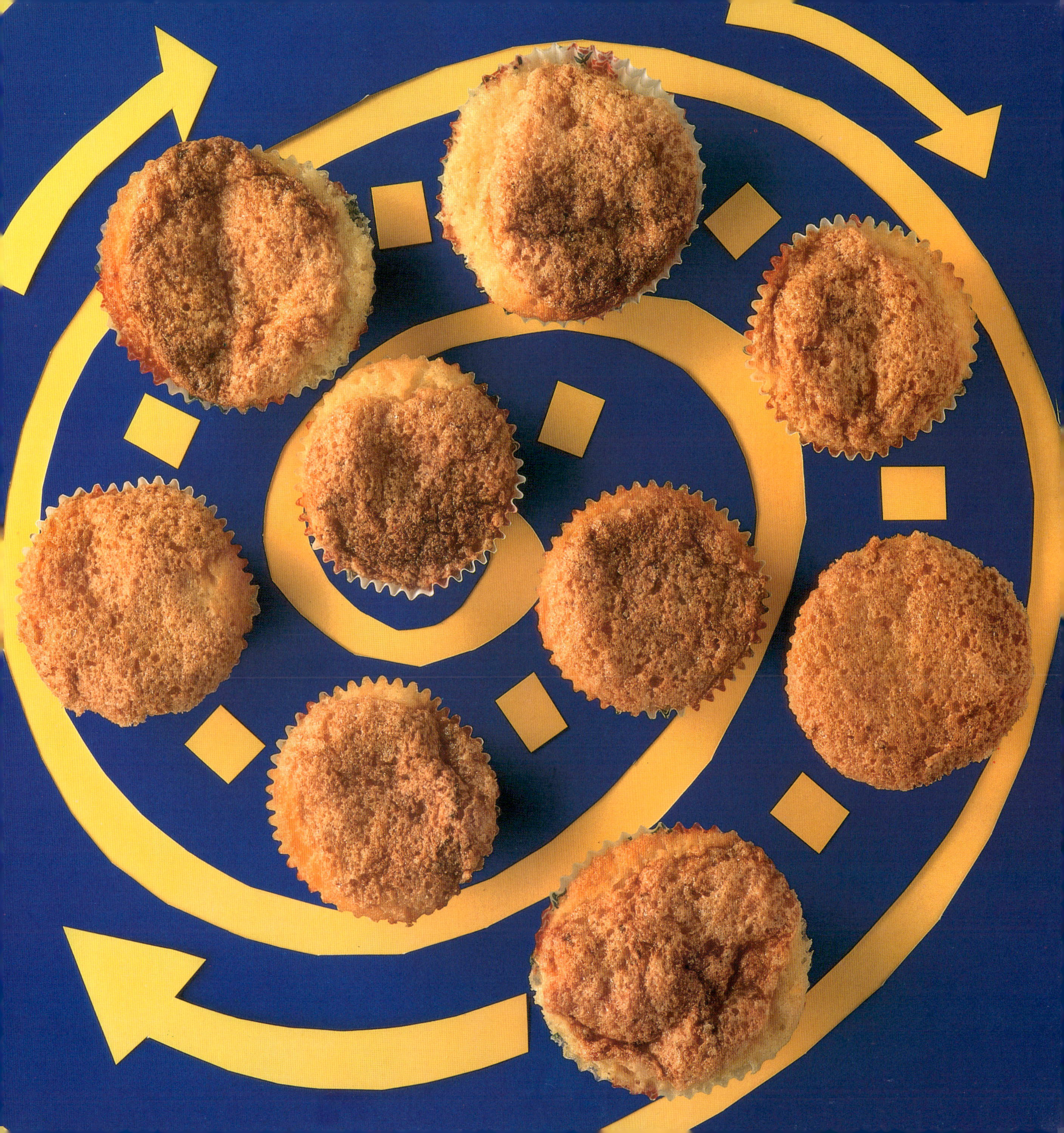

Kooky Cookies

Easy to make and yummy to eat! Let your imagination run wild with the decorating. If it's easier, you can use coloured icing pens.

Makes about 15

INGREDIENTS
115 g/4 oz/1 cup self-raising (rising) flour
5 ml/1 tsp ground ginger
5 ml/1 tsp bicarbonate of soda (baking soda)
50 g/2 oz/4 tbsp granulated sugar
50 g/2 oz/4 tbsp softened butter
25 g/2 tbsp golden syrup (corn syrup)

ICING
115 g/4 oz/½ cup softened butter
250 g/8 oz/2 cups sifted icing (confectioners') sugar
5 ml/1 tsp lemon juice
few drops of food colouring (optional)
coloured icing pens
brightly coloured sweets (candies)

IMPORTANT SAFETY NOTE

Ask an adult to remove the cookies from the oven and do not touch the cookies until completely cool.

1 Sift the flour, ginger and bicarbonate of soda (baking soda) into a bowl. Add the sugar, then rub in the butter with your fingertips until the mixture resembles fine breadcrumbs.

2 Add the golden syrup (light corn syrup) and mix to a dough. Preheat the oven to 190°C/375°F/Gas 5.

3 Roll out to 3 mm (⅛ in) thick on a lightly floured surface. Stamp out the shapes with biscuit (cookie) cutters and transfer to a lightly greased baking sheet. Bake for 5–10 minutes before transferring to a wire rack to cool.

4 To make the icing, beat the butter in a bowl until light and fluffy. Add the icing (confectioners') sugar a little at a time and continue beating. Add lemon juice and food colouring (if using).

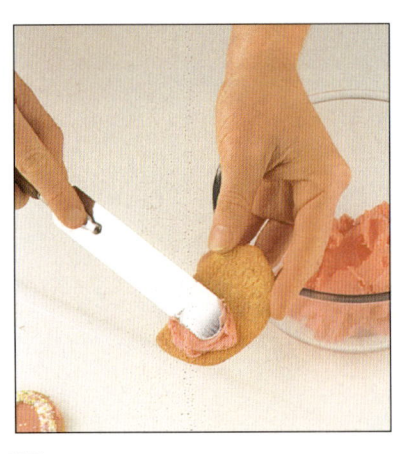

5 Spread the icing over the cooled cookies and leave to set.

6 When the icing has set, make patterns on the icing with coloured icing pens and decorate with coloured sweets (candies).

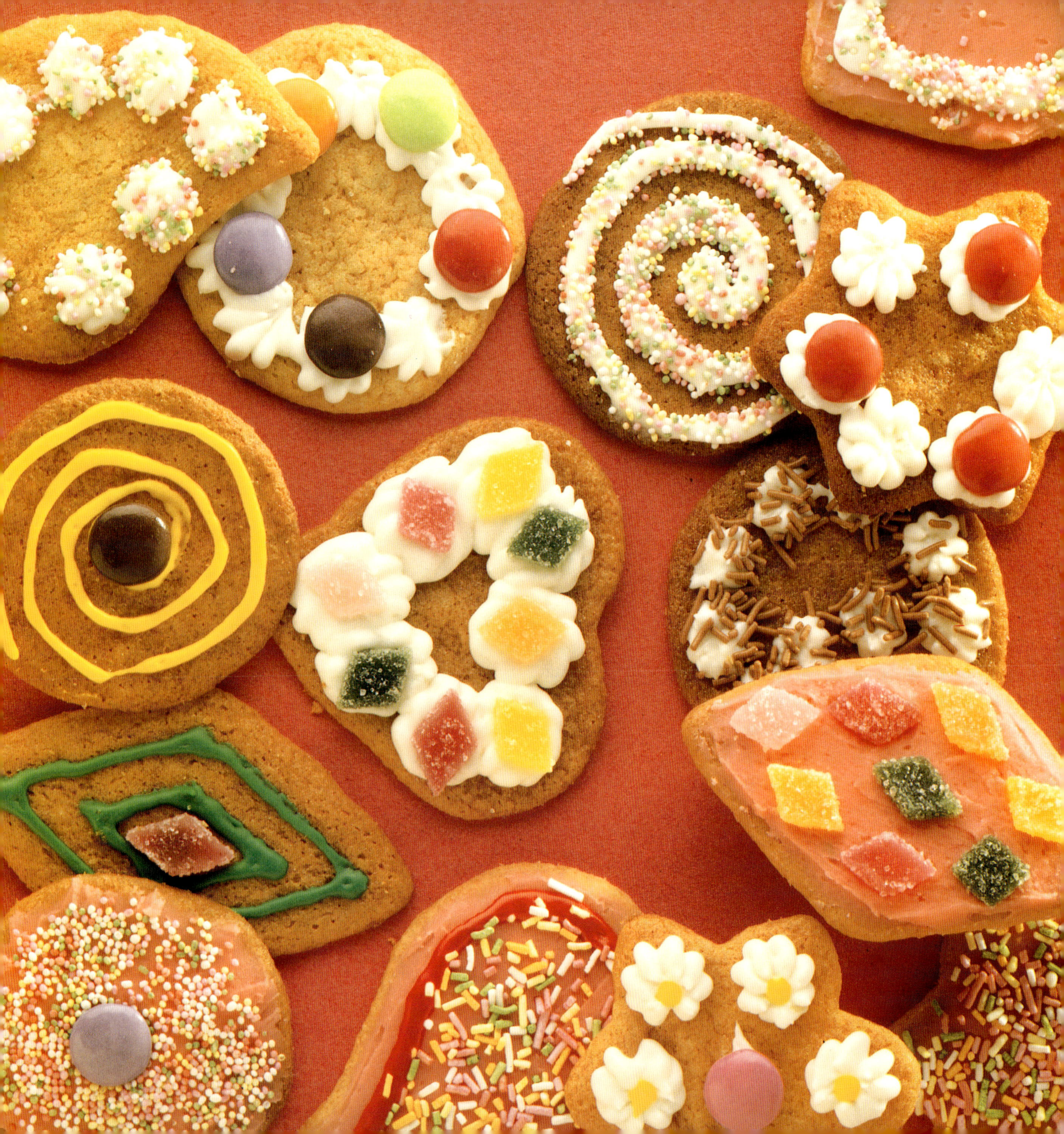

COOKING FUN

Jolly Orange Boats

These are so easy to make and fun to eat. The only difficult thing is waiting for the jelly (gelatine) to set! These boats make a yummy dessert or party treat. You could serve with ice cream for something extra special.

Serves 4

INGREDIENTS
2 oranges
1 packet orange-flavoured jelly (gelatine)
4 sheets rice paper or coloured paper

orange

jelly (gelatine)

rice paper

1 Cut the oranges in half lengthways. Scrape out the flesh, taking care not to pierce the skins. Chop up the flesh.

2 Make the jelly (gelatine) according to the packet instructions. Add the orange flesh while the jelly cools.

3 Place the orange shells onto a baking sheet and pour in the jelly mixture. Leave for 1 hour to set. Once set, cut the skins in half again using a sharp knife to create little boats.

4 Cut the rice paper or coloured paper sheets into eight squares. Pierce each corner with a toothpick and attach the sail to the middle of the orange boat.

IMPORTANT SAFETY NOTE

You may need an adult's help cutting the oranges. Be very careful whenever you handle knives.

COOKING FUN

Chocolate Witchy Apples

These chocolate witches are great fun. Be careful with the melted chocolate, though, as it has a nasty habit of getting everywhere!

Serves 6

INGREDIENTS
6 small eating apples
6 wooden lollipop sticks
250 g/8 oz/8 squares milk chocolate
6 ice cream cones
sweets (candies) for decorating

apple

milk chocolate

sweets (candies)

lollipop stick

ice cream cone

1 Peel and thoroughly dry the apples. Press a wooden lollipop stick into the core of each one.

2 In the microwave or over a pan of boiling water, gently melt the chocolate.

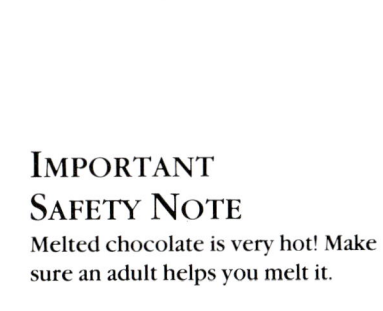

IMPORTANT SAFETY NOTE

Melted chocolate is very hot! Make sure an adult helps you melt it.

3 When melted, tilt the pan and dip the apple into it, coating it thoroughly. Place it on a baking sheet lined with baking paper. Press the sweets (candies) into the chocolate to decorate before the chocolate sets.

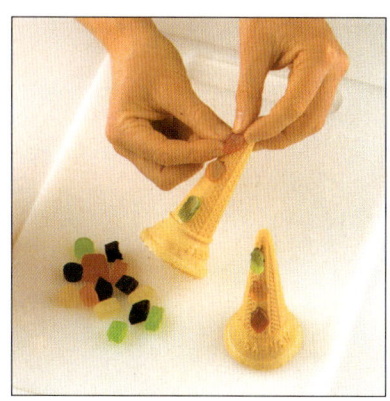

4 Holding the stick, use a little melted chocolate to attach the cone for a hat. The cone can also be decorated by sticking sweets on with spare melted chocolate. Repeat with the other five apples.

Fruit Crush & Fruit Kebabs

Fruit crush is just the ticket on a hot summer's day, served with mouth-watering fruit kebabs.

Serves 6

INGREDIENTS
FOR THE FRUIT CRUSH
300 ml/½ pint/1¼ cups orange juice
300 ml/½ pint/1¼ cups pineapple juice
300 ml/½ pint/1¼ cups tropical fruit juice
475 ml/16 fl oz/2 cups lemonade
fresh pineapple slices and fresh cherries, to decorate

FOR THE FRUIT KEBABS
24 small strawberries
24 green seedless grapes
12 marshmallows
1 kiwi fruit, peeled and cut in 12 wedges
1 banana
15 ml/1 tbsp lemon juice

1 To make the fruit crush, put the orange juice and the pineapple juice into ice-cube trays and freeze them until solid.

2 Mix together the tropical fruit juice and lemonade in a large jug (pitcher). Put a mixture of the ice cubes in each glass and pour the fruit crush over. Decorate the glasses with the pineapple slices and cherries.

3 To make the fruit kebabs, thread two strawberries, two grapes, a marshmallow and a wedge of kiwi fruit onto each of twelve wooden skewers.

4 Peel the banana and cut it into twelve slices. Toss it in the lemon juice and thread onto the skewers. Serve immediately.

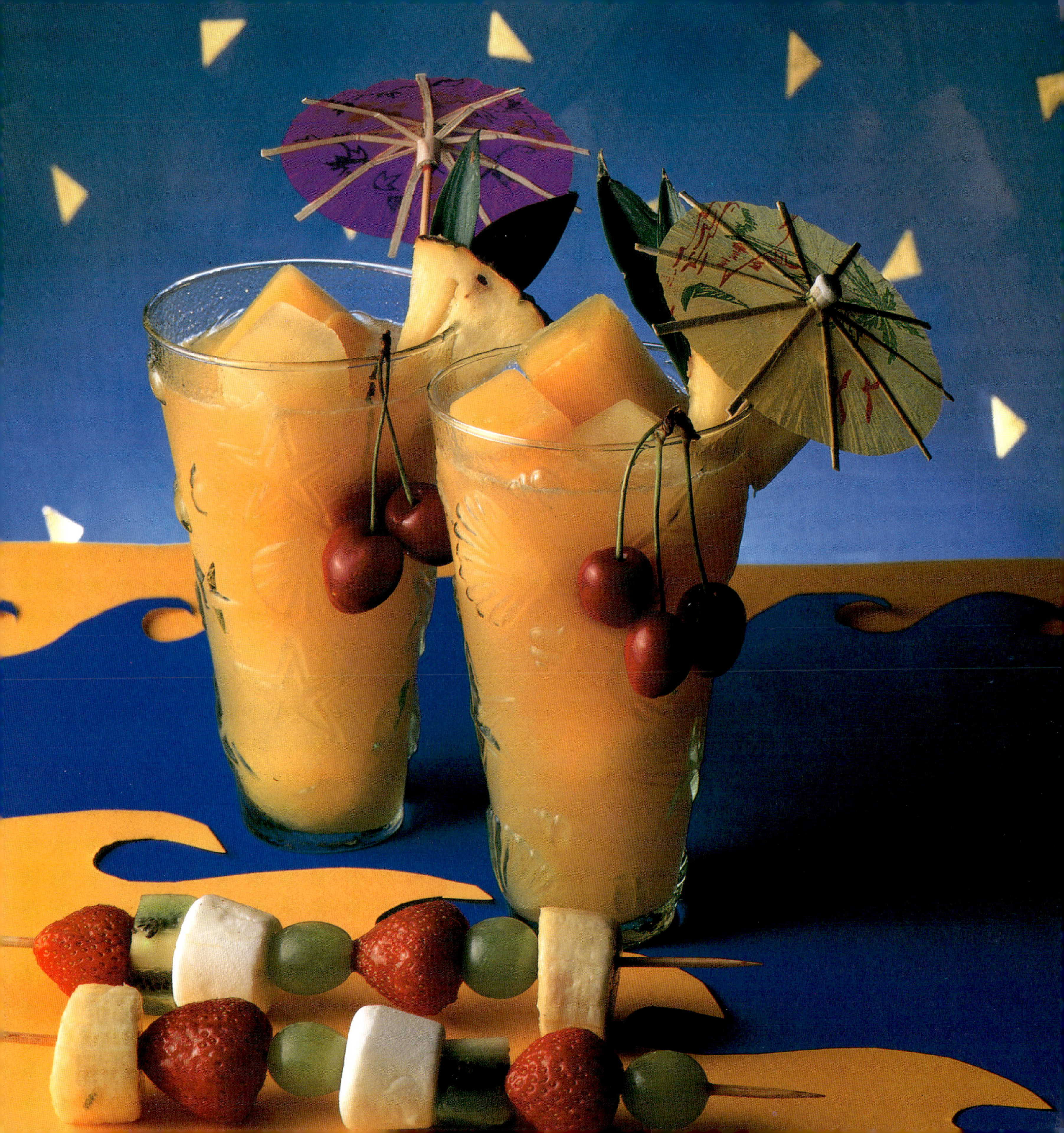

TEMPLATES

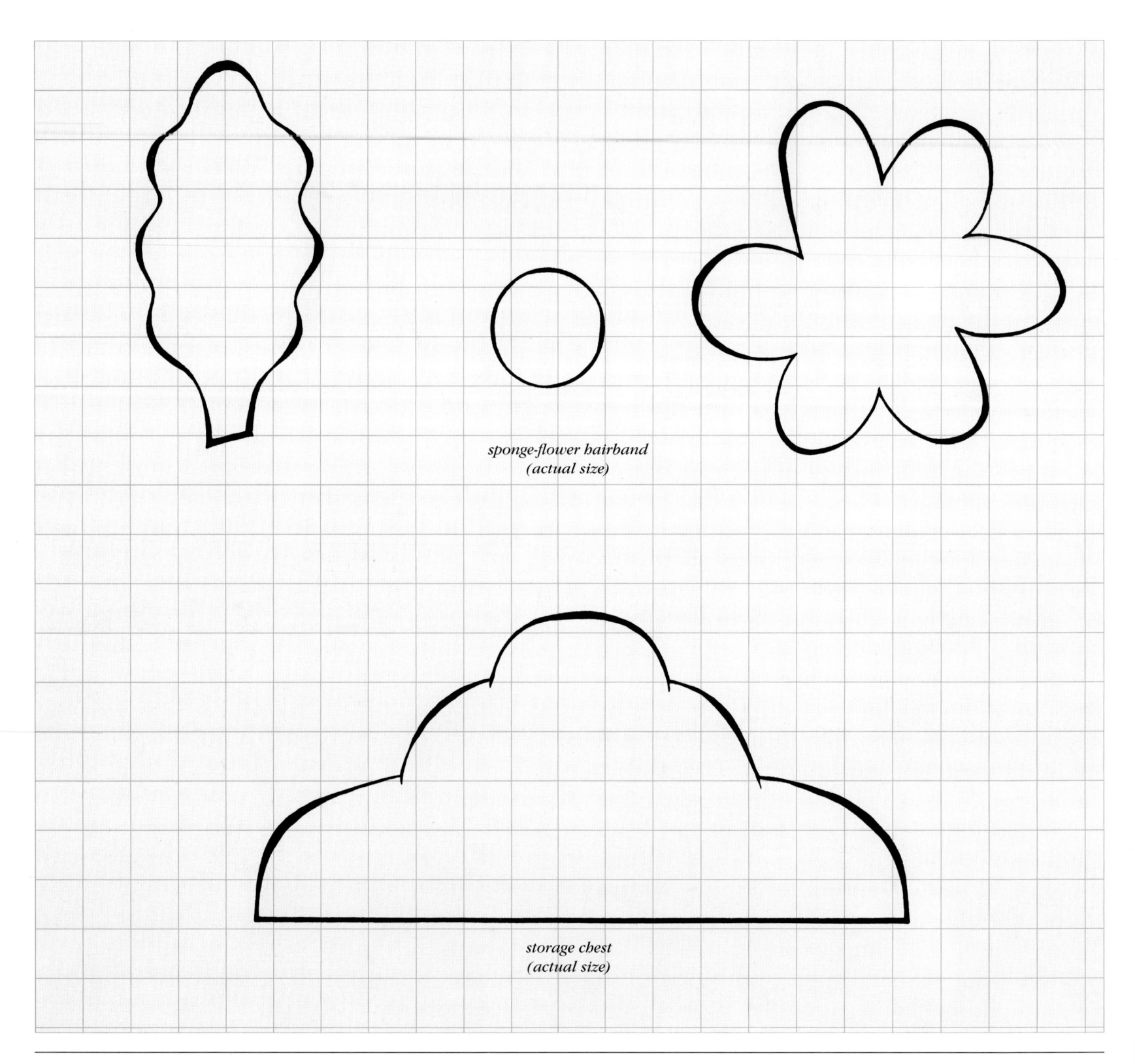

sponge-flower hairband
(actual size)

storage chest
(actual size)

186

TEMPLATES

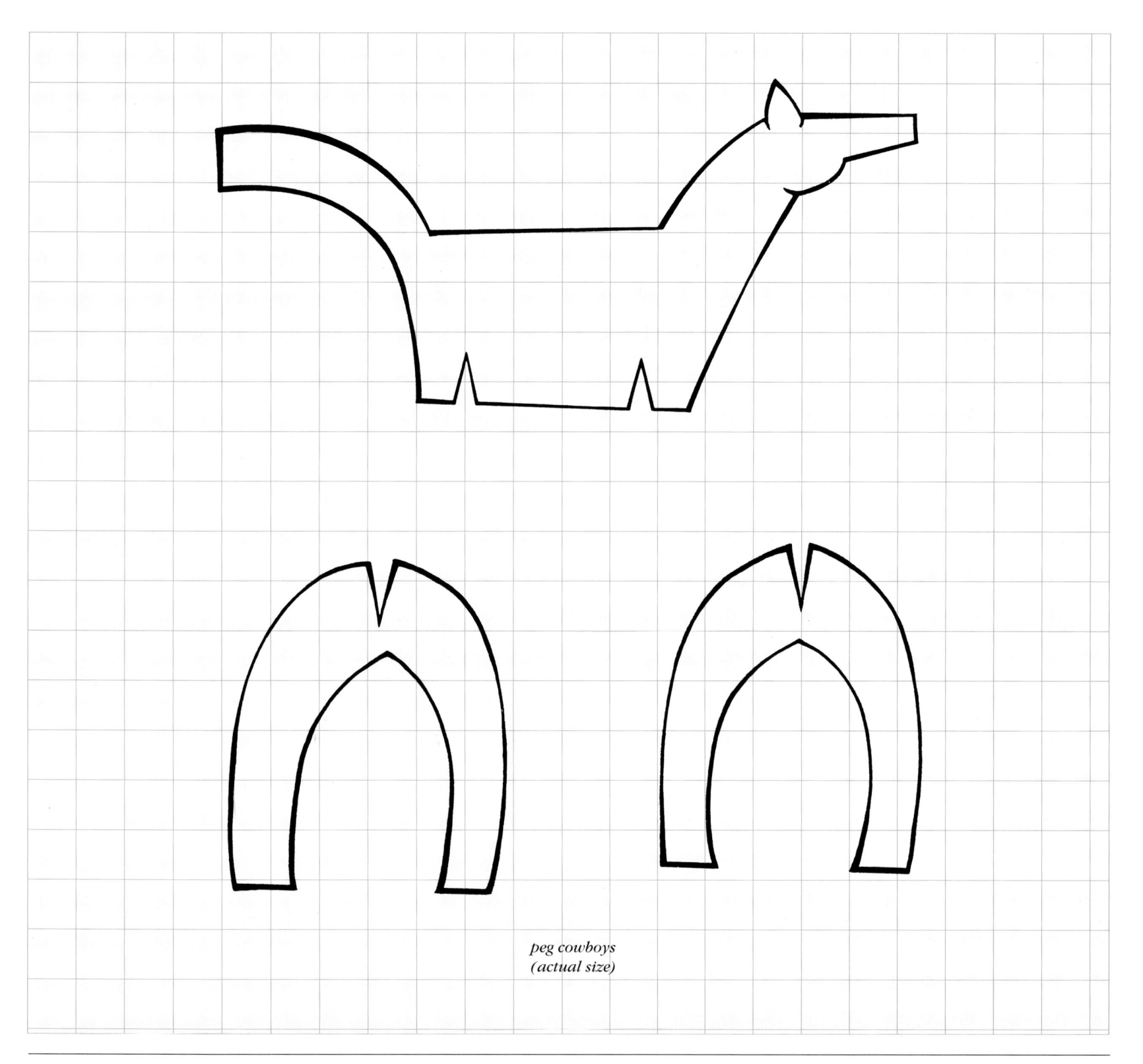

*peg cowboys
(actual size)*

187

Templates

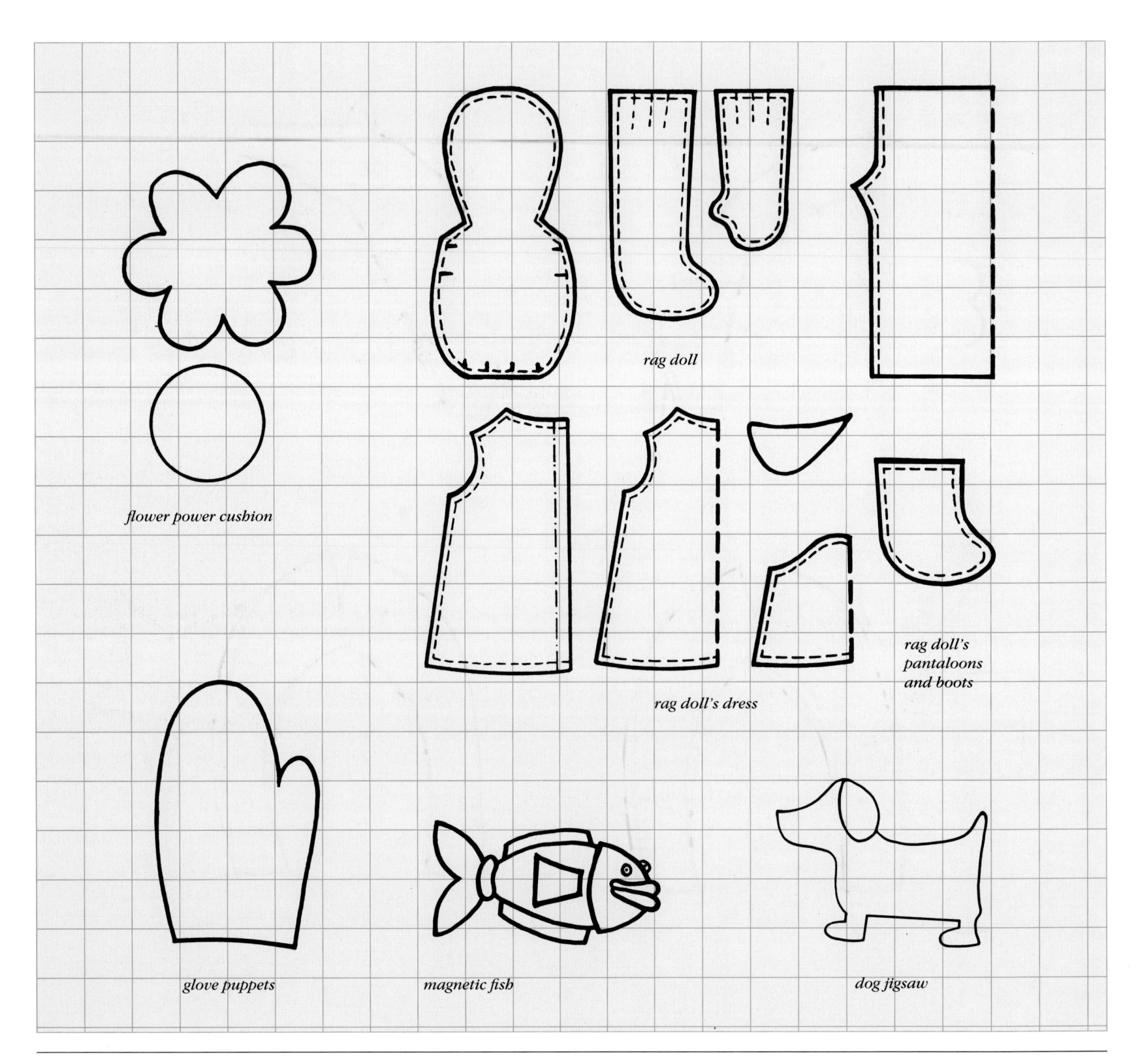

flower power cushion

rag doll

rag doll's dress

rag doll's pantaloons and boots

glove puppets

magnetic fish

dog jigsaw

TEMPLATES

dog and bone mobile

felt picture book

paper fastener puppet

felt game

toy bag

INDEX

A

Activity blanket, 54
Ageing make-up, 85
Animal masks, paper bag, 44
Aphids, 119
Apples, chocolate witchy, 183
Astronaut, 100

B

Badges, jamjar lid, 42
Bag, toy, 72
Balls, catch-the-ball game, 20
Bees, 118
Beetles, 118
Big foot stilts, 74
Biscuits (cookies):
  five-spice fingers, 167
  kooky cookies, 180
  peanut cookies, 166
Blackboard, sunny flower, 78
Blanket, activity, 54
Blanket stitch, 49
Blueberry muffins, 174
Boats, jolly orange, 182
Book, felt picture, 58
Book-ends, squeezy bottle dog, 28
Boots:
  growing plants in, 126
  rag doll's, 53
Bottles:
  bottle maracas, 56
  removing labels, 13
Boxes:
  decoupage toy box, 80
  flattening and cutting up, 13 
  nature box, 36
Bracelets, squeezy bottle, 43
Brownies, chocolate, 172
Bugs, gardening, 118
Butterfly, 96

C

Cacti, growing, 134
Cakes:
  chocolate brownies, 172
  chunky choc bars, 176
  lemon meringue cakes, 178
Cans, making holes in, 49
Carrots:
  dressing-up, 108
  preparing, 154
Catch-the-ball game, 20
Caterpillars, 119
Character skittles, 60
Cheesy salad, chunky, 162
Chest, storage, 34 
Chicken, yellow, 163
Chilli cheese nachos, 159
Chimes, nail, 30
Chocolate:
  chocolate brownies, 172
  chocolate puffs, 170
  chocolate witchy apples, 183
  chunky choc bars, 176
Christmas decorations:
  paper clip, 40
  pasta-shape, 41
Clay doll, Mexican, 76
Clock, toy, 66
Cookies:
  kooky cookies, 180
  peanut cookies, 166
Cooking, 152–85
  blueberry muffins, 174
  chilli cheese nachos, 159
  chocolate brownies, 172
  chocolate puffs, 170
  chocolate witchy apples, 183
  chunky cheesy salad, 162
  chunky choc bars, 176
  equipment, 152
  five-spice fingers, 167
  fruit crush and fruit kebabs, 184
  honey chop, 165
  jolly orange boats, 182
  kooky cookies, 180
  lemon meringue cakes, 178
  let's get tropical!, 171
  minty tea, 136
  monster meringues, 168
  pancake parcels, 160
  peanut cookies, 166
  pizza faces, 156
  roly poly porcupines, 157
  tasty toasts, 158
  techniques, 154
  tiny toads, 164
  yellow chicken, 163
Cowboys, peg, 16
Crazy grass-head, 148
Crown, regal, 112
Cushion, flower power, 70

D

Decoupage toy box, 80
Desert garden, 134
Detective, turn, 133
Dogs:
  dog and bone mobile, 68
  dog jigsaw, 65
  squeezy bottle dog book-ends, 28
Dolls:
  Mexican clay doll, 76
  rag doll, 50
  rag doll's dress, 52
  rag doll's pantaloons and boots, 53
Dress, rag doll's, 52
Dressing-up, 82–113 
  astronaut, 100
  butterfly, 96
  carrot, 108
  Egyptian mummy, 99
  Frankenstein's monster, 92
  ghost, 98
  gremlin, 87
  lion, 94
  make-up, 84
  materials, 82
  monkey, 89
  owl, 90
  pumpkin, 104
  purple monster, 93
  regal crown, 112
  skeleton, 106
  spectacular sea-face, 88
  sunflower, 102
  super hero, 110
  super heroine, 111
  tattoo, 97
  zombie, 86
Drilling wood, 48
Drinks:
  fruit crush, 184
  minty tea, 136
Drum, 24

E

Eggs, separating, 155
Egyptian mummy, 99
Equipment:
  cooking, 152
  gardening, 114

F

Feet, monster, 81
Felt game, 62
Felt picture book, 58
Fish, magnetic, 64
Five-spice fingers, 167

Index

Flower blackboard, sunny, 78
Flower power cushion, 70
Flowers, pressing, 139
Foam rubber stamps, 12
Foil robot, 45
Foil wrappers, 13
Frankenstein's monster, 92
French knots, 49
Fridge magnets, 55
Fruit crush, 184
Fruit kebabs, 184
Fruit salad, tropical, 171

G
Games:
  felt game, 62
  star board game, 77
Gardening projects, 114–51
  a bag of potatoes, 120
  blooming old boots, 126
  crazy grass-head, 148
  desert garden, 134
  equipment, 114
  glass gardening, 144
  good enough to eat!, 122
  grow spaghetti!, 130
  labels, 143
  long-lasting lavender, 138
  lovely lilies, 125
  minty tea, 136
  monkey nuts, 142
  pot of herbs, 135
  pressing flowers, 139
  rock gardens, 146
  scare them off!, 140
  sprouting seeds, 128
  the tallest sunflower, 124
  turn detective, 133
  wigwam runners, 132
  wonderful worms, 150
Ghost, 98
Glass gardening, 144
Glove puppets, 79
Grass-head, crazy, 148
Grating, 155
Greenflies, 119
Gremlin, 87
Groovy guitar, 32

H
Hairband, sponge-flower, 37

Hat, pom-pom, 26
Herbs, growing, 135
Hero, super, 110
Heroine, super, 111
Honey chops, 165

J
Jamjar lid badges, 42
Jelly (gelatine): jolly orange
  boats, 182
Jigsaw, dog, 65
Jolly orange boats, 182
Junk robot, 14

K
Kebabs, fruit, 184
Kooky cookies, 180

L
Labels:
  removing from bottles, 13
  seeds, 143

Lacewings, 118
Ladybirds, 119
Long-lasting lavender, 138
Lemon meringue cakes, 178
Lettuces, growing, 122
Lilies, growing, 125
Lily beetles, 119
Lion, 94
Lipstick, 85

M
Magnets:
  magnetic fish, 64
  fridge magnets, 55

Make-up, 82–5
Maracas, bottle, 56
Masks, paper bag animal, 44
Materials:
  dressing up, 82
  making toys, 46
  recycling, 10
Meringues:
  lemon meringue
    cakes, 178
  monster meringues, 168
Mexican clay doll, 76
Minty tea, 136
Mobiles:
  dog and bone
    mobile, 68
  straw mobile, 38
Monkey, 89
Monkey nuts, growing, 142
Monsters:
  Frankenstein's monster, 92
  monster feet, 81
  purple monster, 93
Muffins, blueberry, 174
Mummy, Egyptian, 99
Musical instruments:
  drum, 24
  bottle maracas, 56
  groovy guitar, 32
  nail chimes, 30
  shaker, 22
  tambourine, 22

N
Nachos, chilli cheese, 159
Nail chimes, 30
Nasturtiums, growing, 122
Nature box, 36

O
Onions, preparing, 154
Orange boats, jolly, 182
Owl, 90

P
Painting, on plastic, 12
Painting lips, 85
Pancake parcels, 160
Pantaloons, rag doll's, 53
Paper bag animal masks, 44
Paper clip Christmas 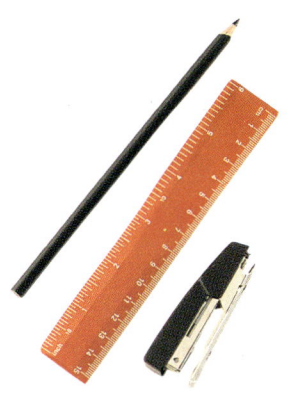
  decorations, 40
Paper fastener puppet, 73
Papier-mâché, 9
Pasta-shape Christmas tree
  decorations, 41
Peanut cookies, 166
Peanuts, growing, 142
Peg cowboys, 16
Picture book, felt, 58
Pizza faces, 156
Plastic, painting on, 12
Pom-pom hat, 26
Porcupines, roly poly, 157
Pork: honey chops, 165
Pot of herbs, 135
Potatoes, growing in a
  bag, 120
Pressing flowers, 139
Printing, foam rubber
  stamps, 12
Puffs, chocolate, 170
Pumpkin, dressing-up, 104
Puppets:
  glove puppets, 79
  paper fastener puppet, 73
  snake sock puppets, 18
  wooden spoon
    puppets, 19
Purple monster, 93

191

Index

R
Radishes, growing, 122
Rag doll, 50
Rag doll's dress, 52
Rag doll's pantaloons
 and boots, 53
Recycling projects, 14–45
 catch-the-ball game, 20
 drum, 24
 foil robot, 45
 groovy guitar, 32
 jamjar lid badges, 42
 junk robot, 14
 nail chimes, 30
 nature box, 36
 paper bag animal
  masks, 44
 paper clip Christmas
  decorations, 40
 pasta-shape Christmas
  tree decorations, 41
 peg cowboys, 16
 pom-pom hat, 26
 shaker, 22
 snake sock puppets, 18
 sponge-flower
  hairband, 37
 squeezy bottle
  bracelets, 43
 squeezy bottle dog
  book-ends, 28
 storage chest, 34
 straw mobile, 38
 tambourine, 22
 wooden spoon
  puppets, 19
Regal crown, 112
Removing make-up, 85
Robots:
 foil robot, 45
 junk robot, 14
Rock gardens, 146
Roly poly porcupines, 157
Rope:
 sealing rope ends, 48
 skipping rope, 59
Runner beans,
 growing, 132

S
Salad, chunky cheesy, 162
Sanding wood, 48
Sausages:
 roly poly
  porcupines, 157
 tiny toads, 164
Scaling-up, 8
Scare them off!, 140
Sea-face, spectacular, 88
Seeds:
 labels, 143
 sprouting seeds, 128
Shaker, 22
Skeleton, 106
Skipping rope, 59
Skittles, character, 60
Slugs, 119
Snake sock puppets, 18
Soft toys, stuffing, 48
Spaghetti!, grow, 130
Spectacular sea-face, 88
Sponge-flower
 hairband, 37
Spoon puppets,
 wooden, 19
Sprouting seeds, 128
Squeezy bottle
 bracelets, 43
Squeezy bottle dog
 book-ends, 28
Stamps, foam rubber, 12
Star board game, 77
Stilts, big foot, 74
Stitches, 49
Storage chest, 34
Straw mobile, 38
Strawberries,
 growing, 122
Stuffing soft toys, 48
Succulents, growing, 133
Sunflowers:
 dressing-up, 102
 growing, 124
Sunny flower
 blackboard, 78
Super hero, 110
Super heroine, 111

T
Tambourine, 22
Tattoo, 97
Tea, minty, 136
Templates, 186–9
Tiny toads, 164
Toasts, tasty, 158
Tomatoes, growing, 122
Toy bag, 72
Toy box, decoupage, 80
Toy clock, 66
Tracing, 8
Tropical!, let's get, 171
Turn detective, 133

V
Vine weevils, 119

W
Wigwam runners, 132
Wire, bending, 49
Witchy apples,
 chocolate, 183
Wonderful worms, 150
Wood:
 drilling, 48
 sanding, 48
Wooden spoon
 puppets, 19

Y
Yellow chicken, 163

Z
Zombie, 86